Estimating and Costing in Civil Engineering

Estimating and Costing in Civil Engineering

Abdullah Sheikh

RANDOM PUBLICATIONS
NEW DELHI (INDIA)

Estimating and Costing in Civil Engineering

ISBN 978-93-5111-434-5

Published in 2014 in India by

RANDOM PUBLICATIONS

4376-A/4B, Gali Murari Lal, Ansari Road
New Delhi-110 002
Phone : +91-11-43580356, +91-11-23289044
e-mail: randomexports@gmail.com, sales@randompublications.com, info@randompublications.com

Reprinted 2023

Type Setting by: Friends Media, Delhi-110089
Printed at : Replika Press Pvt. Ltd.

Preface

A cost estimate is the approximation of the cost of a program, project, or operation. The cost estimate is the product of the cost estimating process. The cost estimate has a single total value and may have identifiable component values. A problem with a cost overrun can be avoided with a credible, reliable, and accurate cost estimate. An estimator is the professional who prepares cost estimates. There are different types of estimators, whose title may be preceded by a modifier, such as building estimator, or electrical estimator, or chief estimator. Other professional titles may also prepare estimates or contribute to estimates, such as quantity surveyors, cost engineers, etc. In the US, there were 185,400 cost estimators in 2010. There are around 75,000 professional quantity surveyors working in the UK. In project management, project cost management is a major functional division. Cost estimating is one of three activities performed in project cost management. In cost engineering, cost estimation is a basic activity. A cost engineering reference book has chapters on capital investment cost estimation and operating cost estimation. The fixed capital investment provides the physical facilities. The working capital investment is a revolving fund to keep the facilities operating. In system, product, or facility acquisition planning, a cost estimate is used to evaluate the required funding and to compare with bids or tenders. In construction contracting, a cost estimate is usually prepared to submit a bid or tender to compete for a contract award. In facility maintenance and operation, cost estimates are used to establish funding or budgets. In an attempt to manage liability risk, some firms avoid the use of the word estimate and instead refer to the estimate as an "Opinion of Probable Cost.

Estimate quality refers to the fulfillment of quality requirements for the estimate. This is in accordance with formal quality assurance. There may also be other expectations for the estimate which are not specific requirements, but may reflect on the perceived quality of the estimate. Published quality requirements generally have to do with credibility, accuracy, confidence level, precision, risk, reliability, and validity of the estimate, as well as thoroughness, uniformity, consistency, verification, and documentation. Estimating methods may vary by type and class of estimate. The method used for most definitive estimates is to fully define and understand the scope, take off or quantify the scope, and apply costing to the scope, which can then be summed to a total cost. Proper documentation and review are also important. Pricing transforms the cost estimate into what the firm wishes to charge for the scope. Early estimates may employ various means of cost modelling. The basic characteristics of effective estimating include: clear identification of task, broad participation in preparing estimates, availability of valid data, standardized structure for the estimate, provision for program uncertainties, recognition of inflation, recognition of excluded costs, independent review of estimates, and revision of estimates for significant program changes. Application of best practices helps ensure a high-quality estimate. "Certain best practices should be followed if accurate and credible cost estimates are to be developed. These best practices represent an overall process of established, repeatable methods that result in high-quality cost estimates that are comprehensive and accurate and that can be easily and clearly traced, replicated, and updated.

This book explores innovative ideas in this subject.

I thank all members of my team who have helped in the preparation of the book. My special thanks go to "Random Publication" who have published the book.

—Abdullah Sheikh

Contents

1

Cost Estimate

A cost estimate is the approximation of the cost of a programme, project, or operation. The cost estimate is the product of the cost estimating process. The cost estimate has a single total value and may have identifiable component values. A problem with a cost overrun can be avoided with a credible, reliable, and accurate cost estimate. An estimator is the professional who prepares cost estimates. There are different types of estimators, whose title may be preceded by a modifier, such as building estimator, or electrical estimator, or chief estimator. Other professional titles may also prepare estimates or contribute to estimates, such as quantity surveyors, cost engineers, etc. In the US, there were 185,400 cost estimators in 2010. There are around 75,000 professional quantity surveyors working in the UK.

Overview

The U.S. Government Accountability Office (GAO) defines a cost estimate as, "the summation of individual cost elements, using established methods and valid data, to estimate the future costs of a programme, based on what is known today." The GAO reports that "realistic cost estimating was imperative when making wise decisions in acquiring new systems." A cost estimate is often needed to support evaluations of project feasibility or funding requirements in support of planning. A cost estimate is often used to establish a budget as the cost constraint for a project or operation.

In project management, project cost management is a major functional division. Cost estimating is one of three activities performed in project cost management. In cost engineering, cost estimation is a basic activity. A cost engineering reference book has chapters on capital investment cost estimation and operating cost estimation. The fixed capital investment provides the physical facilities. The working capital investment is a revolving fund to keep the facilities operating.

In system, product, or facility acquisition planning, a cost estimate is used to evaluate the required funding and to compare with bids or tenders.

In construction contracting, a cost estimate is usually prepared to submit a bid or tender to compete for a contract award.

In facility maintenance and operation, cost estimates are used to establish funding or budgets.

In an attempt to manage liability risk, some firms avoid the use of the word estimate and instead refer to the estimate as an "Opinion of Probable Cost."

Cost Estimate Types

Various projects and operations have distinct types of cost estimating, which vary in their composition and preparation methods. Some of the major areas include:

- Construction Cost
- Manufacturing Cost
- Software Development Cost
- Aerospace Mission Cost
- Resource Exploration Cost
- Facility Operation Cost
- Facility Maintenance & Repair Cost
- Facility Rehabilitation & Renewal Cost
- Facility Retirement Cost

Cost Estimate Classifications

Common cost estimate classifications historically used are

- Order of Magnitude
- Preliminary
- Definitive

These correspond to modern published classes 5, 3, and 1, respectively. The U.S. Department of Energy and many others use a system of five classes of estimates:

Estimate Class		***Name***	***Purpose Project Definition Level***
Class 5	Order of Magnitude	Screening or Feasibility	0% to 2%
Class 4	Intermediate	Concept Study or Feasibility	1% to 15%
Class 3	Preliminary	Budget, Authorization, or Control	10% to 40%
Class 2	Intermediate	Control or Bid/Tender	30% to 70%
Class 1	Definitive	Check Estimate or Bid/Tender	50% to 100%

Methods used to prepare the estimates range from stochastic or judgement at early definition to deterministic at later definition. Some estimates use mixed methods. Cost estimate classifications have been published by ASTM and AACE International. The American Society of Professional Estimators (ASPE) defines estimate levels in the reverse order as Level 1 – Order (Range) of Magnitude, Level 2 – Schematic/ Conceptual Design, Level 3- Design Development, Level 4 – Construction Document, and Level 5 – Bid.>."ACostE defines a Class I Estimate as definitive, a Class II Estimate as semi-detailed, and a Class III Estimate as pre-budget. Other names for estimates of different classes include:

Class 1	***Class 3***	***Class 5***
Detailed Estimate	Semi-Detailed Estimate	Conceptual Estimate
Final Estimate	Scope Estimate	Pre-Design Estimate
Control Estimate	Sanction Estimate	Preliminary Estimate
As-Bid Estimate		Pre-Budget Estimate
As-Sold Estimate		Evaluation Estimate
CD Estimate	DD Estimate	SD Estimate
		Parametric Estimate
		Rough Order-of-Magnitude (ROM) Estimate
		Very Rough Order-of-Magnitude (VROM) Estimate
		SWAG (Scientific, Wild-Ass Guess) Estimate
		PIDOOMA (Pulled It Directly Out Of My Ass) Estimate

Estimate Quality

Estimate quality refers to the fulfillment of quality requirements for the estimate. This is in accordance with formal quality assurance. There may also be other expectations for the estimate which are not specific requirements, but may reflect on the perceived quality of the estimate. Published quality requirements generally have to do with credibility, accuracy, confidence level, precision, risk, reliability, and validity of the estimate, as well as thoroughness, uniformity, consistency, verification, and documentation.''''''

> *"The result of bidding without good estimates is certain: jobs that end up with less profit, no profit, or a loss. The bidder ultimately will go out of business; the only question is how long will it take."*

Since a cost estimate is the approximation of the cost of a project or operation, then estimate accuracy is a measure of how closely the estimate is able to predict the actual expenditures for the project or operation. This can only be known after the project is completed. If, for example, a project estimate was \$1,252,000 for a specific scope and conditions, and at completion the records showed that \$1,172,451.26 was expended, the estimate was 6.8% too high. If the project ended up having a different scope or conditions, an unadjusted computation does not fairly assess the estimate accuracy. Predictions of the estimate accuracy may accompany the estimate. "Estimate accuracy is traditionally represented as a +/- percentage range around the point estimate; with a stated confidence level that the actual cost outcome will fall within this range." An example for a definitive estimate might be that the estimate has a -5/+10% range of accuracy with a 90% confidence that the final value will fall in that range. "The accuracy of an estimate is measured by how well the estimated cost compares to the actual total installed cost. The accuracy of an early estimate depends on four determinants: (1) who was involved in preparing the estimate; (2) how the estimate was prepared; (3) what was known about the project; and (4) other factors considered while preparing the estimate." For the same project, the range of uncertainty about the total estimate decreases, as illustrated in the cone of uncertainty diagram.

Credible cost estimates can be produced by following a rigor of 12 steps outlined by the U.S. GAO. Detailed documentation is recommended to accompany the estimate. "The documentation addresses the purpose of the estimate, the programme background and system description, its schedule, the scope of the estimate (in terms of time and what is and is not included), the ground rules and assumptions, all data sources, estimating methodology and rationale, the results of the risk analysis, and a conclusion about whether the cost estimate is reasonable. Therefore, a good cost estimate—while taking the form of a single number—is supported by detailed documentation that describes how it was derived and how the expected funding will be spent in order to achieve a given objective." This documentation is often titled Basis of Estimate (or BOE). Additional documentation may accompany the estimate, including quantity takeoff documentation and supporting calculations, quotes, etc.

Contingency

A contingency may be included in an estimate to provide for unknown costs which are indicated as likely to occur by experience, but are not identifiable. When using an estimate which has no contingency to set a budget or to set aside funding, a contingency is often added to improve the probability that the budget or funding will be adequate to complete the project. Being unable to complete a project risks public ridicule. The estimate or budget contingency is not intended to compensate for poor estimate quality, and is not intended to fund design growth, owner changes, or anything else unrelated to delivering the scope as defined in the estimate documentation. Generally more contingency is needed for earlier estimates due to the higher uncertainty of estimate accuracy.

Cost Estimating Methods and Best Practices

Estimating methods may vary by type and class of estimate. The method used for most definitive estimates is to fully define and understand the scope, take off or quantify the scope, and apply costing to the scope, which can then be summed to a total cost. Proper documentation and review are also important. Pricing transforms the cost estimate into what the firm wishes to charge for the scope. Early estimates may employ various means of cost modelling. The basic characteristics of effective estimating include: clear identification of task, broad participation in preparing estimates, availability of valid data, standardized structure for the estimate, provision for programme uncertainties, recognition of inflation, recognition of excluded costs, independent review of estimates, and revision of estimates for significant programme changes. Application of best practices helps ensure a high-quality estimate. "Certain best practices should be followed if accurate and credible cost estimates are to be developed. These best practices represent an overall process of established, repeatable methods that result in high-quality cost estimates that are comprehensive and accurate and that can be easily and clearly traced, replicated, and updated."

Tools that may be part of costs estimation are cost indexes. These factors promote time adjustment of capital costs, following changes in technology, availability of materials and labour, and inflation. Due to the inherent unavailability of up-to-date cost literature, several inflation or cost indexes are available.

Construction Cost Estimates

Estimates for the cost of facility construction are a major part of the cost estimate domain. A construction general contractor or subcontractor must normally prepare definitive cost estimates to prepare bids in the construction bidding process to compete for award of the contract. Although many estimators participate in the bidding and procurement processes, those are not a necessary function of cost estimate preparation. Earlier estimates are prepared by differing methods by estimators and others to support the planning process and to compare with bids.

Definitive Estimates (Class 1)

A definitive estimate is prepared from fully designed plans and specifications (or nearly so), preferably what are called contract documents (CD). The contract documents also establish the Scope of Work (SOW). The standard method is to review and understand the design package and take off (or perform a quantity survey of) the project scope by itemizing it into line items with measured quantities. RSMeans refers to this as, "Scope out the project," and, "Quantify." Some jurisdictions or areas of practice define the itemization and measuration in certain terms, such as RICS and may have specific rules for development of a Bill of quantities, or BOQ. The ASPE proposes a best practice standard method for the quantity survey. This includes using the Construction Specifications Institute Uniform Numbering System (MasterFormat) to ensure that all work is accounted for.

Then costs are applied to the quantified line items. This may be called costing or pricing. In estimating for contracting, the cost is what something costs you to build, and price is what you charge another party for building it. RSMeans refers to this as, "Price the quantities." ASPE recommends the "quantity times material and labour costs format" for the compilation of the estimate. This format is illustrated in the handwritten spreadsheet sample. For labour, the estimator should, "Determine basic production rates and multiply them by the units of work to determine total hours for the work." and then multiply the hours by the per hour average labour cost. Labour burdens, material costs, construction equipment costs, and, if applicable, subcontractor costs are also extended on the estimate detail form. Other costs and pricing are added, such as overhead, profit, sales or use taxes, payment and performance bonds, escalation, and contingency.

The costs which are applied to the line-item quantities may come from a cost book (either internal or external) or cost database. For construction contractors or construction managers it is important to track and compile past data of trends, completed projects, production factors, equipment changes, and various labour markets.

The labour requirements are often the most variable and are a primary focus of construction cost estimators. The labour hours required to construct each installation item are calculated by using a man-hour rate times the take-off quantity (a similar method is to divide the take-off quantity by the production rate). Many estimators use a man-hour norm reference for standard man-hours and apply an adjustment factor for project or task conditions, location, methods, equipment, labour skill, etc. to adjust for the anticipated effect on labour.

Direct costs are itemized for all necessary parts of the project. Direct costs are all of the costs which can be attributed directly to the project. Direct costs include costs for general requirements (Division 1 of MasterFormat), which includes such items as project management and coordination, quality control, temporary facilities and controls, cleaning and waste management. Direct costs may also include the costs of project planning, investigation, studies, and design; land or right of way acquisition, and other non-construction costs. Usually, a subtotal of total direct costs is provided in the estimate.

Provisions are made for Indirect costs in addition to the direct costs. Indirect costs include overhead, profit, sales or use taxes, payment and performance bonds, escalation, and contingency. Profit is cost to the buyer, but is not a cost to the provider, rather a projection of anticipated income.

A well documented cost estimate includes a Basis of Estimate (BOE), which describes the scope basis, pricing basis, methods, assumptions, inclusions, and exclusions.

Order-of-Magnitude Estimates (Class 5)

An order-of-magnitude estimate is prepared when little or no design information is available for the project. It is called order of magnitude because that may be all that can be determined at an early stage. In other words, perhaps we can only determine that it is of a 10,000,000 magnitude as opposed to a 1,000,000 magnitude. Various techniques are employed for these estimates, including experience and judgement, historical values and charts, rules of thumb, and simple mathematical calculations. Factor estimating is one of the more popular methods. This involves taking the known cost of a similar facility and factoring the cost for size, place, and time. Cost modelling is another common technique. In cost modelling the estimator models the various parameters of the facility and applies costs to the derived scope.

Building estimators or architects may use the Uniformat system of breaking down the building into functional systems or assemblies during the schematic design (SD) phase of planning and design. The RSMeans Square Foot Costs book organizes building costs according to the 7 divisions of the UNIFORMAT II classification system. The 7 divisions are:

- A Substructure
- B Shell
- C Interiors
- D Services
- E Equipment & Furnishings
- F Special Construction
- G Building Site Work

Allowance (Money)

An allowance is an amount of money given or allotted usually at regular intervals for a specific purpose. In the context of children, parents may provide an allowance (British English: pocket money) to their child for their miscellaneous personal spending. In the construction industry it may be an amount allocated to a specific item of work as part of an overall contract.

The person providing the allowance is usually trying to control how or when money is spent by the recipient so that it meets the aims of the person providing the money. For example an allowance by a parent might be motivated to teach the child money management and may be unconditional or be tied to completion of chores or achievement of specific grades.

The person making the allowance usually specifies the purpose and may put controls in place to make sure that the money is spent for that purpose only. For example a company employee may be given an allowance or per diem to provide for meals and travel when working away from home and may then be required to provide receipts as proof. Or they are provided with specific non-money tokens or vouchers that can be used only for a specific purpose such as a meal voucher.

Types of allowance

Allowances in business:

Construction Contracting: In construction, an allowance is an amount specified and included in the construction contract (or specifications) for a certain item of work (e.g., appliances, lighting, etc.) whose details are not yet determined at the time of contracting. Typically:

1. the allowance amount covers the cost of the contractor's material/equipment delivered to the project plus all taxes less any trade discounts to which the contractor may be entitled with respect to the item of work;
2. the contractor's costs for labour (installation), overhead, profit and other expenses with respect to the allowance item are included in the base contract amount but not in the allowance amount;
3. if the section 1 costs for the item of work are higher (or lower) than the allowance amount, the base contract amount should be increased (decreased) by the difference in the two amounts and by the change (if any) to the contractor's costs under section 2.

The allowance provisions may be handled otherwise in the contract: e.g., the flooring allowance may state that installation costs are part of the allowance. The contractor may be required to produce records of the original takeoff or estimate of the section 2 costs for each allowance item.

Other issues that should be considered in the contract's allowance provision are:

- may the client insist that the contractor use whomever the client wishes to do the allowance work?;
- may the contractor charge the client back for any costs arising from a delay by the client (or client's agent) in selecting the material or equipment of the allowance in question?

Allowances for Children

Parents often give their children an allowance (British English: pocket money) for their miscellaneous personal spending, and also to teach them money management at an early age.

Allowances for Adults

In Japan three quarters of men get a monthly allowance from their wives. Since 1979 Shinsei Bank has been researching the amount of spending money given to husbands by their wives. In 2011 it is 39,600 Yen or about $US 500. This compares to before the bubble burst when the allowance was 76,000 Yen in 1990 ($530 1990 dollars or US$ 930 in 2013)

Bill of Materials

A bill of materials (sometimes bill of material or BOM) is a list of the raw materials, sub-assemblies, intermediate assemblies, sub-components, parts and the quantities of each needed to manufacture an end product. A BOM may be used for communication between manufacturing partners, or confined to a single manufacturing plant.

A BOM can define products as they are designed (engineering bill of materials), as they are ordered (sales bill of materials), as they are built (manufacturing bill of materials), or as they are maintained (service bill of materials). The different types of BOMs depend on the business need and use for which they are intended. In process industries, the BOM is also known as the *formula, recipe,* or *ingredients list.* In electronics, the BOM represents the list of components used on the printed wiring board or printed circuit board. Once the design of the circuit is completed, the BOM list is passed on to the PCB layout engineer as well as component engineer who will procure the components required for the design.

Modular BOMs

In many cases, BOMs are hierarchical in nature with the top level representing the finished product which may be a sub-assembly or a completed item. BOMs that describe the sub-assemblies are referred to as modular BOMs. An example of this is the NAAMS BOM that is used in the automotive industry to list all the components in an assembly line. The structure of the NAAMS BOM is System, Line, Tool, Unit and Detail.

The first hierarchical databases were developed for automating bills of materials for manufacturing organizations in the early 1960s. At present this BOM is used as a data base to identify the many parts and their codes in automobile manufacturing companies.

A bill of materials "implosion" links component pieces to a major assembly, while a bill of materials "explosion" breaks apart each assembly or sub-assembly into its component parts.

A modular BOM can be displayed in the following formats:

- A single-level BOM that displays the assembly or sub-assembly with only one level of children. Thus it displays the components directly needed to make the assembly or sub-assembly.

- An indented BOM that displays the highest-level item closest to the left margin and the components used in that item indented more to the right.
- Modular (planning) BOM

A BOM can also be visually represented by a product structure tree, although they are rarely used in the workplace.

Configurable BOM

A configurable bill of materials (CBOM) is a form of BOM used by industries that have multiple options and highly configurable products (e.g. telecom systems, data-centre hardware (SANS, servers, etc.), PCs, autos).

The CBOM is used to dynamically create "end-items" that a company sells. The benefit of using CBOM structure is it reduces the work-effort needed to maintain product structures. The configurable BOM is most frequently driven by "configurator" software, however it can be enabled manually (manual maintenance is infrequent because it is unwieldy to manage the number of permutations and combinations of possible configurations). The development of the CBOM is dependent on having a modular BOM structure in place. The modular BOM structure provides the assemblies/sub-systems that can be selected to "configure" an end-item.

While most configurators utilize top-down hierarchical rules syntax to find appropriate modular BOMs, maintenance of very similar BOMs (i.e., only one component is different for various voltages) becomes highly excessive. A newer approach, (Bottom-Up/Rules-Based Structuring) utilizing a proprietary search engine scheme transversing through selectable componentry at high speeds eliminates the Planning Modular BOM duplications. The search engine is also used for all combinatorial feature constraints and GUI representations to support specification selections.

To decide which variant of the parts or components are to be chosen, they are attributed by the product options which are the characteristic features of the product (business). If the options of the product build an ideal boolean algebra, it is possible to describe the connection between parts and product variants with an boolean expression, which refers to a subset of the set of products.

Construction Bidding

Construction bidding is the process of submitting a proposal (tender) to undertake, or manage the undertaking of a construction project. The process starts with a cost estimate from blueprints and take offs.

The tender is treated as an offer to do the work for a certain amount of money (firm price), or a certain amount of profit (cost reimbursement or cost plus). The tender which is submitted by the competing firms is generally based on a bill of quantities, a bill of approximate quantities or other specifications which enable the tenders attain higher levels of accuracy, the statement of work.

For instance, a bill of quantities is a list of all the materials (and other work such as amount of excavation) of a project which have sufficient detail to obtain a realistic cost, or rate per described item of work/material. The tenders should not only show the unit cost per material/work, but should also if possible, break it down to labour, plant and material costs. In this way the individual who is selecting the tender will be quite confident that the tender is feasible. Bids are not only chosen on cost alone. Sometimes contractors submit lower tenders to win the contract and win the work. Either the costs that the contractor incurs is greater than the price he is charging the client (as a consequence of a lower tender determining the contract sum), and thus is likely to go insolvent, or he will claim for "loss and/or expense" due to discrepancies in the contract documents (this can be done deliberately). The lowest tender is not always a feasible tender. The lowest tender is the most likely to increase the contract sum, the most throughout the course of the project.

Bid Solicitation

Bid solicitation is the process of making published construction data readily available to interested parties, including construction managers, contractors, and the public. There are several services, including government entities and private planrooms, that allow project owners to release project details to solicit and obtain contractor bids. These services act as a gateway for project owners to release project information to a large group of contractors, general contractors or subcontractors in an attempt to solicit bids. Many of these services are subscription based or charge a flat rate for project data.

Types of Project Delivery

The most common methods of construction project delivery include design-bid-build (DBB), the design-build (DB), the construction manager as constructor approach and a negotiated approach. Each of these methods have advantages and disadvantages and all can be used to successfully plan, design and undertake a given construction project.

Traditional Procurement

The traditional procurement method is the most common construction delivery method. This process begins with an owner selecting an architect to prepare construction documents. These are prepared using drafting standards such as the Institute of Civil Engineers ICE Conditions of Contract, or the NEC Engineering and Construction Contract. In most cases, the architect will release these construction documents publicly, or to a select group of general contractors, who will then place a bid on the project which reflects what they believe cost of construction will total. This bid is inclusive of a multitude of subcontractor bids for each specific trade. The general contractor's fee is generally built into the bid cost. Most government contracts are bid competitively using this method.

Digital Procurement

The digital procurement method is rapidly emerging. There are various web sites that provide electronic bidding, tender calls and other related services.

Design-build

Design-Build (or design/build, and abbreviated D-B or D/B accordingly) is a construction project delivery system where, in contrast to traditional "design-bid-build" (or "design-tender"), the design and construction aspects are contracted for with a single entity known as the design-builder or design-build contractor. The design-builder is usually the general contractor, but in many cases it is also the design professional (architect or engineer). This system is used to minimize the project risk for an owner and to reduce the delivery schedule by overlapping the design phase and construction phase of a project. Where the design-builder is the contractor, the design professionals are typically retained directly by the contractor.

History

The design/build delivery system often cites the original "Master Builder" model used to build most pre-modern projects. Under the Master Builder approach, a central figure of the architect held total project accountability. From inception to completion, the master builder was the key organizational figure and strictly liable to the owner for defects, delays, and losses. The design/build system is a return to some of the fundamentals of the Master Builder approach.

Overview of Process

Design-build focuses on combining the design, permit, and construction schedules in order to streamline the traditional design-bid-build environment. This does not shorten the time it takes to complete the individual tasks of creating construction documents (working drawings and specifications), acquiring building and other permits, or actually constructing the building. Instead, a design-build firm will strive to bring together design and construction professionals in a collaborative environment to complete these tasks at the same time.

Typically the hallmark of a Design/Build project is that one organization is responsible for both design and construction of the project. If this organization is a contractor, the process is known as "Contractor-led Design-Build". If the organization is a design firm, the process is known as "Design-led Design-Build". In either case, the organization employed by the owner rarely handles both aspects of design and construction in-house. In fact, the organization often subcontracts with on-site personnel (if design-led) as well as architects and engineers (if contractor-led).

Potential Problems of Design-Build

Cost estimating for a design-build project is sometimes difficult because design documents are often preliminary and may change over the course of the project. As a result, design-build contracts are often written to allow for unexpected situations without penalizing either the Design-Builder or the owner. Several organizations (such as the Design/Build Institute of America) provide standardized form contracts for design-builders to use, but it is not unusual for the design-builder to provide its own contractual documents.

This uncertainty requires the owner to rely a great deal on the integrity, acumen, and competence of the design-builder. As the certainty of estimates decreases, the opinion of the construction professionals of the Design-Build firm must be trustworthy, accurate, and reasonably verifiable in order to minimize risk.

Benefits of Design-Build

It is important to note that the design-build method, while not focused on saving the owner construction costs, nonetheless often saves the owner money on the overall project. The combined effects of carrying a construction loan (which typically carries a higher interest rate than permanent financing) and an earlier useful on-line date usually yields considerable overall profitability to the project and may make seemingly unfeasible projects into genuine opportunities.

The compression of time is only one important aspect of the implementation of this system.

Other Attributes Include

- Increased accountability by the service provider,
- Single source project delivery, and
- A value based project feedback system

Accountability

Rather than a parcelized level of responsibility of the classic design-bid-build, design-build provides an integrated solution for the owner or client. This moves projects away from the "finger-pointing" that is often commonplace in contemporary construction projects, and allows the owner to look to one entity with any questions or concerns.

Single Source

Instead of having several contractors and consultants, an owner has just one entity to deal with. Design revisions, project feedback, budgeting, permitting, construction issues, change orders, and billing can all be routed through the design-build firm. This single point of contact allows a certain degree of flexibility for the owner. Most design-builders will leverage that flexibility for the owner's benefit by continually refining the construction programme to maximize the owner's value at the completion of the project.

Value-based Project Feedback

Typically, in order for a contractor to bid on a project, very specific details relating to the methods and materials must be given to avoid any ambiguity and to make an "apples to apples" comparison of bids. In a design-build context, the owner, the owner's other consultants, and the design-builder can work together to determine what methods and materials will maximize the owner's value. In instances where marginally more expensive materials, designs, or construction methods might yield a higher return on investment for the owner than those of lower cost, the owner is free to adjust the project's programme without having to re-bid the entire project.

Construction Manager as Constructor

Under this delivery method, a construction manager is hired prior to the completion of the design phase to act as a project coordinator and general contractor. Unlike the DBB method, a construction manager is hired during the design phase, which allows the construction manager to work directly with the architect and circumvent any potential design issues before completion of the construction documents. After documents are completed, the construction manager accepts bids for the various divisions of work from subcontractors or general contractors.

Negotiated

This delivery method is similar to the Design-Bid-Build method in that design and construction are performed by different firms. Unlike the design-bid-build approach, a general contractor and an architect are selected at the project's inception. These firms work together throughout the design phase. When design documents are complete, the final construction costs are negotiated by the general contractor through bids from subcontractors on various scopes of work.

Cost Engineering

"Cost engineering [is] the engineering practice devoted to the project cost management, involving such activities as cost- and control-estimating, which is cost control and cost forecasting, investment appraisal, and risk analysis." "Cost Engineers budget, plan and monitor investment projects. They seek the optimum balance between cost, quality and time requirements."

Skills and Knowledge of Cost Engineers are Similar to Those of Quantity Surveyors.

A cost engineer is "an engineer whose judgement and experience are utilized in the application of scientific principles and techniques to problems of estimation; cost control; business planning and management science; profitability analysis; project management; and planning and scheduling."

Overview

One key objective of cost engineering is to arrive at accurate cost estimates and schedules and to avoid cost overruns and schedule slips. Cost engineering goes beyond preparing cost estimates and schedules by supporting assessment and decisionmaking. "The discipline of 'cost engineering' can be considered to encompass a wide range of cost-related aspects of engineering and programme management, but in particular cost estimating, cost analysis/cost assessment, design-to-cost, schedule analysis/planning and risk assessment." The broad array of cost engineering topics represent the intersection of the fields of project management, business management, and engineering. Most people have a limited view of what engineering encompasses. The most obvious perception is that engineering addresses technical issues such as the physical design of a structure or system. However, beyond the physical manifestation of a design of a structure or system (for example, a building), there are other dimensions to consider such as the money, time, and other resources that were invested in the creation of the building. Cost engineers refer to these investments collectively as "costs".

Cost engineering then can be considered an adjunct of traditional engineering. It recognizes and focuses on the relationships between the physical and cost dimensions of whatever is being "engineered". Cost engineering is most often taught at universities as part of construction engineering, engineering management, civil engineering, and related curricula because it is most often practiced on engineering and construction capital projects. Engineering economics is a core skill and knowledge area of cost engineering.

AACE International "is dedicated to the tenets of furthering the concepts of Total Cost Management and Cost Engineering. Total Cost Management is the effective application of professional and technical expertise to plan and control resources, costs, profitability and risk. Simply stated, it is a systematic approach to managing cost throughout the life cycle of any enterprise, programme, facility, project, product or service. This is accomplished through the application of cost engineering and cost management principles, proven methodologies and the latest technology in support of the management process. ... Total Cost Management is that area of engineering practice where engineering judgement and experience are utilized in the application of scientific principles and techniques to problems of business and programme planning; cost estimating; economic and financial analysis; cost engineering; programme and project management; planning and scheduling; and cost and schedule performance measurement and change control. In summary, the list of practice areas ... are collectively called cost engineering; while the "process" through which these practices are applied is called total cost management or TCM.

History

Cost engineering is a field of engineering practice that began in the 1950s (AACE International was founded in 1956). The skills and knowledge areas of Cost Engineers are similar to those of Quantity

Surveyors. AACE International is one of many international engineering organizations representing practitioners in these fields. The International Cost Engineering Congress (ICEC) was founded in 1976 as a Worldwide Confederation of Cost Engineering, Quantity Surveying and Project Management Societies.

In 2006, AACE published the Total Cost Management (TCM) Framework which outlines an integrated process for applying the skills and knowledge of cost engineering. This has also been called the world's first process for portfolio, programme and project management.

Professional Titles or Positions in Cost Engineering

"Cost engineering practitioners tend to be: a) specialized in function (e.g., cost estimating, planning and scheduling, etc.); b) focused on either the asset management or project control side of the TCM process; and c) focused on a particular industry (e.g., engineering and construction, manufacturing, information technology, etc) or asset type (e.g., chemical process, buildings, software, etc.)... They may work for the business that owns and operates the asset (emphasis on economics and analysis), or they may work for the contractor that executes the projects (emphasis on planning and control)."

Some titles or positions in Cost Engineering practice include:

- Claims and Changes Specialist
- Construction Manager
- Contract Management Specialist
- Cost Analyst
- Cost Engineer
- Cost Estimator (or Estimator)
- Planner/Scheduler (or Scheduling Engineer)
- Pre-Construction Manager
- Project Controls Engineer
- Project Manager
- Quantity Surveyor

Total Cost Management

Total cost management (TCM) is the name given by AACE International to a process for applying the skills and knowledge of cost engineering. It is also the first integrated process or methodology for portfolio, programme and project management. AACE first introduced the concept in the 1990s and published the full presentation of the process in the "Total Cost Management Framework" in 2006.

Overview

Traditionally, the field of project management begins with the "initiation" of a project. The most well known treatment of the project management process is included in the Project Management Institute's Project Management Body of Knowledge (PMBOK). However, the PMBOK does not address what happens before a project is initiated; i.e., how does a project come into being?, how is the project identified and decided upon among other operating, maintenance, or investment options available to an enterprise. Total Cost Management maps the process upstream of project management. In TCM, what precedes project management is referred to as "strategic asset management" or more traditionally, "portfolio and programme management". A unique element of the TCM process is that it integrates all the steps that an organization must take to deploy its business strategy. This includes monitoring and becoming aware of a performance issue with an asset in its asset portfolio (i.e., capital asset base), to completing a project and delivering a modified or new asset to the company's portfolio. It also addresses managing multiple projects as a programme or project portfolio.

TCM has found its widest audience in the companies that make large capital investments in fixed capital assets through construction projects (e.g., oil and gas, chemical, pharmaceuticals, utilities, etc.). However, the process is industry generic and is finding wider use in IT, software and other companies.

Total Cost Management Framework

In 2006, AACE published their Total Cost Management Framework- An Integrated Methodology for Portfolio, Programme and Project Management. In this tested and proven methodology, portfolios of assets are optimized through the use of portfolios of projects, using project management as a delivery system, to support and enhance large, strategic or operational programmes in support of the business and strategic objectives of the organization.

Estimating Road Construction Unit Costs

The unit cost of road construction in dollars per kilometer is the sum of the subunit costs of the road construction activities. Road construction unit costs are estimated by dividing the machine rates by the production rates for the various activities involved in road construction. The road construction activities considered here are surveying, clearing and grubbing, excavation, surfacing, and drainage.

Surveying

Surveying and staking costs vary considerably depending on type and size of the job, access, terrain, and job location. One method of estimating production is to estimate the number of stakes which can be set per hour and the number of stakes which must be set per kilometer. For example, assume about 15 stakes can be set per hour with a two-man crew with the preliminary survey line already in place. A typical five-point section consists of two reference stakes, two slope stakes, and one final centreline stake.

The surveying production rate in km per hour is equal to the number of stakes the crew sets per hour divided by the number of stakes required per km.

Example:

A survey crew is setting 300 stakes per km at a rate of 15 stakes per hour. The cost of a survey crew including transport is \$10 per hr.

P = 15/300 = .05 km/hr

UC = 10/.05 = \$200/km

Clearing and Piling

The clearing and piling cost can be calculated by estimating the number of hectares of right-of way to be cleared and piled per kilometer of road. The clearing and piling production rate in km/hr is the hectares per hour which can be cleared and piled per hour divided by the number of hectares per km to be cleared and piled. Clearing can be accomplished in a number of ways, including men with axes or power saws. Merchantable logs may be removed by skidder or tractor and the remainder piled by tractor for burning or decay. Felling rates and skidding rates for logging can be used for determining the cost of the removal of merchantable logs.

On gentle terrain, if a wide right-of-way is being cleared to permit sunlight to dry the road surface after frequent rains, the project might be estimated as a land clearing project. A method for estimating the total time per hectare required to clear, grub, and pile on gentle terrain with a tractor and shearing blade is shown below. Additional details can be found in the Caterpillar Performance Handbook No. 21, Caterpillar, Inc.

Mechanized Clearing

The clearing time will depend upon the size of tractor and the number and size of the trees. The clearing time, Tc, in machine hours per hectare is

$$Tc = (X/60)\ (AB + M_1N_1 + M_2N_2 + M_3N_3 + M_4N_4 + DF)$$

where X is the hardwood density factor, A is the vine density factor, B is the base minutes per hectare, M is the minutes per tree in each diameter range, N is the number of trees per hectare in each diameter range, D is the sum of the diameters of all trees per hectare larger than 180 cm, and F is the minutes per cm of diameter to cut trees with diameters greater than 180 cm.

Table: *Production factors for felling with Rome KG blade.*

Tractor GHP	*Factors*	*Diameter Range, cm*				*Min per cm of diameter for trees > 180 cm*
		30-60	*61-90*	*91-120*	*121-180*	
	B	M_1	M_2	M_3	M_4	F
140	100	0.8	4.0	9.0	-	-
200	62	0.5	1.8	3.6	11	0.110
335	45	0.2	1.3	2.2	6	0.060
460	39	0.1	0.4	1.3	3	0.033

X = 1.3 if the percentage of hardwoods > 75 and X = 0.7 if percentage of hardwood is < 25, X = 1 otherwise.

A = 2.0 if number of trees/ha > 1500 and A = 0.7 if number of trees/ha < 1000, A = 1.0 otherwise. Increase value of A by 1.0 if there are heavy vines, and by 2.0 for very heavy vines.

For hectares which must be cleared and where stumps must be removed (grubbed), multiply the total time for clearing by a factor of 1.25.

Mechanized Piling

To compute piling time, when a rake or angled shearing blade is used, an equation to calculate the piling time per hectare, Tp, is

$$Tp = (1/60)\ (B + M_1N_1 + M_2N_2 + M_3N_3 + M_4N_4 + DF)$$

where the variables are defined as above.

Table: *Production factors for piling in windrows.*

Tractor GHP	*Factors*	*Diameter Range, cm*				*Min per cm of diameter for trees > 180 cm*
		30-60	*61-90*	*91-120*	*121-180*	
	B	M_1	M_2	M_3	M_4	F
140	185	0.6	1.2	5.0	-	-
200	135	0.4	0.7	2.7	5.4	-
335	111	0.1	0.5	1.8	3.6	0.03
460	97	0.08	0.1	1.2	2.1	0.01

When piling is to include piling of stumps, increase the total piling time by 25 percent.

Example

Five hectares per km of right-of-way in hardwoods are being cleared for a road (extra width is being used to help the road dry after rains). Of the five hectares, 1.2 hectares per km will need to have the stumps removed. Tractor machine rate is $80 per hour. All material will be piled for burning. Work is being done by a 335 HP bulldozer. The average number of trees per hectare less than 180 cm diameter. There is also one tree per hectare with a diameter of approximately 185 cm.

Table: *Data for clearing, grubbing and piling example.*

Number of trees	*Diameter Range, cm*				*Sum of tree diameters for trees*
<30 cm	30-60	61-90	91-120	121-180	> 180 cm
	N_1	N_2	N_3	N_4	D
1100	35	6	6	4	185

Tc = $(X/60)\ (AB + M_1N_1 + M_2N_2 + M_3N_3 + M_4N_4 + DF)$

Tc = $(1.3/60)\ [(1)\ (45) + (.2)\ (35) + (1.3)\ (6) + (2.2)\ (6) + (6)\ (4) + (185)\ (0.06)] = 2.34$ hr/ha

Tp = $(1/60)\ (B + M_1N_1 + M_2N_2 + M_3N_3 + M_4N_4 + DF)$

Tp = $(1/60)\ [111 + (.1)\ (35) + (.5)\ (6) + (1.8)\ (6) + (3.6)\ (4) + (185)\ (0.03)\ ] = 2.47$ hr/ha

Total tractor time/km = $3.8\ (2.34 + 2.47) + 1.2(1.25)\ (2.34 + 2.47) = 25.5$ hr/km

P = $1/25.5 = .039$ km/hr

UC = $80 \times 25.5 = \$\ 2039$/km

Earthwork

The earthwork cost is calculated by estimating the number of cubic metres of common material and rock which must be moved to construct the road. The earthwork production rate is calculated as the cubic metres per hour which can be excavated and placed divided by the number of cubic metres per km to be excavated.

Road construction superintendents can often estimate the number of metres per hour that their equipment can build road based upon local experience after looking at the topography. The engineer's method is to calculate the number of cubic metres to be excavated using formulas or tables for calculating earthwork quantities as a function of sideslope, road width, cut and fill slope ratios. Production rates for bulldozers and hydraulic excavators are available.

For example, a 6.0 metre subgrade on a 30 percent slope with a 1.5:1 fill slope and 0.5:1 cut slope with a one foot ditch and a 20 percent shrinkage factor would be approximately 2100 bank cubic metres per km for a balanced section.

An average production rate in common material (no rock) from an equipment performance handbook might be 150 bank cubic metres per hour for a 300 hp power-shift tractor with ripper. The tractor cost is $80/hr. The rate of excavation would be

$$P = (150\ m^3/hr)/(2100\ m^3/km) = .07\ km/hr$$

$$UC = 80/.07 = \$1143/km$$

If the earthwork is not being placed or sidecast within 50 metres of the cut, the production rate for pushing the material to the placement location must be made. Scrapers or excavators and dump trucks may be used.

Excavation rates in rock vary with the size of job, hardness of rock and other local conditions. Often there is a local market price for blasting. Estimates of blasting production can be made by knowing the size of equipment and the type of job. For example, a 10 cm track-mounted drill and 25 cubic metre per minute air-compressor may prepare 40 cubic metres per hour for small, shallow blasts and 140 cubic metres per hour for larger, deeper blasts including quarry development to produce rock surfacing. A major cost will be explosives. For example, 0.8 kg of explosive such as Tovex might be used per cubic metre of rock at a cost of approximately $2 per kg.

Finish Grading

Finish grading of the subgrade can be estimated by determining the number of passes a grader must make for a certain width subgrade and the speed of the grader. This number can be converted to the number of hours per hectare of subgrade. For example, a 120 hp grader may require about 10 hours of productive machine time without delays per hectare of subgrade or 0.1 hectares per hour. The production rate for final grading of a 6.0 metre subgrade would then be,

$$P = (0.1\ ha/hr)/(0.6\ ha/km) = .17\ km/hr$$

If the grader cost is $30/hr, the unit cost of grading is

$$UC = 30/.17 = \$176/km$$

Similarly, the rate of pulling ditches per kilometre can be estimated.

Surfacing

Surfacing costs are a function of the type of surfacing material, the quantity of surfacing material per square metre, and the length of haul. Local information is the best guide in constructing surfacing costs due to the wide range of conditions that can be encountered.

Natural gravel from streams may require only loading with front-end loaders directly to dump trucks, transporting, spreading, and may or may not be compacted.

Laterite may be ripped by crawler tractor, loaded by front-end loader, transported, spread and grid-rolled with a sheeps-foot roller to produce a sealed running surface. Rock may have to be blasted, loaded into one or more crusher(s), stockpiled, reloaded, transported, spread, and compacted. The costs for each of these operations can be developed by estimating the equipment production rates and machine rates.

Example

A relatively complex surfacing operation requires developing a 20,000 cubic metre solid rock source (26,400 cubic metres in the road prism) to surface 26.4 km of road including shooting and crushing rock, loading, transporting, and spreading rock as follows.

To open up rock source, use data from clearing and common excavation:

(a) To clear and excavate to rock:

Equipment	***Machine Hours***	***Machine Rate***	***Cost***
Tractor	27	72.00	1944.00

Cost per cubic metre solid rock = $0.10

(b) To drill and blast at a production rate of 140 cubic metres per hour

Equipment	***Machine Hours***	***Machine Rate***	***Cost***
Drills	1.0	60.00	60.00
Compressor	1.0	55.00	55.00
Explosives	0.8 kg × $2.0/kg × 140 m^3		224.00
			339.00

Cost per cubic metre solid rock = $2.42

(c) To crush 225 tons per hour (2.6 tons/solid cubic metre):

Equipment	***Machine Hours***	***Machine Rate***	***Cost***
Tractor	0.5	72.00	36.00
Loader	1.0	90.00	90.00
Crusher	1.0	90.00	90.00
Stacker	1.0	15.00	15.00
Generator	1.0	20.00	20.00

A 45 cm culvert, 10 metres long, is being installed. Experience indicates that a small backhoe and operator, and two labourers can install 3 culverts per day. The culvert crew uses a flat-bed truck to transport themselves and the pipe each day.

To install 3 culverts:

Equipment	*Machine Hours*	*Machine Rate*	*Cost*
Backhoe	6	60.00	360.00
Truck	9	12.00	108.88
Pipe Cost	30 metres × $15/metre	450.00	
			918.00

Cost per lineal metre of culvert = $30.60 per metre

Alternatively the cost could be stated as $306 per culvert or if there were an average of 4 culverts per km, then $1224 per km.

Glossary of Construction Cost Estimating

A

- Allocation of costs is the transfer of costs from one cost item to one or more other cost items.
- Allowance - a value in an estimate to cover the cost of known but not yet fully defined work.
- As-sold estimate - the estimate which matches the agreed items and price for the project scope.

B

- Basis of estimate (BOE) - a document which describes the scope basis, pricing basis, methods, qualifications, assumptions, inclusions, and exclusions.
- Bill of materials (BOM) - a list of materials required for the construction of a project or part of a project, which may include quantities.
- Bill of quantities (BOQ) - a document used in tendering in the construction industry in which materials, parts, and labour (and their costs) are itemized. It also (ideally) details the terms and conditions of the construction or repair contract and itemises all work to enable a contractor to price the work for which he or she is bidding.
- Bond - in construction, a performance bond is a surety bond issued by an insurance company or a bank to guarantee satisfactory completion of a project by a contractor.

C

- Chart of accounts (Code of accounts) (COA) - a created list of the accounts used by a business entity to define each class of items for which money or the equivalent is spent or received. It is used to organize the finances of the entity and to segregate expenditures, revenue, assets and liabilities in order to give interested parties a better understanding of the financial health of the entity.
- City cost index. RSMeans publishes a city cost index table.
- Construction is a process that consists of the creation, modification, or demolition of facilities, buildings, civil and monumental works, and infrastructure.
- Construction cost - the total cost to construct a project. This value usually does not include the preplanning, site or right of way acquisition, or design costs, and may not include start-up and commissioning costs. This total or subtotal is usually identified as such in an estimate report. Also known as Total Estimated Contract Cost (TECC).
- Consumables are goods that, according to the 1913 edition of Webster's Dictionary, are capable of being consumed; that may be destroyed, dissipated, wasted, or spent (also known as consumable goods, nondurable goods, or soft goods). In construction, these may include such materials as weld rod, fasteners, tape, glue, etc.
- Contingency - When estimating the cost for a project, product or other item or investment, there is always uncertainty as to the precise content of all items in the estimate, how work will be performed, what work conditions will be like when the project is executed and so on. These uncertainties are risks to the project. Some refer to these risks as "known-unknowns" because the estimator is aware of them, and based on past experience, can even estimate their probable costs. The estimated costs of the known-unknowns is referred to by cost estimators as cost contingency.
- Cost - the value of currency required to obtain a product or service, to expend labour and use equipment and tools, or to operate a business.
- Cost index (or factor) - a value used to adjust the cost of from one time to another. There are various published cost indexes,

listed by year, quarter, or month. RSMeans publishes a historical cost index.

- Costing - the process of applying appropriate costs to the line items after the take off. RSMeans refers to this as, "Price the quantities." May also be called pricing.
- Crew – a group of people (workers) who execute a construction activity. The crew may also include construction equipment required to execute the work.
- Crew hour (ch) – one crew's effort for one hour of time.

D

- Deliverable is a term used in project management to describe a tangible or intangible object produced as a result of the project that is intended to be delivered to a customer (either internal or external).
- Direct costs are directly attributable to the cost object. In construction, the costs of materials, labour, equipment, etc., and all directly involved efforts or expenses for the cost object are direct costs.
- Distributables – a classification of project costs which are not associated with any specific direct account.
- Duration – the amount of clock or calendar time which is required to execute a work activity or task.

E

- Effort - the work done in accomplishing a task or project. May be a measurement of the hours required.
- Equipment - (1) a category of cost for organizing and summarizing costs, (2) construction equipment used to execute the project work, (3) engineered equipment such as pumps or tanks.
- Escalation is defined as changes in the cost or price of specific goods or services in a given economy over a period. In estimates, escalation is an allowance to provide for the anticipated escalation of costs during construction.
- Estimation in project management is the processes of making cost estimates using the appropriate techniques.

F

- Facility - an installation, contrivance, or other thing which facilitates something; a place for doing something. A building, plant, road, reservoir, etc.

- Field Supervision (or field non-manual) - supervisory personnel and all other non-manual staff at the construction site.
- Foreman - the worker or tradesman who is in charge of a construction crew. The foreman may be a hands-on worker who contributes to the work completion or a non-working foreman. A general foreman may be in charge of all or some crews.
- Fringe Benefits - labour cost elements which are provided to pay for benefits received by workers, such as health insurance, pension, training, etc.

G

- General & Administrative Costs (G&A) - the costs of operating a construction business. These costs include such things as office space, office staff, operating facilites, etc. They are not associated with any specific project, but may be allocated across projects in a cost estimate.
- General contractor is responsible for the day-to-day oversight of a construction site, management of vendors and trades, and communication of information to involved parties throughout the course of a building project.
- General requirements - costs for general requirements (Division 1) of the project execution which are actually part of the deliverable. Examples: project management & coordination 47, temporary facilities & controls, cleaning & waste management, commissioning.

I

- Indirect costs are costs that are not directly accountable to a cost object (such as a particular project, facility, function or product).

L

- Labour – a category of cost which is incurred to employ people (workers, crafts, trades, etc.) in the execution of construction work activity.
- Labour burden is the cost of payroll taxes and insurances (such as Workers' compensation) which the employer must pay to employ workers.
- Labour rate (sometimes price) – the amount of currency per unit of time which is required to employ people (workers, crafts, trades, etc.) in the execution of construction work activity. The

rate may represent the wage rate only, or may include various benefits and labour burdens.

- Line item - one element of cost in an estimate which is listed in the estimate spreadsheet.
- Location cost index (or factor) - the ratio of the cost in one location to that in another location. These may include or exclude currency exchange rates. Example: 223 in Boston / 187 in Austin = 1.19. The location cost factor is used to adjust the cost from one location to another. To adjust a known cost in Austin to that in Boston, multiply the Austin cost by 1.19.
- Lump sum – "the complete in-place cost of a system, a subsystem, a particular item, or an entire project."

M

- Man-hour (mh) – one person's (worker, craftsman, tradesman, etc.) effort for one hour of time. Note: some attempt to make this gender neautral, even though there is no need, by renaming this as work hour or job hour or person hour, or something similar.
- Man-hour norms - a set of standard man-hour rates for work tasks, given normal working conditions.
- Man-hour rate – the amount of man-hours which are consumed executing one unit of work activity. Man-hour rate = man-hours required for work / completed work quantity. Example: Excavation 0.125 mh/cy. The man-hour rate is related to the inverse of the production rate times the number of workers in the crew performing the work. Example: Excavation at 80 cy/day (8 hour day) with 2-man crew = 2 x 8 / 80 = 0.2 man-hours/cy.
- Mark-up is the difference between the cost of a good or service and its selling price. A markup is added on to the total cost incurred by the producer of a good or service in order to create a profit.
- Manual labour is physical work done by people involved in construction the project. All of the various trade workers are included in manual labour, including foremen.
- Means & methods - the means and methods used in executing the work.

N

- Non-manual labour - work done by people who are not classified as manual labour.

- Non-productive time - work time which is paid but does not contribute to the production of work. Examples: safety meeting, travel time, clean up time, wash up time, etc.

O

- Open shop is a place of employment at which one is not required to join or financially support a union (closed shop) as a condition of hiring or continued employment. Open shop is also known as a merit shop.
- Overhead - In business, overhead or overhead expense refers to an ongoing expense of operating a business; it is also known as an "operating expense."
- Overtime is the amount of time someone works beyond normal working hours.

P

- Per diem - a daily allowance for expenses, a specific amount of money that an organization gives an individual per day to cover living and travelling expenses (allowance) in connection with work done away from home or on tour. (Latin for "per day" or "for each day")
- Plug number - a value inserted in an estimate as a place holder and an approximation of the cost for a scope element which has not been detailed yet.
- Premium pay - the extra portion of wages paid when a worker works overtime. Example: Wage rate is 10.00/hour, overtime is paid at time and a half, or 15.00/hour, the premium pay is 5.00/ hour.
- Price is the quantity of payment or compensation given by one party to another in return for goods or services.
- Pricing is the function of determining the amount of money asked in consideration for undertaking the project. Depending on the market and profit considerations, etc., the price may be more or less than the cost.
- Production rate – the quantity of work which is completed in one unit of time. Production rate = completed work quantity / duration. Example: Excavation 80 cy/day = 10 cy/hour (in an 8 hour day). RSMeans lists this as Daily Output.
- Productivity is the term which relates one rate to another rate, given two differing sets of conditions for the same work. A

production rate greater than the reference production rate indicates a higher productivity. A production rate less than the reference production rate indicates a lower productivity. A man-hour rate greater than the reference man-hour rate indicates a lower productivity. A man-hour rate less than the reference man-hour rate indicates a higher productivity. (The economic concept of productivity is an average measure of the efficiency of production. Productivity is a ratio of production output to what is required to produce it (inputs).)

- Productivity factor – the ratio of a selected production rate to a reference production rate. Example: selected rate = 102, reference rate = 80, productivity factor = 102/80 = 1.28. Alternatively – the ratio of a reference man-hour rate to a selected man-hour rate. Example: selected rate = 0.104, reference rate = 0.125, productivity factor = 0.125/0.104 = 1.20. A productivity factor is often used to adjust a set of standard or normal (norm) production or man-hour rates to a set of rates for a specific project, location, or set of working conditions. Example: Specific type of excavation – standard = 150 cy/day. For specific project, location, or conditions the productivity factor is 0.80. The resulting production rate for that is 150 x 0.8 = 120 cy/day. The actual productivity factor for a project or subset of production rates (or man-hour rates) is the ratio of the actual production rate to the estimated production rate.
- Profit - in accounting, is the difference between revenue and cost. In estimates, it is an allowance to provide for anticipated profit upon completion of the project.
- Profit margin refers to a measure of profitability. It is calculated by finding the net profit as a percentage of the revenue.
- Project - A temporary endeavour undertaken to create a unique product, service, or result.

Q

- Quality can mean a high degree of excellence ("a quality product") or a degree of excellence or the lack of it ("work of average quality").
- Quantify
- Quantity is a property that can exist as a magnitude or multitude. For example 1200 mm or 10 each.
- Quantity surveyor (QS) is a professional working within the construction industry concerned with building costs, in the U.K.

and some other areas. A QS employs standard methods of measurement to develop a bill of quantities.

R

- Resources are what is required to carry out a project's tasks. They can be people, equipment, facilities, materials, tools, supplies, or anything else capable of definition required for the completion of a project activity.

S

- Schedule of values is a detailed statement furnished by a construction contractor, builder or others outlining the portions of the contract sum. It allocates values for the various parts of the work and is also used as the basis for submitting and reviewing progress payments.
- Scope of a project in project management is the sum total of all of its products and their requirements or features.
- Specification - an explicit set of requirements to be satisfied by a material, product, or service.
- Subcontractor is an individual or in many cases a business that signs a contract to perform part or all of the obligations of another's contract.
- Supplier - A distributor or other company which supplies materials, parts, equipment, etc.

T

- Take off - the process of reviewing and understanding the design package and using the project scope drawings and documents to itemize the scope into line items with measured quantities. RSMeans refers to this as, "Scope out the project," and, "Quantify."
- Task - a distinct piece of work performed.
- Tool - any physical item that can be used to achieve a goal, especially if the item is not consumed in the process.

U

- Unit Cost - the cost for one measured unit of completed work activity.

V

- Virtual Design and Construction (VDC) is the use of integrated multi-disciplinary performance models of design-construction projects, including the Product (i.e., facilities), Work Processes and Organization of the design - construction - operation team in order to support explicit and public business objectives. In VDC (BIM is one method) the modelling consists of the usual three dimensions, plus the time dimension and the cost dimension.

W

- Work (1) is the amount of effort applied to produce a deliverable or to accomplish a task, (2) is everything required or supplied to complete a construction project.
- Work breakdown structure (WBS) - a deliverable oriented decomposition of a project into smaller components. It defines and groups a project's discrete work elements in a way that helps organize and define the total work scope of the project.
- Worker - a person engaged in the accomplishment of work. In cost estimating, the hands-on workers contribute to the production and are counted in calculations of the production rate. Other workers supervise or support the hands-on work in some way.
- Wage rate - The agreed monetary compensation per hour for a person to accomplish work. This is the pay provided to the worker, excluding any fringe benefits or other labour burdens. Labour unions typically have negotiated agreements which define the wage rates for workers, as well as the rates for fringe benefits.

2

Project Planning

Project planning is part of project management, which relates to the use of schedules such as Gantt charts to plan and subsequently report progress within the project environment.

Initially, the project scope is defined and the appropriate methods for completing the project are determined. Following this step, the durations for the various tasks necessary to complete the work are listed and grouped into a work breakdown structure. Project planning is often used to organize different areas of a project, including project plans, work loads and the management of teams and individuals.

The logical dependencies between tasks are defined using an activity network diagram that enables identification of the critical path. Float or slack time in the schedule can be calculated using project management software. Then the necessary resources can be estimated and costs for each activity can be allocated to each resource, giving the total project cost. At this stage, the project schedule may be optimized to achieve the appropriate balance between resource usage and project duration to comply with the project objectives.

Once established and agreed, the project schedule becomes what is known as the baseline schedule. Progress will be measured against the baseline schedule throughout the life of the project. Analyzing progress compared to the baseline schedule is known as earned value management.

The inputs of the project planning phase include the project charter and the concept proposal. The outputs of the project planning phase include the project requirements, the project schedule, and the project management plan.

Gantt Chart

A Gantt chart is a type of bar chart, developed by Henry Gantt in the 1910s, that illustrates a project schedule. Gantt charts illustrate the start and finish dates of the terminal elements and summary elements of a project. Terminal elements and summary elements comprise the work breakdown structure of the project. Some Gantt charts also show the dependency (i.e. precedence network) relationships between activities. Gantt charts can be used to show current schedule status using percent-complete shadings and a vertical "TODAY" line as shown here.

Although now regarded as a common charting technique, Gantt charts were considered revolutionary when first introduced. In recognition of Henry Gantt's contributions, the Henry Laurence Gantt Medal is awarded for distinguished achievement in management and in community service. This chart is also used in information technology to represent data that has been collected.

Historical Development

The first known tool of this type was developed in 1896 by Karol Adamiecki, who called it a *harmonogram*. Adamiecki published his chart in 1931, however, only in Polish, which limited both its adoption and recognition of his authorship. The chart is named after Henry Gantt (1861–1919), who designed his chart around the years 1910–1915.

One of the first major applications of Gantt charts was during World War I. On the initiative of General William Crozier, then Chief of Ordnance these included that of the Emergency Fleet, the Shipping Board, etc.

In the 1980s, personal computers allowed for widespread creation of complex and elaborate Gantt charts. The first desktop applications were intended mainly for project managers and project schedulers. With the advent of the Internet and increased collaboration over networks at the end of the 1990s, Gantt charts became a common feature of web-based applications, including collaborative groupware.

Advantages and Limitations

Gantt charts have become common technique for representing the phases and activities of a project work breakdown structure (WBS), so they can be understood by a wide audience all over the world. The technique is frequently used in Project Management to help break down the project.

A common error made by those who equate Gantt chart design with project design is that they attempt to define the project work breakdown structure at the same time that they define scheduled activities. This practice makes it very difficult to follow the 100% Rule. Instead the WBS should be fully defined to follow the 100% Rule, then the project schedule can be designed.

Although a Gantt chart is useful and valuable for small projects that fit on a single sheet or screen, they can become quite unwieldy for projects with more than about 30 activities. Larger Gantt charts may not be suitable for most computer displays. A related criticism is that Gantt charts communicate relatively little information per unit area of display. That is, projects are often considerably more complex than can be communicated effectively with a Gantt chart.

Gantt charts only represent part of the triple constraints (cost, time and scope) on projects, because they focus primarily on schedule management. Moreover, Gantt charts do not represent the size of a project or the relative size of work elements, therefore the magnitude of a behind-schedule condition is easily miscommunicated. If two projects are the same number of days behind schedule, the larger project has a larger effect on resource utilization, yet the Gantt does not represent this difference.

Although project management software can show schedule dependencies as lines between activities, displaying a large number of dependencies may result in a cluttered or unreadable chart.

Because the horizontal bars of a Gantt chart have a fixed height, they can misrepresent the time-phased workload (resource requirements) of a project, which may cause confusion especially in large projects. In the example shown in this article, Activities E and G appear to be the same size, but in reality they may be different orders of magnitude. A related criticism is that all activities of a Gantt chart show planned workload as constant. In practice, many activities (especially summary elements) have front-loaded or back-loaded work plans, so a Gantt chart with percent-complete shading may actually miscommunicate the true schedule performance status.

Example

In the following example there are seven tasks, labelled *A* through *G*. Some tasks can be done concurrently (*A* and *B*) while others cannot be done until their predecessor task is complete (*C* cannot begin until *A* is complete). Additionally, each task has three time estimates: the optimistic time estimate (*O*), the most likely or normal time estimate (*M*), and the pessimistic time estimate (*P*). The expected time (T_E) is computed using the beta probability distribution for the time estimates, using the formula $(O + 4M + P) \div 6$.

Activity	*Predecessor*	*Time estimates*			*Expected time*
		Opt. (O)	*Normal (M)*	*Pess. (P)*	
A	—	2	4	6	4.00
B	—	3	5	9	5.33
C	*A*	4	5	7	5.17
D	*A*	4	6	10	6.33
E	*B, C*	4	5	7	5.17
F	*D*	3	4	8	4.50
G	*E*	3	5	8	5.17

Project Stakeholder

Project stakeholders are those entities within or outside an organization which:

1. sponsor a project, or
2. have an interest or a gain upon a successful completion of a project;
3. may have a positive or negative influence in the project completion.

Examples of project stakeholders include the customer, the user group, the project manager, the development team, the testers, etc.

Stakeholders are anyone who has an interest in the project. Project stakeholders are individuals and organizations that are actively involved in the project, or whose interests may be affected as a result of project execution or project completion. They may also exert influence over the project's objectives and outcomes. The project management team must identify the stakeholders, determine their requirements and expectations, and, to the extent possible, manage their influence in relation to the requirements to ensure a successful project.

The following are examples of project stakeholders:

- Project leader
- Project team members
- Upper management
- Project customer
- Resource Managers
- Line Managers
- Product user group
- Project testers

There are narrower views of the term stakeholder, focusing on the influencers and decision makers of a business or technological change. In this context, stakeholders are managers who have the organizational authority to allocate resources (people, money, services) and set priorities for their own organizations in support of a change. They are the people who make or break a change.

The rationale for this emphasis on decision maker is reinforced by the views of John Kotter, a professor at the Harvard Business School and the author of numerous books on corporate culture, change and leadership. In an interview published in CIO Insight magazine, Kotter said, "I've seen too many technology projects get dumped on project teams and task forces that simply don't have enough clout, enough credibility, connections, you name it, to be able to do a difficult job, and so, surprise, surprise, they start getting frustrated and the powerful people in the company just ignore them or do what they want to do anyway. Also, on a lot of the IT projects, if you go up to the typical line manager and say to him, 'You've got this big thing going on here. What's the vision? Paint a picture for me. How's the company going to be different in 18 months when this is all done?' They can't even see it. So of course they haven't bought into it. And if they haven't bought into it, are they going to cooperate?"

Delphi method

The Delphi method is a structured communication technique, originally developed as a systematic, interactive forecasting method which relies on a panel of experts. The experts answer questionnaires in two or more rounds. After each round, a facilitator provides an anonymous summary of the experts' forecasts from the previous round as well as the reasons they provided for their judgements. Thus, experts are encouraged to revise their earlier answers in light of the replies of other members of their panel. It is believed that during this process the range of the answers will decrease and the group will converge towards the "correct" answer. Finally, the process is stopped after a pre-defined stop criterion (e.g. number of rounds, achievement of consensus, stability of results) and the mean or median scores of the final rounds determine the results. Delphi is based on the principle that forecasts (or decisions) from a structured group of individuals are more accurate than those from unstructured groups. The technique can also be adapted for use in face-to-face meetings, and is then called mini-Delphi or Estimate-Talk-Estimate (ETE). Delphi has been widely used for business forecasting and has certain advantages over another structured forecasting approach, prediction markets.

History

The name "Delphi" derives from the Oracle of Delphi. The authors of the method were not happy with this name, because it implies "something oracular, something smacking a little of the occult". The Delphi method is based on the assumption that group judgements are more valid than individual judgements.

The Delphi method was developed at the beginning of the Cold War to forecast the impact of technology on warfare. In 1944, General Henry H. Arnold ordered the creation of the report for the U.S. Army Air Corps on the future technological capabilities that might be used by the military.

Different approaches were tried, but the shortcomings of traditional forecasting methods, such as theoretical approach, quantitative models or trend extrapolation, in areas where precise scientific laws have not been established yet, quickly became apparent. To combat these shortcomings, the Delphi method was developed by Project RAND during the 1950-1960s (1959) by Olaf Helmer, Norman Dalkey, and Nicholas Rescher. It has been used ever since, together with various modifications and reformulations, such as the Imen-Delphi procedure.

Experts were asked to give their opinion on the probability, frequency, and intensity of possible enemy attacks. Other experts could anonymously give feedback. This process was repeated several times until a consensus emerged.

Key Characteristics

The following key characteristics of the Delphi method help the participants to focus on the issues at hand and separate Delphi from other methodologies:

Anonymity of the Participants

Usually all participants remain anonymous. Their identity is not revealed, even after the completion of the final report. This prevents the authority, personality, or reputation of some participants from dominating others in the process. Arguably, it also frees participants (to some extent) from their personal biases, minimizes the "bandwagon effect" or "halo effect", allows free expression of opinions, encourages open critique, and facilitates admission of errors when revising earlier judgements.

Structuring of Information Flow

The initial contributions from the experts are collected in the form of answers to questionnaires and their comments to these answers.

The panel director controls the interactions among the participants by processing the information and filtering out irrelevant content. This avoids the negative effects of face-to-face panel discussions and solves the usual problems of group dynamics.

Regular Feedback

Participants comment on their own forecasts, the responses of others and on the progress of the panel as a whole. At any moment they can revise their earlier statements. While in regular group meetings participants tend to stick to previously stated opinions and often conform too much to the group leader; the Delphi method prevents it.

Role of the Facilitator

The person coordinating the Delphi method can be known as a *facilitator* or Leader, and facilitates the responses of their *panel of experts*, who are selected for a reason, usually that they hold knowledge on an opinion or view. The facilitator sends out questionnaires, surveys etc. and if the panel of experts accept, they follow instructions and present their views. Responses are collected and analyzed, then common and conflicting viewpoints are identified. If consensus is not reached, the process continues through thesis and antithesis, to gradually work towards synthesis, and building consensus.

Applications

Use in Forecasting: First applications of the Delphi method were in the field of science and technology forecasting. The objective of the method was to combine expert opinions on likelihood and expected development time, of the particular technology, in a single indicator. One of the first such reports, prepared in 1964 by Gordon and Helmer, assessed the direction of long-term trends in science and technology development, covering such topics as scientific breakthroughs, population control, automation, space progress, war prevention and weapon systems. Other forecasts of technology were dealing with vehicle-highway systems, industrial robots, intelligent internet, broadband connections, and technology in education.

Later the Delphi method was applied in other areas, especially those related to public policy issues, such as economic trends, health and education. It was also applied successfully and with high accuracy in business forecasting. For example, in one case reported by Basu and Schroeder (1977), the Delphi method predicted the sales of a new product during the first two years with inaccuracy of 3–4% compared with actual sales. Quantitative methods produced errors of 10–15%, and traditional unstructured forecast methods had errors of about 20%.

The Delphi method has also been used as a tool to implement multi-stakeholder approaches for participative policy-making in developing countries. The governments of Latin America and the Caribbean have successfully used the Delphi method as an open-ended public-private sector approach to identify the most urgent challenges for their regional ICT-for-developmenteLAC Action Plans. As a result, governments have widely acknowledged the value of collective intelligence from civil society, academic and private sector participants of the Delphi, especially in a field of rapid change, such as technology policies.

Use in Policy-making

From the 1970s, the use of the Delphi technique in public policy-making introduces a number of methodological innovations. In particular:

- the need to examine several types of items (not only *forecasting* items but, typically, *issue* items, *goal* items, and *option* items) leads to introducing different evaluation scales which are not used in the standard Delphi. These often include *desirability*, *feasibility* (technical and political) and *probability*, which the analysts can use to outline different scenarios: the *desired* scenario (from desirability), the *potential* scenario (from feasibility) and the *expected* scenario (from probability);
- the complexity of the issues posed in public policy-making leads to give more importance to the arguments supporting the evaluations of the panelists; so these are often invited to list arguments for and against each option item, and sometimes they are given the possibility to suggest new items to be submitted to the panel;
- for the same reason, the scaling methods, which are used to measure panel evaluations, often include more sophisticated approaches such as multi-dimensional scaling.

Further innovations come from the use of computer-based (and later web-based) Delphi conferences. According to Turoff and Hiltz, in computer-based Delphis:

- the iteration structure used in the paper Delphis, which is divided into three or more discrete rounds, can be replaced by a process of continuous (roundless) interaction, enabling panelists to change their evaluations at any time;

- the statistical group response can be updated in real-time, and shown whenever a panelist provides a new evaluation.

According to Bolognini, web-based Delphis offer two further possibilities, relevant in the context of interactive policy-making and e-democracy. These are:

- the involvement of a large number of participants,
- the use of two or more panels representing different groups (such as policy-makers, experts, citizens), which the administrator can give tasks reflecting their diverse roles and expertise, and make them to interact within ad hoc communication structures. For example, the *policy community* members (policy-makers and experts) may interact as part of the *main conference* panel, while they receive inputs from a *virtual community* (citizens, associations etc.) involved in a *side conference*. These web-based variable communication structures, which he calls *Hyperdelphi* (HD), are designed to make Delphi conferences "more fluid and adapted to the hypertextual and interactive nature of digital communication".

One successful example of a (partially) web-based policy Delphi is the five-round Delphi exercise (with 1,454 contributions) for the creation of the eLAC Action Plans in Latin America. It is believed to be the most extensive online participatory policy-making foresight exercise in the history of intergovernmental processes in the developing world at this time. In addition to the specific policy guidance provided, the authors list the following lessons learned include "(1) the potential of Policy Delphi methods to introduce transparency and accountability into public decision-making, especially in developing countries; (2) the utility of foresight exercises to foster multi-agency networking in the development community; (3) the usefulness of embedding foresight exercises into established mechanisms of representative democracy and international multilateralism, such as the United Nations; (4) the potential of online tools to facilitate participation in resource-scarce developing countries; and (5) the resource-efficiency stemming from the scale of international foresight exercises, and therefore its adequacy for resource-scarce regions."

Online Delphi Systems

A number of Delphi forecasts are conducted using web sites that allow the process to be conducted in real-time. For instance, the TechCast Project uses a panel of 100 experts worldwide to forecast breakthroughs in all fields of science and technology. Another example is the Horizon Project, where educational futurists collaborate online using the Delphi method to come up with the technological advancements to look out for in education for the next few years.

Variations

Traditionally the Delphi method has aimed at a consensus of the most probable future by iteration. Other versions, such as the Policy Delphi, is instead a decision support method aiming at structuring and discussing the diverse views of the preferred future. In Europe, more recent web-based experiments have used the Delphi method as a communication technique for interactive decision-making and e-democracy. The Argument Delphi, was developed by OsmoKuusi, focuses on ongoing discussion and finding relevant arguments rather than focusing on the output. The Disaggregative Policy Delphi, developed by Petri Tapio, uses cluster analysis as a systematic tool to construct various scenarios of the future in the latest Delphi round. The respondent's view on the probable and the preferable future are dealt with as separate cases.

Discussion

Overall the track record of the Delphi method is mixed. There have been many cases when the method produced poor results. Still, some authors attribute this to poor application of the method and not to the weaknesses of the method itself. It must also be realized that in areas such as science and technology forecasting, the degree of uncertainty is so great that exact and always correct predictions are impossible, so a high degree of error is to be expected.

Another particular weakness of the Delphi method is that future developments are not always predicted correctly by consensus of experts. Firstly, the issue of ignorance is important. If panelists are misinformed about a topic, the use of Delphi may only add confidence to their ignorance. Secondly, sometimes unconventional thinking of amateur outsiders may represent the disrupting element the experts could not predict, as described in the black swan theory. One of the initial problems of the method was its inability to make complex forecasts with multiple factors. Potential future outcomes were usually considered as if they had no effect on each other. Later on, several extensions to the Delphi method were developed to address this problem, such as cross impact analysis, that takes into consideration the possibility that the occurrence of one event may change probabilities of other events covered in the survey. Still the Delphi method can be used most successfully in forecasting single scalar indicators.

Despite these shortcomings, today the Delphi method is a widely accepted forecasting tool and has been used successfully for thousands of studies in areas varying from technology forecasting to drug abuse.

Delphi vs. Prediction Markets

Delphi has characteristics similar to prediction markets as both are structured approaches that aggregate diverse opinions from groups. Yet, there are differences that may be decisive for their relative applicability for different problems.

Some advantages of prediction markets derive from the possibility to provide incentives for participation.

1. They can motivate people to participate over a long period of time and to reveal their true beliefs.
2. They aggregate information automatically and instantly incorporate new information in the forecast.
3. Participants do not have to be selected and recruited manually by a facilitator. They themselves decide whether to participate if they think their private information is not yet incorporated in the forecast.

Delphi seems to have these advantages over prediction markets:

1. Participants reveal their reasoning
2. It is easier to maintain confidentiality
3. Potentially quicker forecasts if experts are readily available.

Conspiracy Theory

American conservative Field Searcy has theorized that the Delphi method amounts to a form of attempted mind control. This particular theory was given apparent credence by the Georgia State Senate Majority Leader Chip Rogers. Senator Rogers invited Mr. Searcy to the state Capitol in Atlanta, to speak on the separate conspiracy theories regarding the UN initiative Agenda 21. Mr. Searcy is quoted as saying that liberal groups will attempt to enact Agenda 21 through using the Delphi method as form of mind control: "They do that by a process known as the Delphi technique. The Delphi technique was developed by the Rand Corporation during the Cold War as a mind-control technique. It's also known as 'consensive[sic] process.' But basically the goal of the Delphi technique is to lead a targeted group of people to a pre-determined outcome while keeping the illusion of being open to public input."

Construction Management

Construction management or construction project management (CPM) is the overall planning, coordination, and control of a project from beginning to completion. CPM is aimed at meeting a client's requirement in order to produce a functionally and financially viable project.

CPM is project management that applies to the construction sector. The construction industry is composed of five sectors: residential, commercial, heavy civil, industrial, and environmental. A construction manager holds the same responsibilities and completes the same processes in each sector. All that separates a construction manager in one sector from one in another is the knowledge of the construction site. This may include different types of equipment, materials, subcontractors, and possibly locations.

A contractor is assigned to a construction project once the design has been completed by the architect or is still in progress. This is done by going through a bidding process with different contractors. The contractor is selected by using one of three common selection methods: low-bid selection, best-value selection, or qualifications-based selection.

A construction manager should have the ability to handle public safety, time management, decision making, mathematics, and human resources.

Functions

The functions of Construction management typically include the following:

1. Specifying project objectives and plans including delineation of scope, budgeting, scheduling, setting performance requirements, and selecting project participants.
2. Maximizing the resource efficiency through procurement of labour, materials and equipment.
3. Implementing various operations through proper coordination and control of planning, design, estimating, contracting and construction in the entire process.
4. Developing effective communications and mechanisms for resolving conflicts.:

The Construction Management Association of America (a US construction management certification and advocacy body) says the 120 most common responsibilities of a Construction Manager fall into the following 7 categories: Project Management Planning, Cost Management, Time Management, Quality Management, Contract Administration, Safety Management, and CM Professional Practice. CM professional practice includes specific activities, such as defining the responsibilities and management structure of the project management team, organizing and leading by implementing project controls, defining roles and responsibilities, developing communication protocols, and identifying elements of project design and construction likely to give rise to disputes and claims.

The Five Types of Construction

- Residential: Residential construction includes individual homes, apartments, condominiums, townhouses, and other housing types.
- Commercial: This refers to construction dealing with the needs of commerce, trade, and government. Examples include shopping centres, schools, banks, hospitals, theaters, and government buildings.
- Heavy Civil: The construction of transportation infrastructure such as roads, bridges, railroads, tunnels, and airports. Dams are also included here, but other water-related infrastructure is considered environmental.
- Industrial: Buildings and other constructed items used for product production, including chemical plants, steel mills, oil refineries, manufacturing plants, and pipelines.
- Environmental: Environmental construction used to be part of heavy civil, but is now its own section, dealing with projects that improve the environment. Some examples are sanitary sewers, waste management, and clean water.

Construction Management Jobs

- Planning Engineer
- Project coordinator
- Field Engineer
- Office Engineer
- Quantity Surveyor
- Project Engineer
- Area Superintendent
- Project Superintendent

- Project Manager
- Estimator
- Lead Estimator
- Senior Estimator
- Chief Estimator
- Project Executive.

Obtaining the Project

Bids: A bid is given to the owner by construction managers that are willing to complete their construction project. A bid tells the owner how much money they should expect to pay the construction management company in order for them to complete the project.

- Open Bid: An open bid is used for public projects. Any and all contractors are allowed to submit their bid due to public advertising.
- Closed Bid: A closed bid is used for private projects. A selection of contractors are sent an invitation for bid so only they can submit a bid for the specified project.

Selection Methods

- Low-bid selection: This selection focuses on the price of a project. Multiple construction management companies submit a bid to the owner that is the lowest amount they are willing to do the job for. Then the owner usually chooses the company with the lowest bid to complete the job for them.
- Best-value selection: This selection focuses on both the price and qualifications of the contractors submitting bids. This means that the owner chooses the contractor with the best price and the best qualifications. The owner decides by using a request for proposal (RFP), which provides the owner with the contractor's exact form of scheduling and budgeting that the contractor expects to use for the project.
- Qualifications-based selection: This selection is used when the owner decides to choose the contractor only on the basis of their qualifications. The owner then uses a request for qualifications (RFQ), which provides the owner with the contractor's experience, management plans, project organization, and budget and schedule performance. The owner may also ask for safety records and individual credentials of their members.

Payment Contracts

- Lump-sum: This is the most common type of contract. The construction manager and the owner agree on the overall cost of the construction project and the owner is responsible for paying that amount whether the construction project exceeds or falls below the agreed price of payment.
- Cost-Plus-Fee: This contract provides payment for the contractor including the total cost of the project as well as a fixed fee or percentage of the total cost. This contract is beneficial to the contractor since any additional costs will be paid for even though they were unexpected for the owner.
- Guaranteed Maximum Price: This contract is the same as the cost-plus-fee contract although there is a set price that the overall cost and fee do not go above.
- Unit-Price: This contract is used when the cost cannot be determined ahead of time. The owner provides materials with a specific unit price to limit spending.

Project Stages

Design: The design stage contains a lot of steps: programming and feasibility, schematic design, design development, and contract documents. It is the responsibility of the design team to ensure that the design meets all building codes and regulations. It is during the design stage that the bidding process takes place.

- Programming and feasibility: The needs, goals, and objectives must be determined for the building. Decisions must be made on the building size, number of rooms, how the space will be used, and who will be using the space. This must all be considered to begin the actual designing of the building.
- Schematic design: Schematic designs are sketches used to identify spaces, shapes, and patterns. Materials, sizes, colours, and textures must be considered in the sketches.
- Design development (DD): This step requires research and investigation into what materials and equipment will be used as well as their cost.
- Contract documents (CDs): Contract documents are the final drawings and specifications of the construction project. They are used by contractors to determine their bid while builders use them for the construction process. Contract documents can also be called working drawings.

Pre-Construction

The pre-construction stage begins when the owner gives a notice to proceed to the contractor that they have chosen through the bidding process. A notice to proceed is when the owner gives permission to the contractor to begin their work on the project. The first step is to assign the project team which includes the project manager (PM), contract administrator, superintendent, and field engineer.

- Project manager: The project manager is in charge of the project team.
- Contract administrator: The contract administrator assists the project manager as well as the superintendent with the details of the construction contract.
- Superintendent: It is the superintendent's job to make sure everything is on schedule including flow of materials, deliveries, and equipment. They are also in charge of coordinating on-site construction activities.
- Field Engineer: A field engineer is considered an entry-level position and is responsible for paperwork.

During the pre-construction stage, a site investigation must take place. A site investigation takes place to discover if any steps need to be implemented on the job site. This is in order to get the site ready before the actual construction begins. This also includes any unforeseen conditions such as historical artifacts or environment problems. A soil test must be done to determine if the soil is in good condition to be built upon.

Procurement

The procurement stage is when labour, materials and equipment needed to complete the project are purchased. This can be done by the general contractor if the company does all their own construction work. If the contractor does not do their own work, they obtain it through subcontractors. Subcontractors are contractors who specialize in one particular aspect of the construction work such as concrete, melding, glass, or carpentry. Subcontractors are hired the same way a general contractor would be, which is through the bidding process. Purchase orders are also part of the procurement stage.

- Purchase orders: A purchase order is used in various types of businesses. In this case, a purchase order is an agreement between a buyer and seller that the products purchased meet the required specifications for the agreed price.

Construction

The construction stage begins with a pre-construction meeting brought together by the superintendent. The pre-construction meeting is meant to make decisions dealing with work hours, material storage, quality control, and site access. The next step is to move everything onto the construction site and set it all up.

At this stage, construction monitoring and supervision is of great importance to ensure that a project is completed on time and on budget, while meeting all relevant regulations and quality standards.

Contractor Progress Payment Schedule

A Contractor progress payment schedule is a schedule of when (according to project milestones or specified dates) contractors and suppliers will be paid for the current progress of installed work.

Progress payments are partial payments for work completed during a portion, usually a month, during a construction period. Progress payments are made to general contractors, subcontractors, and suppliers as construction projects progress. Payments are typically made on a monthly basis but could be modified to meet certain milestones. Progress payments are an important part of contract administration for the contractor. Proper preparation of the information necessary for payment processing can help the contractor financially complete the project.

Post-Construction

Once the construction has been completed there are specific steps that must be taken to prepare the building for occupancy.

- Project punchout: A project punchout means that the project must be looked at for any issues before it is considered completely finished. Issues may include replacing a cracked tile on the floor or changing the colour of paint. A list is created containing these issues and it is known as a punch list or a snag list.
- Substantial completion: The architect for the project determines if the building meets every requirement and issues a certificate of substantial completion. This certificate announces the official completion of the project.
- Final inspection: A final inspection is done by the building official once the certificate of substantial completion has been issued.

- Certificate of Occupancy: A certificate of occupancy is issued by the building official which informs the owner that it is now safe to occupy. This is issued by the building official after the final inspection.
- Commissioning: This is the process of testing systems and equipment to ensure that they are working correctly. Then the owner must be trained to properly operate the systems and equipment in the building.
- Final documentation: This provides information on the building to the owner for future references. This includes warranties, operation manuals, inspection and testing reports, and record drawings.
- Final completion: Final completion occurs when all required paperwork and documentation is completed, including payments to the contractor.

Owner Occupancy

Once the owner moves into the building, a warranty period begins. This is to ensure that all materials, equipment, and quality meet the expectations of the owner that are included within the contract.

Dust and Mud

Environmental Protections:

- Storm water pollution: As a result of construction, the soil is displaced from its original location which can possibly cause environmental problems in the future. Runoff can occur during storms which can possibly transfer harmful pollutants through the soil to rivers, lakes, wetlands, and coastal waters.
- Endangered species: If endangered species have been found on the construction site, the site must be shut down for some time. The construction site must be shut down for as long as it takes for authorities to make a decision on the situation. Once the situation has been assessed, the contractor makes the appropriate accommodations to not disturb the species.
- Vegetation: There may often be particular trees or other vegetation that must be protected on the job site. This may require fences or security tape to warn builders that they must not be harmed.
- Wetlands: The contractor must make accommodations so that erosion and water flow are not affected by construction. Any

liquid spills must be maintained due to contaminants that may enter the wetland.

- Historical or Cultural artifacts:Artifacts may include arrowheads, pottery shards, and bones. All work comes to a halt if any artifacts are found and will not resume until they can be properly examined and removed from the area.

Construction Activity Documentation

Project Meetings: Project meetings take place at scheduled intervals to discuss the progress on the construction site and any concerns or issues. The discussion and any decisions made at the meeting must be documented.

Diaries, Logs, and Daily Field Reports

Diaries, logs, and daily field reports keep track of the daily activities on a job site each day.

- Diaries: Each member of the project team is expected to keep a project diary. The diary contains summaries of the day's events in the member's own words. They are used to keep track of any daily work activity, conversations, observations, or any other relevant information regarding the construction activities. Diaries can be referred to when disputes arise and a diary happens to contain information connected with the disagreement. Diaries that are handwritten can be used as evidence in court.
- Logs: Logs keep track of the regular activities on the job site such as phone logs, transmittal logs, delivery logs, and RFI (Request for Information) logs.
- Daily Field Reports: Daily field reports are a more formal way of recording information on the job site. They contain information that includes the day's activities, temperature and weather conditions, delivered equipment or materials, visitors on the site, and equipment used that day.

Resolving Disputes

- Mediation:Mediation uses a third party mediator to resolve any disputes. The mediator helps both disputing parties to come to a mutual agreement. This process ensures that no attorneys become involved in the dispute and is less time-consuming.
- Minitrial: A minitrial takes more time and money than a mediation. The minitrial takes place in an informal setting and

involves some type of advisor or attorney that must be paid. The disputing parties may come to an agreement or the third party advisor may offer their advice. The agreement is nonbinding and can be broken.

- Arbitration:Arbitration is the most costly and time-consuming way to resolve a dispute. Each party is represented by an attorney while witnesses and evidence are presented. Once all information is provided on the issue, the arbitrator makes a ruling which provides the final decision. The arbitrator provides the final decision on what must be done and it is a binding agreement between each of the disputing parties.

Terminology

The following terms are commonly used in the industry:

- Construction management (CM) refers to form of delivery and (in the UK) management of the site.
- Real estate management (REM) is professional property advice (a continuous process, as opposed to a process).
  - o Corporate real estate management (CREM) is a company-focused variant.
- Management contracting (MC):
  - o UK: form of delivery
  - o US: CM at risk
- Programme management (ProgM) is concerned with management of a client's portfolio (the programme, in this sense, is equivalent to a client's brief) or (in the UK) managing time in a project.
- Project control (PC) is the tracking and reporting of the progress, time, cost and quality of a project. This function can be characterized as passive, whereas construction project management (CPM) is active.
- Project leader (PL): The person responsible for achieving the project's objectives; acts as a manager "in-line".
- Project director (PD): The leader of a large project that can be broken down into sub-projects (e.g. the Channel tunnel) or the head of a PM organization
- Owner representative (OR): The representative of the owner; may be internal or external to the company
- Document Control (DC): Key function of a project manager

- Build operate transfer (BOT)
  - Finance build operate transfer (FBOT)
  - Design build operate transfer (DBOT)
- Build own operate (BOO)
- Engineering procurement construction (EPC)
- Private finance initiative (PFI)
- General contract (GC)
- Joint Venture (JV): A collaboration between two or more companies from the same or different backgrounds and/or fields to complete a common project. Joint Ventures typically have a lead contractor that deals with most of the business aspects. The lead will usually have a bigger stake in the partnership (ie. the lead will have a 65% stake while the second contractor might have 30% and a third might have 5%).
- Guaranteed maximum price (GMP): A contract-specified upper limit to the project's final price
- Multiple prime contracts (MPC)
  - UK: One contractor takes responsibility for the development (package deal).
  - US: A client may have five or six prime contractors.

Study and Practice

Construction Management education comes in a variety of formats: formal degree programmes (Two-year associate degree; four-year baccalaureate degree, masters degree, project management, operations management engineer degree, doctor of philosophy degree, postdoctoral researcher); on-the-job-training; and continuing education and professional development. Information on degree programmes is available from the American Council for Construction Education (ACCE) or the Associated Schools of Construction (ASC).

According to the American Council for Construction Education (the academic accrediting body of construction management educational programmes in the U.S.), the academic field of construction management encompasses a wide range of topics. These range from general management skills, through management skills specifically related to construction, to technical knowledge of construction methods and practices. There are many schools offering Construction Management programmes, including some offering a Masters degree.

Estimation Theory

Estimation theory is a branch of statistics and Signal processing that deals with estimating the values of parameters based on measured/ empirical data that has a random component. The parameters describe an underlying physical setting in such a way that their value affects the distribution of the measured data. An estimator attempts to approximate the unknown parameters using the measurements.

For example, it is desired to estimate the proportion of a population of voters who will vote for a particular candidate. That proportion is the parameter sought; the estimate is based on a small random sample of voters.

Or, for example, in radar the goal is to estimate the range of objects (airplanes, boats, etc.) by analyzing the two-way transit timing of received echoes of transmitted pulses. Since the reflected pulses are unavoidably embedded in electrical noise, their measured values are randomly distributed, so that the transit time must be estimated.

In estimation theory, two approaches are generally considered.

- The probabilistic approach (described in this article) assumes that the measured data is random with probability distribution dependent on the parameters of interest
- The set-membership approach assumes that the measured data vector belongs to a set which depends on the parameter vector.

For example, in electrical communication theory, the measurements which contain information regarding the parameters of interest are often associated with a noisysignal. Without randomness, or noise, the problem would be deterministic and estimation would not be needed.

Estimation Process

The entire purpose of estimation theory is to arrive at an estimator — preferably an easily implementable one. The estimator takes the measured data as input and produces an estimate of the parameters with the corresponding accuracy.

It is also preferable to derive an estimator that exhibits optimality. Estimator optimality usually refers to achieving minimum average error over some class of estimators, for example, a minimum variance unbiased estimator. In this case, the class is the set of unbiased estimators, and the average error measure is variance (average squared error between the value of the estimate and the parameter). However, optimal estimators do not always exist.

These are the general steps to arrive at an estimator:

- In order to arrive at a desired estimator, it is first necessary to determine a probability distribution for the measured data, and the distribution's dependence on the unknown parameters of interest. Often, the probability distribution may be derived from physical models that explicitly show how the measured data depends on the parameters to be estimated, and how the data is corrupted by random errors or noise. In other cases, the probability distribution for the measured data is simply "assumed", for example, based on familiarity with the measured data and/or for analytical convenience.
- After deciding upon a probabilistic model, it is helpful to find the theoretically achievable (optimal) precision available to any estimator based on this model. The Cramér–Rao bound is useful for this.
- Next, an estimator needs to be developed, or applied (if an already known estimator is valid for the model). There are a variety of methods for developing estimators; maximum likelihood estimators are often the default although they may be hard to compute or even fail to exist. If possible, the theoretical performance of the estimator should be derived and compared with the optimal performance found in the last step.
- Finally, experiments or simulations can be run using the estimator to test its performance.

After arriving at an estimator, real data might show that the model used to derive the estimator is incorrect, which may require repeating these steps to find a new estimator. A non-implementable or infeasible estimator may need to be scrapped and the process started anew.

Estimation theory can be applied to both linear and nonlinear models and is closely related to system identification and nonlinear system identification.

In summary, the estimator estimates the parameters of a physical model based on measured data.

Basics

To build a model, several statistical "ingredients" need to be known. These are needed to ensure the estimator has some mathematical tractability instead of being based on "good feel".

The first is a set of statistical samples taken from a random vector (RV) of size N. Put into a vector,

$$\mathrm{x} = \begin{bmatrix} x[0] \\ x[1] \\ \vdots \\ x[N-1] \end{bmatrix}.$$

Secondly, there are the corresponding M parameters

$$\theta = \begin{bmatrix} \theta_1 \\ \theta_2 \\ \vdots \\ \theta_M \end{bmatrix},$$

which need to be established with their continuous probability density function (pdf) or its discrete counterpart, the probability mass function (pmf)

$$p(\mathrm{x} \mid \theta).$$

It is also possible for the parameters themselves to have a probability distribution (e.g., Bayesian statistics). It is then necessary to define the Bayesian probability

$$\pi(\theta).$$

After the model is formed, the goal is to estimate the parameters, commonly denoted $\hat{\theta}$, where the "hat" indicates the estimate.

One common estimator is the minimum mean squared error estimator, which utilizes the error between the estimated parameters and the actual value of the parameters

$$\mathrm{e} = \hat{\theta} - \theta$$

as the basis for optimality. This error term is then squared and minimized for the MMSE estimator.

Estimators

Commonly used estimators and estimation methods, and topics related to them:

- Maximum likelihood estimators
- Bayes estimators
- Method of moments estimators
- Cramér–Rao bound
- Minimum mean squared error (MMSE), also known as Bayes least squared error (BLSE)

- Maximum a posteriori (MAP)
- Minimum variance unbiased estimator (MVUE)
- nonlinear system identification
- Best linear unbiased estimator (BLUE)
- Unbiased estimators
- Particle filter
- Markov chain Monte Carlo (MCMC)
- Kalman filter, and its various derivatives
- Wiener filter

Examples

Unknown constant in additive white Gaussian noise:

Consider a received discrete signal, $x[n]$, of N independentsamples that consists of an unknown constant A with additive white Gaussian noise (AWGN) $w[n]$with known variance σ^2 (*i.e.*, $\mathcal{N}(0,\sigma^2)$). Since the variance is known then the only unknown parameter is A.

The model for the signal is then

$$x[n] = A + w[n] \quad n = 0,1,\ldots,N-1$$

Two possible (of many) estimators are:

- $\hat{A}_1 = x[0]$
- $\hat{A}_2 = \frac{1}{N}\sum_{n=0}^{N-1} x[n]$ which is the sample mean

Both of these estimators have a mean of A, which can be shown through taking the expected value of each estimator

$$\mathrm{E}\left[\hat{A}_1\right] = \mathrm{E}\left[x[0]\right] = A$$

and

$$\mathrm{E}\left[\hat{A}_2\right] = \mathrm{E}\left[\frac{1}{N}\sum_{n=0}^{N-1} x[n]\right] = \frac{1}{N}\left[\sum_{n=0}^{N-1} \mathrm{E}\left[x[n]\right]\right] = \frac{1}{N}[NA] = A$$

At this point, these two estimators would appear to perform the same. However, the difference between them becomes apparent when comparing the variances.

$$\mathrm{var}\left(\hat{A}_1\right) = \mathrm{var}\left(x[0]\right) = \sigma^2$$

and

$$\operatorname{var}\left(\hat{A}_2\right)=\operatorname{var}\left(\frac{1}{N}\sum_{n=0}^{N-1}x[n]\right)\overset{independence}{=}\frac{1}{N^2}\left[\sum_{n=0}^{N-1}\operatorname{var}(x[n])\right]=\frac{1}{N^2}\left[N\sigma^2\right]=\frac{\sigma^2}{N}$$

It would seem that the sample mean is a better estimator since its variance is lower for every N>1.

Maximum likelihood

Continuing the example using the maximum likelihood estimator, the probability density function (pdf) of the noise for one sample $w[n]$ is

$$p(w[n])=\frac{1}{\sigma\sqrt{2\pi}}\exp\left(-\frac{1}{2\sigma^2}w[n]^2\right)$$

and the probability of $x[n]$ becomes ($x[n]$ can be thought of a $\mathcal{N}(A,\sigma^2)$)

$$p(x[n];A)=\frac{1}{\sigma\sqrt{2\pi}}\exp\left(-\frac{1}{2\sigma^2}(x[n]-A)^2\right)$$

By independence, the probability of x becomes

$$p(\mathrm{x};A)=\prod_{n=0}^{N-1}p(x[n];A)=\frac{1}{\left(\sigma\sqrt{2\pi}\right)^N}\exp\left(-\frac{1}{2\sigma^2}\sum_{n=0}^{N-1}(x[n]-A)^2\right)$$

Taking the natural logarithm of the pdf

$$\ln p(\mathrm{x};A)=-N\ln\left(\sigma\sqrt{2\pi}\right)-\frac{1}{2\sigma^2}\sum_{n=0}^{N-1}(x[n]-A)^2$$

and the maximum likelihood estimator is

$$\hat{A}=\arg\max\ln p(\mathrm{x};A)$$

Taking the first derivative of the log-likelihood function

$$\frac{\partial}{\partial A}\ln p(\mathrm{x};A)=\frac{1}{\sigma^2}\left[\sum_{n=0}^{N-1}(x[n]-A)\right]=\frac{1}{\sigma^2}\left[\sum_{n=0}^{N-1}x[n]-NA\right]$$

and setting it to zero

$$0=\frac{1}{\sigma^2}\left[\sum_{n=0}^{N-1}x[n]-NA\right]=\sum_{n=0}^{N-1}x[n]-NA$$

This results in the maximum likelihood estimator

$$\hat{A}=\frac{1}{N}\sum_{n=0}^{N-1}x[n]$$

which is simply the sample mean. From this example, it was found that the sample mean is the maximum likelihood estimator for N samples of a fixed, unknown parameter corrupted by AWGN.

Cramér–Rao lower bound

To find the Cramér–Rao lower bound (CRLB) of the sample mean estimator, it is first necessary to find the Fisher information number

$$\mathcal{I}(A) = \mathrm{E}\left(\left[\frac{\partial}{\partial A}\ln p(\mathrm{x};A)\right]^2\right) = -\mathrm{E}\left[\frac{\partial^2}{\partial A^2}\ln p(\mathrm{x};A)\right]$$

and copying from above

$$\frac{\partial}{\partial A}\ln p(\mathrm{x};A) = \frac{1}{\sigma^2}\left[\sum_{n=0}^{N-1} x[n] - NA\right]$$

Taking the second derivative

$$\frac{\partial^2}{\partial A^2}\ln p(\mathrm{x};A) = \frac{1}{\sigma^2}(-N) = \frac{-N}{\sigma^2}$$

and finding the negative expected value is trivial since it is now a deterministic constant $-\mathrm{E}\left[\frac{\partial^2}{\partial A^2}\ln p(\mathrm{x};A)\right] = \frac{N}{\sigma^2}$

Finally, putting the Fisher information into $\mathrm{var}\left(\hat{A}\right) \geq \frac{1}{\mathcal{I}}$ results in

$$\mathrm{var}\left(\hat{A}\right) \geq \frac{\sigma^2}{N}$$

Comparing this to the variance of the sample mean (determined previously) shows that the sample mean is *equal to* the Cramér–Rao lower bound for all values of N and A. In other words, the sample mean is the (necessarily unique) efficient estimator, and thus also the minimum variance unbiased estimator (MVUE), in addition to being the maximum likelihood estimator.

Maximum of a Uniform Distribution

One of the simplest non-trivial examples of estimation is the estimation of the maximum of a uniform distribution. It is used as a hands-on classroom exercise and to illustrate basic principles of estimation theory. Further, in the case of estimation based on a single sample, it demonstrates philosophical issues and possible misunderstandings in the use of maximum likelihood estimators and likelihood functions.

Given a discrete uniform distribution $1, 2, \ldots, N$ with unknown maximum, the UMVU estimator for the maximum is given by

$$\frac{k+1}{k}m - 1 = m + \frac{m}{k} - 1$$

where *m* is the sample maximum and *k* is the sample size, sampling without replacement. This problem is commonly known as the German tank problem, due to application of maximum estimation to estimates of German tank production during World War II.

The formula may be understood intuitively as:

"The sample maximum plus the average gap between observations in the sample", the gap being added to compensate for the negative bias of the sample maximum as an estimator for the population maximum.

This has a variance of

$$\frac{1}{k}\frac{(N-k)(N+1)}{(k+2)} \approx \frac{N^2}{k^2} \text{ for small samples } k \ll N$$

so a standard deviation of approximately N/k, the (population) average size of a gap between samples; compare $\frac{m}{k}$ above. This can be seen as a very simple case of maximum spacing estimation.

The sample maximum is the maximum likelihood estimator for the population maximum, but, as discussed above, it is biased.

Applications of Cost Indices to Estimating

In the screening estimate of a new facility, a single parameter is often used to describe a cost function. For example, the cost of a power plant is a function of electricity generating capacity expressed in megawatts, or the cost of a sewage treatment plant as a function of waste flow expressed in million gallons per day.

The general conditions for the application of the single parameter cost function for screening estimates are:

1. Exclude special local conditions in historical data
2. Adjust for inflation index
3. Determine new facility cost on basis of specified size or capacity (using the methods described in Sections 5.3 to 5.6)
4. Adjust for local index of construction costs
5. Adjust for different regulatory constraints
6. Adjust for local factors for the new facility

Some of these adjustments may be done using compiled indices, whereas others may require field investigation and considerable professional judgement to reflect differences between a given project and standard projects performed in the past.

Example 5-13: Screening estimate for a refinery

The total construction cost of a refinery with a production capacity of 200,000 bbl/day in Gary, Indiana, completed in 2001 was $100 million. It is proposed that a similar refinery with a production capacity of 300,000 bbl/day be built in Los Angeles, California, for completion in 2003. For the additional information given below, make an order of magnitude estimate of the cost of the proposed plant.

1. In the total construction cost for the Gary, Indiana, plant, there was an item of $5 million for site preparation which is not typical for other plants.
2. The variation of sizes of the refineries can be approximated by the exponential rule, Equation (5.4), with $m = 0.6$.
3. The inflation rate is expected to be 8% per year from 1999 to 2003.
4. The location index was 0.92 for Gary, Indiana and 1.14 for Los Angeles in 1999. These indices are deemed to be appropriate for adjusting the costs between these two cities.
5. New air pollution equipment for the LA plant costs $7 million in 2003 dollars (not required in the Gary plant).
6. The contingency cost due to inclement weather delay will be reduced by the amount of 1% of total construction cost because of the favourable climate in LA (compared to Gary).

On the basis of the above conditions, the estimate for the new project may be obtained as follows:

1. Typical cost excluding special item at Gary, IN is

   $100 million - $5 million = $ 95 million
2. Adjustment for capacity based on the exponential law yields

   $(\$95)(300{,}000/200{,}000)^{0.6} = (95)(1.5)^{0.6} = \$121.2$ million
3. Adjustment for inflation leads to the cost in 2003 dollars as

   $(\$121.2)(1.08)^4 = \$164.6$ million
4. Adjustment for location index gives

   $(\$164.6)(1.14/0.92) = \$204.6$ million

5. Adjustment for new pollution equipment at the LA plant gives

   \$204.6 + \$7 = \$211.6 million

6. Reduction in contingency cost yields

   (\$211.6)(1-0.01) = \$209.5 million

Since there is no adjustment for the cost of construction financing, the order of magnitude estimate for the new project is \$209.5 million.

Example 5-14: Conceptual estimate for a chemical processing plant

In making a preliminary estimate of a chemical processing plant, several major types of equipment are the most significant parameters in affecting the installation cost. The cost of piping and other ancillary items for each type of equipment can often be expressed as a percentage of that type of equipment for a given capacity. The standard costs for the major equipment types for two plants with different daily production capacities. It has been established that the installation cost of all equipment for a plant with daily production capacity between 100,000 bbl and 400,000 bbl can best be estimated by using linear interpolation of the standard data.

Table: Cost Data for Equipment and Ancillary Items

Equipment type	***Equipment Cost (\$1000)***		***Cost of ancillary items as % of equipment cost (\$1000)***	
	100,000 bbl	400,000 bbl	100,000 bbl	400,000 bbl
Furnace	3,000	10,000	40%	30%
Tower	2,000	6,000	45%	35%
Drum	1,500	5,000	50%	40%
Pump, etc.	1,000	4,000	60%	50%

A new chemical processing plant with a daily production capacity of 200,000 bbl is to be constructed in Memphis, TN in four years. Determine the total preliminary cost estimate of the plant including the building and the equipment on the following basis:

1. The installation cost for equipment was based on linear interpolation, and adjusted for inflation for the intervening four years. We expect inflation in the four years to be similar to the period 1990-1994 and we will use the GNP Deflator index.
2. The location index for equipment installation is 0.95 for Memphis, TN, in comparison with the standard cost.
3. An additional cost of \$500,000 was required for the local conditions in Memphis, TN.

The solution of this problem can be carried out according to the steps as outlined in the problem statement:

1. The costs of the equipment and ancillary items for a plant with a capacity of 200,000 bbl can be estimated by linear interpolation of the data and the results.

Table: Results of Linear Interpolation for an Estimation Example		
Equipment type	***Equipment Cost (in $1,000)***	***Percentage for ancillary items***
Furnace	$3,000 + (1/3)($10,000-$3,000) = $5,333	40% - (1/3)(40%-30%) = 37%
Tower	$2,000 + (1/3)($6,000-$2,000) = $3,333	45% - (1/3)(45%-35%) = 42%
Drum	$1,500 + (1/3)($5,000-$1,500) = $2,667	50% - (1/3)(50%-40%) = 47%
Pumps, etc.	$1,000 + (1/3)($4,000-$1,000) = $2,000	60% - (1/3)(60%-50%) = 57%

2. Hence, the total project cost in thousands of current dollars is given by Equation (5.8) as:
3. ($5,333)(1.37) + ($3,333)(1.42) +($2,667)(1.47) + ($2,000)(1.57) = $2,307 + $4,733 + $3,920 + $3,140 = $ 19,000
4. The corresponding cost in thousands of four year in the future dollars using Equation and Table is:

   ($19,100)(105/94) = $21,335
5. The total cost of the project after adjustment for location is

   (0.95)($21,335,000) + $500,000 ≈ $20,800,000

Estimate Based on Engineer's List of Quantities

The engineer's estimate is based on a list of items and the associated quantities from which the total construction cost is derived. This same list is also made available to the bidders if unit prices of the items on the list are also solicited from the bidders. Thus, the itemized costs submitted by the winning contractor may be used as the starting point for budget control.

In general, the progress payments to the contractor are based on the units of work completed and the corresponding unit prices of the work items on the list. Hence, the estimate based on the engineers' list of quanitities for various work items essentially defines the level of detail to which subsequent measures of progress for the project will be made.

Example: Bid Estimate Based on Engineer's List of Quantities

Using the unit prices in the bid of contractor 1 for the quantitites specified by the engineer, we can compute the total bid price of contractor 1 for the roadway project. The itemized costs for various work items as well as the total bid price.

Table: *Bid Price of Contractor 1 in a Highway Project*

Items	***Unit***	***Quantity***	***Unit price***	***Item cost***
Mobilization	ls	1	115,000	115,000
Removal, berm	lf	8,020	1.00	8.020
Finish subgrade	sy	1,207,500	0.50	603,750
Surface ditches	lf	525	2.00	1,050
Excavation structures	cy	7,000	3.00	21,000
Base course, untreated, 3/4"	ton	362,200	4.50	1,629,900
Lean concrete, 4" thick	sy	820,310	3.10	2,542,961
PCC, pavement, 10" thick	sy	76,010	10.90	7,695,509
Concrete, ci AA (AE)	ls	1	200,000	200,000
Small structure	cy	50	500	25,000
Barrier, precast	lf	7,920	15.00	118,800
Flatwork, 4" thick	sy	7,410	10.00	74,100
10" thick	sy	4,241	20.00	84,820
Slope protection	sy	2,104	25.00	52,600
Metal, end section, 15"	ea	39	100	3,900
18"	ea	3	150	450
Post, right-of-way, modification	lf	4,700	3.00	14,100
Salvage and relay pipe	lf	1,680	5.00	8,400
Loose riprap	cy	32	40.00	1,280
Braced posts	ea	54	100	5,400
Delineators, type I	lb	1,330	12.00	15,960
type II	ea	140	15.00	2,100
Constructive signs fixed	sf	52,600	0.10	5,260
Barricades, type III	lf	29,500	0.20	5,900
Warning lights	day	6,300	0.10	630
Pavement marking, epoxy				
material Black	gal	475	90.00	42,750
Yellow	gal	740	90.00	66,600
White	gal	985	90.00	88,650
Plowable, one-way white	ea	342	50.00	17,100
Topsoil, contractor furnished	cy	260	10.00	2,600
Seedling, method A	acr	103	150	15,450
Excelsior blanket	sy	500	2.00	1,000
Corrugated, metal pipe, 18"	lf	580	20.00	11,600
Polyethylene pipe, 12"	lf	2,250	15.00	33,750
Catch basin grate and frame	ea	35	350	12,250

Contd...

Items	*Unit*	*Quantity*	*Unit price*	*Item cost*
Equal opportunity training	hr	18,000	0.80	14,400
Granular backfill borrow	cy	274	10.00	2,740
Drill caisson, 2'x6"	lf	722	100	72,200
Flagging	hr	20,000	8.25	165,000
Prestressed concrete member				
type IV, 141'x4"	ea	7	12,000	84,000
132'x4"	ea	6	11,000	66,000
Reinforced steel	lb	6,300	0.60	3,780
Epoxy coated	lb	122,241	0.55	67,232.55
Structural steel	ls	1	5,000	5,000
Sign, covering	sf	16	10.00	160
type C-2 wood post	sf	98	15.00	1,470
24"	ea	3	100	300
30"	ea	2	100	200
48"	ea	11	200	2,200
Auxiliary	sf	61	15.00	915
Steel post, 48"x60"	ea	11	500	5,500
type 3, wood post	sf	669	15.00	10,035
24"	ea	23	100	2,300
30"	ea	1	100	100
36"	ea	12	150	1,800
42"x60"	ea	8	150	1,200
48"	ea	7	200	1,400
Auxiliary	sf	135	15.00	2,025
Steel post	sf	1,610	40.00	64,400
12"x36"	ea	28	100	2,800
Foundation, concrete	ea	60	300	18,000
Barricade, 48"x42"	ea	40	100	4,000
Wood post, road closed	lf	100	30.00	3,000
Total				***$14,129,797.55***

Allocation of Construction Costs Over Time

Since construction costs are incurred over the entire construction phase of a project, it is often necessary to determine the amounts to be spent in various periods to derive the cash flow profile, especially for large projects with long durations. Consequently, it is important to examine the percentage of work expected to be completed at various time periods to which the costs would be charged. More accurate estimates may be accomplished once the project is scheduled as described in Chapter 10, but some rough estimate of the cash flow may be required prior to this time.

Consider the basic problem in determining the percentage of work completed during construction. One common method of estimating percentage of completion is based on the amount of money spent relative to the total amount budgeted for the entire project. This method has the obvious drawback in assuming that the amount of money spent has been used efficiently for production. A more reliable method is based on the concept of *value of work completed* which is defined as the product of the budgeted labour hours per unit of production and the actual number of production units completed, and is expressed in budgeted labourhours for the work completed. Then, the percentage of completion at any stage is the ratio of the value of work completed to date and the value of work to be completed for the entire project. Regardless of the method of measurement, it is informative to understand the trend of work progress during construction for evaluation and control.

In general, the work on a construction project progresses gradually from the time of mobilization until it reaches a plateau; then the work slows down gradually and finally stops at the time of completion. The rate of work done during various time periods (expressed in the percentage of project cost per unit time) which ten time periods have been assumed. The solid line A represents the case in which the rate of work is zero at time t = 0 and increases linearly to 12.5% of project cost at t = 2, while the rate begins to decrease from 12.5% at t = 8 to 0% at t = 10. The dotted line B represents the case of rapid mobilization by reaching 12.5% of project cost at t = 1 while beginning to decrease from 12.5% at t = 7 to 0% at t = 10. The dash line C represents the case of slow mobilization by reaching 12.5% of project cost at t = 3 while beginning to decrease from 12.5% at t = 9 to 0% at t = 10.

The value of work completed at a given time (expressed as a cumulative percentage of project cost). In each case (A, B or C), the value of work completed can be represented by an "S-shaped" curve. The effects of rapid mobilization and slow mobilization are indicated by the positions of curves B and C relative to curve A, respectively.

While the curves represent highly idealized cases, they do suggest the latitude for adjusting the schedules for various activities in a project.

While the rate of work progress may be changed quite drastically within a single period, such as the change from rapid mobilization to a slow mobilization in periods 1, 2 and 3, the effect on the value of work completed over time will diminish in significance as indicated by the cumulative percentages for later periods. Thus, adjustment of the scheduling of some activities may improve the utilization of labour, material and equipment, and any delay caused by such adjustments for individual activities is not likely to cause problems for the eventual progress toward the completion of a project.

In addition to the speed of resource mobilization, another important consideration is the overall duration of a project and the amount of resources applied. Various strategies may be applied to shorten the overall duration of a project such as overlapping design and construction activities or increasing the peak amounts of labour and equipment working on a site. However, spatial, managerial and technical factors will typically place a minimum limit on the project duration or cause costs to escalate with shorter durations.

Computer Aided Cost Estimation

Numerous computer aided cost estimation software systems are now available. These range in sophistication from simple spreadsheet calculation software to integrated systems involving design and price negotiation over the Internet. While this software involves costs for purchase, maintenance, training and computer hardware, some significant efficiencies often result. In particular, cost estimates may be prepared more rapidly and with less effort.

Some of the common features of computer aided cost estimation software include:

- Databases for unit cost items such as worker wage rates, equipment rental or material prices. These databases can be used for any cost estimate required. If these rates change, cost estimates can be rapidly re-computed after the databases are updated.
- Databases of expected productivity for different components types, equiptment and construction processes.
- Import utilities from computer aided design software for automatic quantity-take-off of components. Alternatively, special user interfaces may exist to enter geometric descriptions of components to allow automatic quantity-take-off.
- Export utilities to send estimates to cost control and scheduling software. This is very helpful to begin the management of costs during construction.

- Version control to allow simulation of different construction processes or design changes for the purpose of tracking changes in expected costs.
- Provisions for manual review, over-ride and editing of any cost element resulting from the cost estimation system
- Flexible reporting formats, including provisions for electronic reporting rather than simply printing cost estimates on paper.
- Archives of past projects to allow rapid cost-estimate updating or modification for similar designs.

A typical process for developing a cost estimate using one of these systems would include:

1. If a similar design has already been estimated or exists in the company archive, the old project information is retreived.
2. A cost engineer modifies, add or deletes components in the project information set. If a similar project exists, many of the components may have few or no updates, thereby saving time.
3. A cost estimate is calculated using the unit cost method of estimation. Productivities and unit prices are retrieved from the system databases. Thus, the latest price information is used for the cost estimate.
4. The cost estimation is summarized and reviewed for any errors.

Estimation of Operating Costs

In order to analyze the life cycle costs of a proposed facility, it is necessary to estimate the operation and maintenance costs over time after the start up of the facility. The stream of operating costs over the life of the facility depends upon subsequent maintenance policies and facility use. In particular, the magnitude of routine maintenance costs will be reduced if the facility undergoes periodic repairs and rehabilitation at periodic intervals.

Since the tradeoff between the capital cost and the operating cost is an essential part of the economic evaluation of a facility, the operating cost is viewed not as a separate entity, but as a part of the larger parcel of life cycle cost at the planning and design stage. The techniques of estimating life cycle costs are similar to those used for estimating capital costs, including empirical cost functions and the unit cost method of estimating the labour, material and equipment costs. However, it is the interaction of the operating and capital costs which deserve special attention.

As suggested earlier in the discussion of the exponential rule for estimating, the value of the cost exponent may influence the decision whether extra capacity should be built to accommodate future growth. Similarly, the economy of scale may also influence the decision on rehabilitation at a given time. As the rehabilitation work becomes extensive, it becomes a capital project with all the implications of its own life cycle. Hence, the cost estimation of a rehabilitation project may also involve capital and operating costs.

While deferring the discussion of the economic evaluation of constructed facilities to Chapter 6, it is sufficient to point out that the stream of operating costs over time represents a series of costs at different time periods which have different values with respect to the present. Consequently, the cost data at different time periods must be converted to a common base line if meaningful comparison is desired.

Example : Maintenance Cost on a Roadway

Maintenance costs for constructed roadways tend to increase with both age and use of the facility. As an example, the following empirical model was estimated for maintenance expenditures on sections of the Ohio Turnpike:

$$C = 596 + 0.0019\,V + 21.7\,A$$

where C is the annual cost of routine maintenance per lane-mile (in 1967 dollars), V is the volume of traffic on the roadway (measured in equivalent standard axle loads, ESAL, so that a heavy truck is represented as equivalent to many automobiles), and A is the age of the pavement in years since the last resurfacing. According to this model, routine maintenance costs will increase each year as the pavement service deteriorates. In addition, maintenance costs increase with additional pavement stress due to increased traffic or to heavier axle loads, as reflected in the variable V.

For example, for V = 500,300 ESAL and A = 5 years, the annual cost of routine maintenance per lane-mile is estimated to be:

$$C = 596 + (0.0019)(500{,}300) + (21.7)(5)$$

$$= 596 + 950.5 + 108.5 = 1{,}655 \text{ (in 1967 dollars)}$$

Example: Time Stream of Costs over the Life of a Roadway

The time stream of costs over the life of a roadway depends upon the intervals at which rehabilitation is carried out. If the rehabilitation strategy and the traffic are known, the time stream of costs can be estimated.

Using a life cycle model which predicts the economic life of highway pavement on the basis of the effects of traffic and other factors, an optimal schedule for rehabilitation can be developed. For example, a time stream of costs and resurfacing projects for one pavement section. As described in the previous example, the routine maintenance costs increase as the pavement ages, but decline after each new resurfacing. As the pavement continues to age, resurfacing becomes more frequent until the roadway is completely reconstructed at the end of 35 years.

Construction (Design and Management)

The Construction (Design and Management) Regulations 2007, also known as CDM Regulations or CDM 2007, define legal duties for the safe operation of UK construction sites. The regulations place specific duties on clients, designers and contractors, to plan their approach to health and safety. They apply throughout the life of a construction project, from its inception to its subsequent final demolition and removal.

It was introduced by the Health and Safety Executive's Construction Division to help:

- Improve planning and management of projects from the very start of the project;
- Assign the right people for the right job at the right time to manage the risks on site;
- Target effort where it can do most good in terms of health and safety;
- Discourage unnecessary bureaucracy.

These regulations were a result of an EU Directive 92/57/EEC (OJ L245, 26.8.92), the so-called 'Construction Sites Directive'. They came into force on April 6, 2007 and replaced the Construction (Design and Management) Regulations 1994, Construction (Design and Management) (Amendment) Regulations 2000 and the Construction (Health, Safety and Welfare) Regulations 1996.

The regulations are divided into 5 parts:

- Part 1 deals with matters of interpretation and application of the regulations.
- Part 2 covers general management duties of the duty holders that apply to all construction projects including those that are non-notifiable.
- Part 3 sets out additional management duties of the duty holders that apply to notifiable projects.

- Part 4 of the regulations apply to all construction work carried out on construction sites, and covers physical safeguards that must be provided to prevent danger. This was covered previously by the Construction (Health, Safety and Welfare) Regulations 1996, which are revoked by CDM2007.
- Part 5 covers issues of civil liability, transitional provisions that apply during the period when the regulations come into force, and amendments and revocations of other legislation.

CDM 2007 applies to all construction work and covers a very broad range of construction activities such as building, civil engineering, engineering construction work, demolition, site preparation and site clearance, except for Part 3, which only applies if the project is notifiable. On a notifiable project, the client must additionally appoint a competent CDM co-ordinator and a competent Principal Contractor, a Construction Phase Plan ("Construction Phase" – incorporating Mobilisation (let the building contract, appoint contractor, issue production information, arrange site hand-over, and review contractor's proposals), Construction to Practical Completion (administer the building contract and provide contractor with further information as necessary), After Practical Completion (administer the building contract after practical completion, resolve defects and make final inspections). The importance of this phase is in the inspection of expected performance standards to ensure compliance).and a Health & Safety File must be produced. Additional duties are also placed on the Client, Designers and Contractors for notifiable projects. The CDM Co-ordinator is the new title for the Planning Supervisor under CDM 1994, with increased duties and responsibilities.

Approved Code of Practice 2007 (ACoP)

The HSE's Approved Code of Practice (ACoP): Managing Health and Safety in Construction, gives practical advice on how comply with the law. It states that if you follow the advice given you comply with the law as far as CDM regulations are concerned. If you are prosecuted for breach of health and safety law, and it is proved that you did not follow relevant provisions of the Approved Code, you must show that you have complied with the law in some other way, or a Court may find you at fault.

The ACoP came into force in April 2007. This edition is a complete re-write from the original and revised ACoP's that were written for the CDM regulations 1994.

Notifiable and Non-notifiable Projects

Projects are classified as 'notifiable' if they take longer than 30 days or longer than 500 person days (e.g., 50 people working 10 days on the construction project). Under the CDM regulation, the client appoints a competent Principal Contractor and CDM co-ordinator, who notifies the Health and Safety Executive (HSE) by using Form 10 (F10). Failure to do so means the client must take the duties of Principal Contractor and CDM co-ordinator assigned to the parties under CDM 2007.

Non-notifiable projects are those that are likely to take less than 30 days of construction time. Although there is no legal requirement for a formal appointment of a Principle Contractor or CDM co-ordinator or a construction phase plan for non-notifiable projects, regulation does require co-operation and co-ordination between all members of the project team.

Duty Holders

Persons with specific duties under the regulations are the client, designer, principal contractor, other contractors, and a new duty holder introduced by the regulations: 'CDM co-ordinator'.

Each of these duty holders, apart from the client, must be "competent" to act in the project. Details of the duties of each principal and issues about competence follow.

Client

The client is the person for whom the project is carried out. On a project, the client is the most influential person, having control over the duration, budget and appointment of various parties to carry out the work. As such they have a key role to play in the promotion of a systematic approach to the management of health and safety in construction. They set the tone of the project and make decisions crucial to its development. The legal duties of a client under CDM 2007 are:

- Verify the competence and resources of all organisations and internal teams the client engages or allocates to the project (e.g., principal contractor, CDM co-ordinator, designers, contractors)
- Ensure that suitable management arrangements are made for the project (although client doesn't have to carry out the management themselves)
- Ensure sufficient time and resources are allowed for all stages of the project including site set up

- Provide pre-construction information to the designers and contractors, or co-operate with CDM co-ordinator to collect and compile relevant pre-construction information
- Ensure co-operation and co-ordination between the client's employees and client contractors with the project contractors where the client's work activities overlap the construction work

On notifiable projects the client's additional duties are to:

- Select and appoint a competent and resourced CDM co-ordinator and principal contractor
- Cerify the sufficiency of the construction phase plan prior to construction commencement
- Cerify that suitable welfare facilities are in place prior to construction commencement and co-operate with the principal contractor to provide suitable welfare facility
- Compile and retain health and safety file from the CDM co-ordinator, keep information up to date and provide access to any person who needs to see it for health and safety purposes

Often, clients have little knowledge of managing a construction project. The regulation recognises this and doesn't require the client to manage the project themselves. Clients without construction expertise must rely on the CDM co-ordinator's advice on how best to meet their duties, and subsequently the CDM co-ordinator needs the clients support and input to work effectively. The client remains responsible for ensuring client duties are met. Note that domestic clients having work done on a property they intend to live in have no duties under CDM 2007 and are exempt from the regulations.

CDM Co-ordinator

A CDM co-ordinator is only required on notifiable projects. Their primary roles and duties are to provide the client with a key project advisor in respect of construction health and safety risk management matters and to ensure compliance of the design and the designers with CDM 2007. Through early involvement with clients and designers, a CDM co-ordinator can make a significant contribution to reducing risks to workers during construction, and to contractors and end users who work in, or on, the structure after construction. As such, the client must appoint a CDM co-ordinator as soon as it is practicably possible. The legal duties of a CDM co-ordinator under CDM 2007 are as follow:

- Notify the project to the Health & Safety Executive when the project is notifiable

- Advise and assist the client with their duties for engaging or appointing competent and adequately resourced organisations (e.g., CDM co-ordinator and Principal Contractor)
- Assist the client with suitable management arrangements for the project (This may include design audits and construction site audits and inspections)
- Identify and collect pre-construction information and provide it in a convenient form to designers, the principal contractor, and other contractors who need it to carry out their duties
- Advise the client on the sufficiency of the time allocated for all phases of the project
- ensure that the design complies with the requirements of the regulations, paying particular attention to any late design changes
- Ensure that the designers and principal contractor co-operate and co-ordinate with each other and with those involved in the project
- Help the client verify the sufficiency of the construction phase plan to commence construction and adequacy of welfare provisions
- Prepare the health and safety file, or review and update an existing health and safety file, and give it to the client at end of construction for maintenance work

Designers

In CDM 2007, 'designer' has a broad meaning and covers person or organisations who prepare drawings, design details and those who specifies a particular method of construction or material. Therefore, by default anyone involved in the project is a potential designer, including the clients, architects, civil and structural engineers, building surveyors, building service designers, landscape architects, contractors, interior designers and shop fitters, temporary work engineers, and anyone purchasing materials where the choice has been left open.

Designers are in a unique position to reduce construction risks, and play a key role in CDM 2007. Designs develop from initial concepts through to a detailed specification, often involving different teams and people at various stages. At each stage, designers from all disciplines can contribute significantly by identifying and eliminating hazards, and reducing risks from hazards where elimination is not possible. Designers' earliest decisions fundamentally affect the health and safety of construction work. These decisions influence later design choices, and considerable work may be required if it is necessary to unravel earlier decisions. It is vital to address health and safety from the very start.

Designers' responsibilities extend beyond the construction phase of a project. The regulation places legal duties for them to consider the health and safety of those who maintain, repair, clean, refurbish, and eventually remove or demolish all or part of the structure, as well as the health and safety of users of workplaces. For most designers, buildability considerations, and ensuring the structure can be easily maintained and repaired is part of their normal work. Considering the health and safety of those who do this work should not be an onerous duty. Failure to address these issues adequately at the design stage usually increass running costs, because clients are then faced with more costly solutions when repairs and maintenance become necessary. Where significant risks remain despite available remedies, designers must provide information with the design that ensures that the CDM co-ordinator, other designers and contractors are aware of these risks.

Designers also have duties under other legislation, including those parts of the Management of Health and Safety at Work Regulations 1999 that require risk assessment.

The legal duties of a designer under CDM 2007 are:

- Ensure that the client is aware of the client's duties prior to commencing any design work
- Ensure that personnel allocated to their design team from internal resources are competent and adequately resourced
- Ensure that any designers or contractors that are engaged on the project are competent and adequately resourced
- Ensure that the design and the designers' duties are complied with by any designers engaged by them, including any designers who are based outside UK
- Eliminate or reduce health and safety risks to constructors, users, maintainers, repairers, commissioners, testers, cleaners, demolishers etc. when preparing the design
- Co-operate and communicate with other designers, including temporary works designers, to ensure adequate co-ordination of the design
- Provide information about risks that cannot be satisfactorily addressed by their designs to the client, other designers and contractors

On notifiable projects the designers' additional duties are to:

- verify that the project has been notified and that the CDM co-ordinator has been appointed as soon as possible after commencement of initial or preliminary design;
- co-operate with the CDM co-ordinator for the verification of design and designer compliance and the co-ordination of the design;
- provide any information requested by the CDM co-ordinator for the health and safety file.

Principal Contractor

The principal contractor has a central role in managing health and safety during the construction phase. It is achieved mainly by developing a health and safety plan from the pre-construction information identified and collated by the CDM co-ordinator and provided by the client and designers, and by ensuring that the plan is followed. The principal contractor must be a contractor. A contractor is someone who performs or manages construction work and has been formally appointed as principal contractor by the client. The principal contractor is then also a contractor and must also comply with the contractor's duties. The principal contractor has the major responsibility for safety and health during the construction phase on notifiable projects only, and has the duties to:

- Demonstrate their organisation's competence and adequacy of resources to perform the principal contractor's duties on the particular project
- Verify competence and resources allocation of any sub-contracted designers or contractors
- Prepare, develop, communicate, implement and amend the construction phase plan
- Plan and manage the construction processes and ensure other contractors manage their work, including inspections and audits
- Ensure the provision of adequate welfare facilities, prevent unauthorised access to the site, prepare and enforce the site rules and manage effective co-operation and co-ordination between contractors
- Make available to the other contractors key documents, e.g., health and safety file information, site surveys, designers' information, risk assessments, and the construction phase plan

- Inform other contractors of their mobilisation time, which should be sufficient
- Ensure the workforce is consulted on health and safety matters and provided with suitable inductions, information, and training
- Liaise with the CDM co-ordinator for any design undertaken during the construction phase and provide information for the health and safety file
- Display the project notification on the site

Contractors

Contractors and those actually doing the construction work are most at risk of injury and ill health. They have a key role to play, in co-operation with the principal contractor, in planning and managing the work to ensure that risks are properly controlled On all projects contractors must:

- Plan, manage and monitor their own work to make sure that workers under their control are safe from the start of their work on site
- Ensure that any contractor who they appoint or engage to work on the project is with the permission of the Estates project manager/supervisor and are informed of the minimum amount of time for them to plan and prepare before they start work on the site
- Provide workers under their control (whether employed or self-employed) with any necessary information, including about relevant aspects of other contractors' work, and site induction (where not provided by a principal contractor or Estates safety officer) which they need to work safely, to report problems or to respond appropriately in an emergency
- Co-operate with others and co-ordinate their work with others working on the project
- Ensure that there are adequate welfare facilities for their workers

In addition, where projects are notifiable under the Regulations, contractors must:

- Check that the client is aware of their duties, check that a CDM co-ordinator has been appointed and ensure that HSE has been notified before the work starts
- Co-operate with the principal contractor in planning and managing work, including reasonable directions and site rules

- Provide details to the principal contractor of any contractor engaged in connection with carrying out work
- Provide any information needed for the health and safety file
- Inform the principal contractor of any problems with the plan
- Inform the principal contractor of reportable accidents, diseases and dangerous occurrences

Workers

The CDM2007 places legal duties on workers to ensure they carry out the work as safely as possible and that they do not endanger the visitors/ members of the public. They must:

- Ensure they only carry out construction work they are competent to do
- Report obvious risks and hazards to the contractor
- Co-operate with others and co-ordinate work so as to ensure their own health and safety and others who may be affected by the work
- Follow site health and safety rules and procedures

The Statutory Documents

This section covers mandatory documents for a CDM project, including project notification, pre-construction information, construction phase plan, and health and safety plan. Whilst pre-construction information should be produced for all projects, some form of the other documents must be produced for both notifiable and non-notifiable projects. Project notification is only needed for notifiable project. The Construction Phase Plan is also only required on notifiable projects, but something similar would still be required on non-notifiable projects to provide for effective health and safety management during construction. The Health and Safety File must be produced on notifiable projects, and is prepared by the CDM Co-ordinator. However, if a Health and Safety File exists for a structure the project modifies, the existing Health and Safety File must be amended to reflect changes. The client must establish who updates any existing Health and Safety Files. Even if a Health and Safety File is not required on a non-notifiable project, as-built and operational and maintenance information are still required.

Project Notification (Form 10)

The regulations require the CDM co-ordinator to notify the local HSE office of all construction work expected to last more than 30 working days and also all work which may not last this long but is expected to involve more than 500 person days or shifts of construction work. The initial notification should be made as soon as possible after appointment of the CDM co-ordinator. Further notifications would be required by changes in the information required on the notification. An additional notification would be required subsequent to the appointment of the principal contractor, if this appointment had not been made at the time of the initial notification, a change in the client or CDM co-ordinator, or a significant change in workscope and/or duration. Additional notifications are not required where designers and contractors change. This notification may be performed using the HSE Form 10(rev) or by other means, including electronic, providing it contains the information specified by Schedule 1 of CDM2007, which consists of:

1. Date of Forwarding and exact address of the construction site
2. A brief description of the project and the construction work it includes
3. Contact details of the client, CDM co-ordinator and principal contractor (name, address, telephone number and e-mail address)
4. Date planned for start of the construction phase
5. The time allowed by the client to the principal contractor referred to in regulation 15(b) for planning and preparation for construction work
6. Planned duration of the construction phase
7. Estimated maximum number of people at work on the construction site
8. Planned number of contractors on the construction site
9. Name and address of any designer and contractor already appointed
10. A declaration signed by or on behalf of the client that he is aware of his duties under these regulations

Pre-construction Information

The pre-construction information (PCI) provides information for those designing, bidding for, or planning work and for the development of the construction phase plan. The client has a duty to obtain this information for all projects. On non-notifiable projects the client must provide all relevant information to the designers and contractors. On notifiable projects, the CDM co-ordinator assists the client with identifying what is required and collection of that information. The CDM co-ordinator also ensures the pre-construction information is in a convenient format and provide the relevant parts to designers, the principal contractor and other contractors.

The 'pre-construction information' is information regarding the project, site and other relevant issues required by the designers and contractors working on the project. This information is useful for the designers in their attempts to eliminate or reduce risks in design decisions, for bidding contractors to properly evaluate the work and associated risks, and for the contractors performing the work in their management of health and safety on the site. The client must provide all information that pertains to the site, and any other information that could be reasonably obtained. They must provide this information as soon as possible in the project so the designers can consider the information in design and planning decisions. Some of this information is also supplied to bidding contractors so they can make informed tenders for the work, or allow the construction team, in a situation where tenders are not required, to effectively plan the construction work. The pre-construction information may be discrete pieces of information in the form of drawings, reports, surveys, etc., either in electronic or hard copy format, with an index provided to all of the project team so information available to all. Alternatively, though not preferred, the 'pre-construction information' may be a single document.

Construction Phase Plan

On notifiable projects, the client must ensure the construction phase plan is sufficiently developed by the principal contractor before construction begins. A sufficient construction phase plan must contain the health and safety management systems and arrangements for the specific project and site, and the risk assessments and method statements for initial work activities. The CDM co-ordinator assists the client in assessing the construction phase plan prior to construction commencement. On non-notifiable projects involving demolition or sites or activities involving high levels of risk it is recommended that a written plan, approximating the construction phase plan should be produced and reviewed. The client must establish the need for this, probably with assistance from the designers.

Welfare Facilities

On notifiable projects the client must ensure the principal contractor has made suitable arrangements for site welfare facilities, taking into account the numbers of workers expected to work on the site, the site conditions and the project tasks, prior to allowing construction to commence. The CDM co-ordinator helps the client with this. The principal contractor has an absolute duty to prepare the construction phase plan prior to construction commencement, and develop, communicate, implement and amend the plan as necessary to maintain its sufficiency to effectively plan, manage and monitor the construction work. This should ensure that the work is performed, so far as reasonably practicable, without risks to health and safety.

Health and Safety File

A health and safety file is only required on notifiable projects however, if a health and safety file exists for a structure involved in a non-notifiable project, this file still must be updated. The health and safety file should contain the information needed to allow future construction work safely, including cleaning, maintenance, alterations refurbishment, and demolition. The file scope, structure, and format must be agreed between the client and the CDM Co-ordinator at the start of the project. Under CDM 2007 the CDM co-ordinator must prepare the health and safety file, or review and update an existing health and safety file, and pass it the client at the end of construction. This is an expansion on the requirement previously on the planning supervisor under CDM 1994, as that only required the planning supervisor to ensure that the file was prepared. On notifiable projects, contractors must promptly provide information regarding their own work that has been identified as necessary include in the health and safety file to the principal contractor for his submissions to the CDM co-ordinator. What is required, in what format and when should have been provided within the pre-construction information.

File Content

1. Description of Works: Give a brief description of the structural / building work carried out in the project to which this health & safety file relates.
2. Residual Hazards: Describe or list the residual hazards and how they have been dealt with (for example surveys or other information concerning asbestos, contaminated land, water bearing strata, buried services etc.).
3. Structural Design Principles: Description of the key structural principles incorporated in the design of the structure (e.g., bracing, sources of substantial stored energy, including pre or post-tensioned members) and safe working loads for floors and

roofs, particularly where these may preclude placing scaffolding or heavy machinery there.

4. Hazardous Materials: List any hazards associated with the materials used (for example hazardous substances, lead paint, special coatings which should not be burnt off).
5. Installed Plant: Give information regarding the removal or dismantling of installed plant and equipment (for example lifting arrangements).
6. Cleaning & Maintenance: Give health & safety information about any equipment provided for cleaning or maintaining the structure.
7. Services: Give the nature, location, and markings of significant services, including fire-fighting services.
8. Access Drawings: Give information and as-built drawings of the structures, its plant and equipment (e.g., means of safe access to and from service voids, fire doors, and compartmentation).

3

Pricing Preliminaries

When it comes to the pricing of Prelims or oncost expenses, much thought is to be applied to determining the extent of this allowance when tendering. Preliminaries and General by virtue of its scope and broad definition can easily contribute or result in huge losses if not correctly understood or determined at the tender stage.

There are many schools of thought on this subject, and all of them follow some sort of predefined checklist to ensure that all aspects are accounted for. When pricing preliminaries always start with your supervision, site establishment, methodology of construction, access restrictions, plant and programme requirements, doing this will determine the basic plan of construction and reveal all the obvious elements to price. In getting the preliminaries correct, careful attention to detail is required. Reading through the specifications and guidelines might show obligations to allow for in your preliminaries.

Once all of these variables are established, the information needs to be priced in a logical manner which allows quick and logical calculation adjustments.For example, if you change the price of diesel in a certain cell then in an instant all the preliminaries should be adjusted taking into account the effect of all other diesel related calculations.

In order to build such a spreadsheet takes years of experience and understanding of Excel and pricing. We do however offer a solution in this regard that is we have included such a template as part of the Tendering package. This template (view template) simplyfies the entire process and also calculates the cashflow in terms of Fixed, Value and Time related costs as required by the FIDIC Contract. All of the following categories are completely linked, priced and tabled in a logical manner.

- Salaries (Management & supervision per category)
- Establishment (offices, telephones, infrastructure, etc)
- Plant (Plant utilization, fuel consumption and operators)
- Protection,
- Safety,
- Scaffolding,
- Financial (Bonds, insurance, etc)

Completing this template certainly provides more science in calculating P&G's and will leave you assured that the price accounted for meets your obligations. All contractors use some sort of process in establishing their P&G's and this template document certainly provide a tried and tested solution in reducing this risk when tendering. Refer to the Tendering / Estimating Package.

Labour Costing

Labour productivity is fundamental to the success of any Construction project. The best method to control and monitor this resource is to understand the actual expenditure of each activity in accordance with the priced tender allowable.

Bill of Quantity rates are normally made up of the following components;

- Labour
- Material
- Plant
- Subcontractors
- Mark-up

The labour component is usually broken down into a team size (eg. 1 Carpenter + 2 Helpers) that can execute work at a determined productivity. Various % factors can be applied to increase or reduce the productivity as difficulty is decided at the tendering stage. Once this information is extracted from the BOQ rates then the labour allowable for all trades can be entered into a spreadsheet; that is the team size, productivity and quantity for each activity. This information will be used to compare against actual costs.

Should you however not have the team detail in your priced BOQ then simply enter the labour component and quantity into the template.

This information will still allow you to calculate the actual efficiency but will not assist you in determining team sizes or productivity required at the start of a project.(This will have to be established manually on site)

Once the allowables, productivity outputs and team sizes are captured we can start feeding in the daily costing and progress measurement into the template. The site foreman is required to record the actual manpower used each day and identify the activities and quantity of work that was executed. For example the following information will be recorded.

Placing concrete 11/03/10 1 artisan 8hrs 4 helpers 8hrs 35m3

Once all the daily record sheets are received, first check that the number of labour and hours correspond with the clock in card information. It is very important to make sure all labour and hours of work are accounted for, and that the labour not taking part in the direct works is removed from the calculation. Failure in checking this will result in a fruitless exercise with meaningless results.

By entering the number of labour and hours worked against the recorded activity, the spreadsheet (view template) will calculate the labour cost for the day based on the actual labour hourly rates. The quantity of the work measured is then entered and the allowable value is generated. These sums compared against each other will determine the profit or loss value for that activity.

Work Breakdown Structure

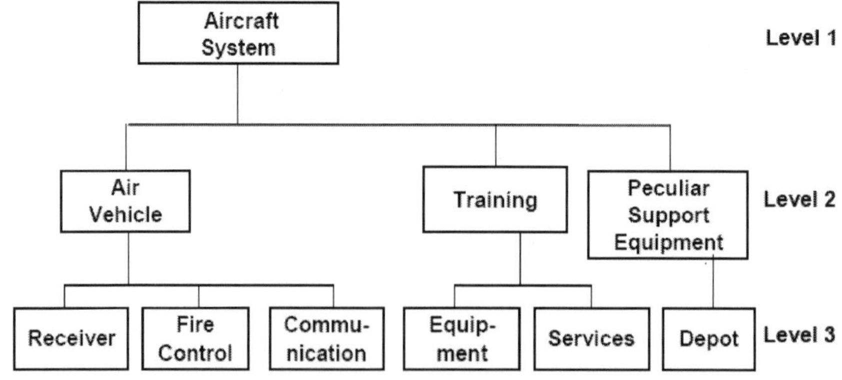

Figure: *Example of a product oriented work breakdown structure of an aircraft system.*

A work breakdown structure (WBS), in project management and systems engineering, is a deliverable oriented decomposition of a project into smaller components. A work breakdown structure element may be a product, data, service, or any combination thereof. A WBS also provides the necessary framework for detailed cost estimating and control along with providing guidance for schedule development and control.

Overview

WBS is a hierarchical and incremental decomposition of the project into phases, deliverables and work packages. It is a tree structure, which shows a subdivision of effort required to achieve an objective; for example a programme, project, and contract. In a project or contract, the WBS is developed by starting with the end objective and successively subdividing it into manageable components in terms of size, duration, and responsibility (e.g., systems, subsystems, components, tasks, subtasks, and work packages) which include all steps necessary to achieve the objective.

The work breakdown structure provides a common framework for the natural development of the overall planning and control of a contract and is the basis for dividing work into definable increments from which the statement of work can be developed and technical, schedule, cost, and labour hour reporting can be established.

A work breakdown structure permits summing of subordinate costs for tasks, materials, etc., into their successively higher level "parent" tasks, materials, etc. For each element of the work breakdown structure, a description of the task to be performed is generated. This technique (sometimes called a *system breakdown structure*) is used to define and organize the total scope of a project.

The WBS is organised around the primary products of the project (or planned outcomes) instead of the work needed to produce the products (planned actions). Since the planned outcomes are the desired ends of the project, they form a relatively stable set of categories in which the costs of the planned actions needed to achieve them can be collected. A well-designed WBS makes it easy to assign each project activity to one and only one terminal element of the WBS. In addition to its function in cost accounting, the WBS also helps map requirements from one level of system specification to another, for example a requirements cross reference matrix mapping functional requirements to high level or low level design documents.

History

The concept of work breakdown structure developed with the Programme Evaluation and Review Technique (PERT) by the United

States Department of Defence (DoD). PERT was introduced by the U.S. Navy in 1957 to support the development of its Polaris missile programme. While the term "work breakdown structure" was not used, this first implementation of PERT did organize the tasks into product-oriented categories.

By June 1962, DoD, NASA and the aerospace industry published a document for the PERT/COST system which described the WBS approach. This guide was endorsed by the Secretary of Defence for adoption by all services. In 1968, the DoD issued "Work Breakdown Structures for Defence Materiel Items" (MIL-STD-881), a military standard requiring the use of work breakdown structures across the DoD.

The document has been revised several times, most recently in 2011. The current version of this document can be found in "Work Breakdown Structures for Defence Materiel Items" (MIL-STD-881C). It includes WBS definitions for specific defence material commodity systems, and addresses WBS elements that are common to all systems. Elements of each WBS Element:

1. The scope of the project, "deliverables" of the project.
2. Start and end time of the scope of project.
3. Budget for the scope of the project.
4. Name of the person related to the scope of project.

Defence Materiel Item categories from MIL-STD-881C are:

- Aircraft Systems WBS
- Electronic Systems WBS
- Missile Systems WBS
- Ordnance Systems WBS
- Sea Systems WBS
- Space Systems WBS
- Surface Vehicle Systems WBS
- Unmanned Air Vehicle Systems WBS
- Unmanned Maritime Systems WBS
- Launch Vehicle Systems WBS
- Automated Information Systems WBS

The common elements identified in MIL-STD-881C, Appendix L are: Integration, assembly, test, and checkout; Systems engineering; Programme management; System test and evaluation; Training; Data;

Peculiar support equipment; Common support equipment; Operational/ Site activation; Industrial facilities; Initial spares and repair parts. The standard also includes additional common elements unique to Space Systems, Launch Vehicle Systems and Automated Information Systems.

In 1987, the Project Management Institute (PMI) documented the expansion of these techniques across non-defence organizations. The *Project Management Body of Knowledge* (PMBOK) Guide provides an overview of the WBS concept, while the "Practice Standard for Work Breakdown Structures" is comparable to the DoD handbook, but is intended for more general application.

Design Principles

100% Rule: An important design principle for work breakdown structures is called the 100% rule. It has been defined as follows:

The 100% rule states that the WBS includes 100% of the work defined by the project scope and captures all deliverables – internal, external, interim – in terms of the work to be completed, including project management. The 100% rule is one of the most important principles guiding the development, decomposition and evaluation of the WBS. The rule applies at all levels within the hierarchy: the sum of the work at the "child" level must equal 100% of the work represented by the "parent" and the WBS should not include any work that falls outside the actual scope of the project, that is, it cannot include more than 100% of the work... It is important to remember that the 100% rule also applies to the activity level. The work represented by the activities in each work package must add up to 100% of the work necessary to complete the work package.

Mutually Exclusive Elements

Mutually exclusive: In addition to the 100% rule, it is important that there is no overlap in scope definition between different elements of a work breakdown structure. This ambiguity could result in duplicated work or mis-communications about responsibility and authority. Such overlap could also cause confusion regarding project cost accounting. If the WBS element names are ambiguous, a WBS dictionary can help clarify the distinctions between WBS elements. The WBS Dictionary describes each component of the WBS with milestones, deliverables, activities, scope, and sometimes dates, resources, costs, quality.

Plan Outcomes, Not Actions

If the work breakdown structure designer attempts to capture any action-oriented details in the WBS, s/he will likely include either too many actions or too few actions. Too many actions will exceed 100% of the parent's scope and too few will fall short of 100% of the parent's scope. The best way to adhere to the 100% rule is to define WBS elements in terms of outcomes or results, not actions. This also ensures that the WBS is not overly prescriptive of methods, allowing for greater ingenuity and creative thinking on the part of the project participants. For new product development projects, the most common technique to ensure an outcome-oriented WBS is to use a product breakdown structure. Feature-driven software projects may use a similar technique which is to employ a feature breakdown structure. When a project provides professional services, a common technique is to capture all planned deliverables to create a deliverable-oriented WBS. Work breakdown structures that subdivide work by project phases (e.g. preliminary design phase, critical design phase) must ensure that phases are clearly separated by a deliverable also used in defining entry and exit criteria (e.g. an approved preliminary or critical design review).

Level of Detail

One must decide when to stop dividing work into smaller elements. This will assist in determining the duration of activities necessary to produce a deliverable defined by the WBS. There are several heuristics or "rules of thumb" used when determining the appropriate duration of an activity or group of activities necessary to produce a specific deliverable defined by the WBS.

- The first is the "80 hour rule" which means that no single activity or group of activities at the lowest level of detail of the WBS to produce a single deliverable should be more than 80 hours of effort.
- The second rule of thumb is that no activity or group of activities at the lowest level of detail of the WBS should be longer than a single reporting period. Thus if the project team is reporting progress monthly, then no single activity or series of activities should be longer than one month long.
- The last heuristic is the "if it makes sense" rule. Applying this rule of thumb, one can apply "common sense" when creating the duration of a single activity or group of activities necessary to produce a deliverable defined by the WBS.

A work package at the activity level is a task that:

- can be realistically and confidently estimated;
- makes no sense practically to break down any further;

- can be completed in accordance with one of the heuristics defined above;
- produces a deliverable which is measurable; and
- forms a unique package of work which can be outsourced or contracted out.

Terminal Element

The lowest elements in a tree structure, a terminal element is one that is not further subdivided. In a Work Breakdown Structure such (activity or deliverable) elements are the items that are estimated in terms of resource requirements, budget and duration; linked by dependencies; and scheduled. At the juncture of the WBS element and organization unit, control accounts and work packages are established and performance is planned, measured, recorded, and controlled. A WBS can be expressed down to any level of interest. Three levels are the minimum recommended, with additional levels for and only for items of high cost or high risk, and two levels of detail at cases such as systems engineering or programme management, with the standard showing examples of WBS with varying depth such as software development at points going to 5 levels or fire-control system to 7 levels.

Consistent to Norms

The higher WBS structure should be consistent to whatever norms or template mandates exist within the organization or domain. For example, shipbuilding for the U.S. Navy must respect that the nautical terms and their hierarchy structure put into MIL-STD are embedded in Naval Architecture and that matching Navy offices and procedures have been built to match this naval architecture structure, so any significant change of WBS element numbering or naming in the hierarchy would be unacceptable.

Example

At WBS Level 1 it shows 100 units of work as the total scope of a project to design and build a custom bicycle. At WBS Level 2, the 100 units are divided into seven elements. The number of units allocated to each element of work can be based on effort or cost; it is not an estimate of task duration.

The three largest elements of WBS Level 2 are further subdivided at Level 3. The two largest elements at Level 3 each represent only 17% of the total scope of the project. These larger elements could be further subdivided using the *progressive elaboration* technique described above.

WBS design can be supported by software (e.g. a spreadsheet) to allow automatic rolling up of point values. Estimates of effort or cost can be developed through discussions among project team members. This collaborative technique builds greater insight into scope definitions, underlying assumptions, and consensus regarding the level of granularity required to manage the project.

Misconceptions

- A WBS is not an exhaustive list of work. It is instead a comprehensive classification of project scope.
- A WBS is neither a project plan, a schedule, nor a chronological listing. It specifies what will be done, not how or when.
- A WBS is not an organizational hierarchy, although it may be used when assigning responsibilities.

Estimating Concrete Pricing

Estimating concrete pricing is no easy task. There are so many variables when you are estimating concrete pricing that one single error could represent a huge impact on your company's finances. Let's understand how we can breakdown and generate a reliable concrete pricing.

Concrete Pricing: Concrete

The most important item to consider is essential the ready-mixed concrete. The ready-mix concrete supplier could offer you a quote once you explain them the place where you will be placing the concrete, the formwork used and the amount of concrete that you will be using. Concrete is essentially quoted per cubic yard or cubic metre, and as an average you could use $77 per cubic yard. But always have your ready mix concrete quoted by a local supplier.

Concrete Pricing: Leveling

If you are placing concrete over ground surface, you will need to grade or prepare the surface the concrete. Pricing this item is a little bit difficult as you might want to cover expenses related to grading, compacting soil, excavating, trenching and other components that might affect your concrete pricing calculation. As a good average you can use $65 per hour of work needed to prepare the surface assuming that the surface is more than 75% levelled and no huge amount of work is needed to prepare the surface.

Concrete Pricing: More than Levelling

If your surface is not levelled, then you will need additional work to provide with an accurate concrete pricing. Depending on how much work you need to do, this item will significantly affect you concrete pricing. Sometimes you need to do a surcharge, excavate and fill with suitable material, or just remove soft spot on the terrain to make it suitable to withstand structure loads. Depending on the distance from where you will be providing sand or any other suitable fill material, this could be adding over $10 per cubic metre or cubic yard in your estimate.

Concrete Pricing: Forms

Concrete forms will affect the concrete pricing as it is one of the most labour-intensive related activities that need to be considered on a reliable concrete pricing. First you need to identify the type of formwork that will be used, how it will be installed, do you need to buy the formwork, or rent it? As you see there are many variables but for a good estimate, one that will be safe for you and good for your client, you could be pricing it at $1.10 per square feet. A square or rectangular shape area will not be the same as a rounded area or any other irregular shape.

Concrete Pricing: Finishing

Concrete pricing and appearance will likely be affected by the way concrete is being finished. Concrete could be finished in many different ways such as smooth surface, exposed aggregate surface or stamped concrete finish. Some surfaces may require only strikeoff and screeding to proper contour and elevation, while for other surfaces a broomed, floated, or troweled finish may be specified. To consider this in your concrete pricing analysis you could add $0.75 per square feet or maybe higher depending on the complexity of the finished being requested.

Concrete Pricing: Rebars

Sometimes concrete will need different types or rebars, or reinforcement. Rebars could be plain, corrugated, epoxy coated, fibreglass, or many different types of reinforcement such as wire mesh, plastic mesh and/or fibre might be added to increase concrete strength and resistance. All of these materials should be adding about $0.14 cents per square foot, depending on the amount of reinforcement being requested that number could go up or slightly less.

Contract

In common law legal systems, a contract is an agreement having a lawful object entered into voluntarily by two or more parties, each of whom intends to create one or more legal obligations between them. The elements of a contract are “offer” and “acceptance” by “competent persons" having legal capacity who exchange "consideration" to create "mutuality of obligation."

Proof of some or all of these elements may be done in writing, though contracts may be made entirely orally or by conduct. The remedy for breach of contract can be "damages" in the form of compensation of money or specific performance enforced through an injunction. Both of these remedies award the party at loss the "benefit of the bargain" or expectation damages, which are greater than mere reliance damages, as in promissory estoppel. The parties may be natural persons or juristic persons. A contract is a legally enforceable promise or undertaking that something will or will not occur. The word promise can be used as a legal synonym for contract, although care is required as a promise may not have the full standing of a contract, as when it is an agreement without consideration.

Contract law varies greatly from one jurisdiction to another, including differences in common law compared to civil law, the impact of received law, particularly from England in common law countries, and of law codified in regional legislation. Regarding Australian Contract Law for example, there are 40 relevant acts which impact on the interpretation of contract at the Commonwealth (Federal / national) level, and an additional 26 acts at the level of the state of NSW. In addition there are 6 international instruments or conventions which are applicable for international dealings, such as the United Nations Convention on Contracts for the International Sale of Goods.

Contents

History:

Figure: *Bill of sale of a male slave and a building in Shuruppak, Sumerian tablet, circa 2600 BC*

Contract law is based on the principle expressed in the Latin phrase *pacta sunt servanda,* which is usually translated "agreements must be kept" but more literally means "pacts must be kept". Contract law can be classified, as is habitual in civil law systems, as part of a general law of obligations, along with tort, unjust enrichment, and restitution. The common law of contract originated with the writ of assumpsit, which was originally a tort action based on reliance.

Jurisdictions vary in their principles of freedom of contract. In common law jurisdictions such as the United Kingdom and the United States, a high degree of freedom is expected. For example, in American law, it was determined in the 1901 case of *Hurley v. Eddingfield* that a physician was permitted to deny treatment to a patient despite the lack of other available medical assistance and the patient's subsequent death. This is in contrast to the civil law, which typically applies certain overarching principles to disputes arising out of contract, as in the French Civil Code. Other legal systems such as Islamic law, socialist legal systems, and customary law have their own variations.

However, in the case of the United States the principle of freedom of contract has eroded over time due to judicial deference to legislation affecting contracts. For example, the Civil Rights Act of 1964 restricted private racial discrimination against African-Americans. In the early 20th century the United States underwent the "Lochner era", in which the Supreme Court of the United States struck down economic regulations on the basis of freedom of contract and the Due Process Clause; these decisions were eventually overturned and the Supreme Court established a deference to legislative statutes and regulations which restrict freedom of contract. The U.S. Constitution contains a Contract Clause, but this has been interpreted as only restricting the retroactive impairment of contracts.

Not all agreements are necessarily contractual, as the parties must have an intention to be legally bound. In American English, a gentlemen's agreement is one which is not intended to be legally enforceable.

Commercial use

Contracts are widely used in commercial law, and form the legal foundation for transactions across the world. Common examples include construction contracts, product purchases (with associated warranties of quality), software licenses, employment contracts, insurance policies, real estate deeds to transfer title, professional services, wholesale merchandise supply, and various other uses.

Online contracts have common. E-signature laws have made the electronic contract and signature as legally valid as a paper contract. It has been estimated that roughly one hundred and ten electronic contracts are signed every second.

Elements

At common law, the elements of a contract are offer, acceptance, intention to create legal relations, and consideration.

Offer and Acceptance

In order for a contract to be formed, the parties must reach mutual assent (also called a meeting of the minds). This is typically reached through offer and an acceptance which does not vary the offer's terms, which is known as the "mirror image rule". If a purported acceptance does vary the terms of an offer, it is not an acceptance but a counteroffer and, therefore, simultaneously a rejection of the original offer. The Uniform Commercial Code disposes of the mirror image rule in §2-207, although the UCC only governs transactions in goods in the USA. As a court cannot read minds, the intent of the parties is interpreted objectively from the perspective of a reasonable person, as determined in the early English case of *Smith v Hughes* [1871].

Contracts may be bilateral or unilateral. A bilateral contract is an agreement in which each of the parties to the contract makes a promise or set of promises to each other. For example, in a contract for the sale of a home, the buyer promises to pay the seller $200,000 in exchange for the seller's promise to deliver title to the property. These common contracts take place in the daily flow of commerce transactions, and in cases with sophisticated or expensive promises may involve extensive negotiation and various condition precedent requirements, which are requirements that must be met for the contract to be fulfilled.

Less common are unilateral contracts in which one party makes a promise, but the other side does not promise anything. In these cases, those accepting the offer are not required to communicate their acceptance to the offeror. In a reward contract, for example, a person who has lost a dog could promise a reward if the dog is found, through publication or orally. The payment could be additionally conditioned on the dog being returned alive. Those who learn of the reward are not required to search for the dog, but if someone finds the dog and delivers it, the promisor is required to pay. In the similar case of advertisements of deals or bargains, a general rule is that these are not contractual offers but merely an "invitation to treat" (or bargain), but the applicability of this rule is disputed and contains various exceptions. The High Court of Australia stated that the term unilateral contract is "unscientific and misleading".

In certain circumstances, an implied contract may be created. A contract is implied in fact if the circumstances imply that parties have reached an agreement even though they have not done so expressly. For example, a patient may implicitly enter a contract by visiting a doctor and being examined; if the patient refuses to pay after being examined, the patient has breached a contract implied in fact. A contract which is implied in law is also called a quasi-contract, because it is not in fact a contract; rather, it is a means for the courts to remedy situations in which one party would be unjustly enriched were he or she not required to compensate the other. Quantum meruit claims are an example.

Intention to be Legally Bound

In commercial agreements it is presumed that parties intend to be legally bound unless the parties expressly state the opposite as in a heads of agreement document. For example, in *Rose & Frank Co v JR Crompton & Bros Ltd* an agreement between two business parties was not enforced because it contained an 'honour clause' which stated the parties wish that the agreement not be reviewed or enforced by a court.

In contrast, domestic and social agreements such as those between children and parents are typically unenforceable on the basis of public policy. For example, in the English case *Balfour v. Balfour* a husband agreed to give his wife £30 a month while he was away from home, but the court refused to enforce the agreement when the husband stopped paying. In contrast, in *Merritt v Merritt* the court enforced an agreement between an estranged couple.

Consideration

Consideration is something of value given by a promissor to a promisee in exchange for something of value given by a promisee to a promissor. Typically, the thing of value is a payment, although it may be an act, or forbearance to act, when one is privileged to do so, such as an adult refraining from smoking. This thing of value or forbearance from some legal right is considered to be a legal detriment. In the exchange of legal detriments, a bargain is created. In the United States, the emphasis has shifted to the process of bargaining as exemplified by *Hamer v. Sidway* (1891). Roman law-based systems (including Scotland) do not require consideration, and some commentators have suggested that consideration be abandoned, and estoppel be used to replace it as a basis for contracts.

However, legislation, rather than judicial development, has been touted as the only way to remove this entrenched common law doctrine. Lord Justice Denning famously stated that "The doctrine of consideration is too firmly fixed to be overthrown by a side-wind."

Courts will typically not weigh the "adequacy" of consideration as long as the consideration is determined to be "sufficient", with sufficiency defined as meeting the test of law, whereas "adequacy" is the subjective fairness or equivalence For instance, agreeing to sell a car for a penny may constitute a binding contract if a party desires the penny. This is known as the *peppercorn rule*, but in some jurisdictions, the penny may constitute legally insufficient *nominal consideration*. Parties may do this for tax purposes, attempting to disguise gift transactions as contracts. Transferring money may be sufficient, particularly if there is accord and satisfaction.

However, consideration must be given as part of entering the contract, not prior as in past consideration. For example, in the early English case of *Eastwood v. Kenyon* [1840], the guardian of a young girl took out a loan to educate her. After she was married, her husband promised to pay the debt but the loan was determined to be past consideration. The insufficiency of past consideration is related to the *preexisting duty rule*. In the early English case of *Stilk v. Myrick* [1809], a captain promised to divide the wages of two deserters among the remaining crew if they agreed to sail home short-handed; however, this promise was found unenforceable as the crew were already contracted to sail the ship. The preexisting duty rule also extends to general legal duties; for example, a promise to refrain from committing a tort or crime is not sufficient.

Formation

In addition to the elements of a contract:

- A party must have capacity to contract
- The purpose of the contract must be lawful
- The form of the contract must be legal
- The parties must intend to create a legal relationship
- The parties must consent

As a result, there are a variety of affirmative defences that a party may assert to avoid his obligation.

Affirmative Defences

Vitiating factors constituting defences to purported contract formation include:

- Mistake (such as *non est factum*)
- Incapacity, including mental incompetence and infancy/minority
- Duress
- Undue influence
- Unconscionability
- Misrepresentation or fraud
- Frustration of purpose

Such defences operate to determine whether a purported contract is either (1) void or (2) voidable. Void contracts cannot be ratified by either party. Voidable contracts *can* be ratified.

In the United States, persons under 18 are typically minor and their contracts are considered voidable; however, if the minor voids the contract, benefits received by the minor must be returned. The minor can enforce breaches of contract by an adult while the adult's enforcement may be more limited under the bargain principle. Promissory estoppel or unjust enrichment may be available, but generally are not.

Formalities and Writing

Typically, contracts are oral or written, but written contracts have typically been preferred in common law legal systems; in 1677 England passed the Statute of Frauds which influenced similar statute of frauds laws in the United States and other countries such as Australia. In general, the Uniform Commercial Code as adopted in the United States requires a written contract for tangible product sales in excess of $500, and real estate contracts are required to be written. If the contract is not required by law to be written, an oral contract is valid and therefore legally binding. The United Kingdom has since replaced the original Statute of Frauds, but written contracts are still required for various circumstances such as land (through the Law of Property Act 1925).

If a contract is in a written form, and somebody signs it, then the signer is typically bound by its terms regardless of whether he has actually read it provided the document is contractual in nature. However, affirmative defences such as duress or unconscionability may enable the signer to avoid the obligation. Further, reasonable notice of a contract's terms must be given to the other party prior to their entry into the contract.

An unwritten, unspoken contract, also known as "a contract implied by the acts of the parties", which can be either an implied-in-fact contract or implied-in-law contract, may also be legally binding. Implied-in-fact contracts are real contracts under which the parties receive the "benefit of the bargain". However, contracts implied in law are also known as quasi-contracts, and the remedy is quantum meruit, the fair market value of goods or services rendered.

Invitation to Treat

Where a product in large quantities is advertised in a newspaper or on a poster, it generally is not considered an offer but instead will be regarded as an invitation to treat, since there is no guarantee that the store can provide the item for everyone who might want one. However, an exception to this rule may be made if an advertisement includes a reward, which is what happened in the famous case of *Carlill v. Carbolic Smoke Ball Company*, decided in nineteenth-century England.

In *Carlill*, a medical firm, advertised a smoke ball marketed as a wonder drug that would, according to the instructions, protect users from catching the flu. If it did not work, buyers would receive £100 and the company said that they had deposited £1,000 in the bank to show their good faith. When sued, Carbolic argued the ad was not to be taken as a serious, legally bindingoffer. It was merely an invitation to treat, and a gimmick (a "mere puff"). But the court of appeal held that it would appear to a reasonable man that Carbolic had made a serious offer, and determined that the reward was a contractual promise.

Third Parties

The doctrine of privity of contract means that only those involved in striking a bargain would have standing to enforce it. In general this is still the case, only parties to a contract may sue for the breach of a contract, although in recent years the rule of privity has eroded somewhat and third party beneficiaries have been allowed to recover damages for breaches of contracts they were not party to. In cases where facts involve third party beneficiaries or debtors to the original contracting party have been allowed to be considered parties for purposes of enforcement of the contract. A recent advance has been seen in the case law as well as statutory recognition to the dilution of the doctrine of privity of contract. The recent tests applied by courts have been the test of benefit and the duty owed test. The duty owed test looks to see if the third party was agreeing to pay a debt for the original party, and whereas the benefit test looks to see if circumstances indicate that the promisee intends to give the beneficiary the benefit of the promised performance. Any defence allowed to parties of the original contract extend to third party beneficiaries. A recent example is the UK's Contracts (Rights of Third Parties) Act 1999.

Performance

Performance varies according to the particular circumstances. While a contract is being performed, it is called an executory contract, and when it is completed it is an executed contract. In some cases there may be substantial performance but not complete performance, which allows the performing party to be partially compensated.

Uncertainty, Incompleteness and Severance

If the terms of the contract are uncertain or incomplete, the parties cannot have reached an agreement in the eyes of the law. An agreement to agree does not constitute a contract, and an inability to agree on key issues, which may include such things as price or safety, may cause the entire contract to fail. However, a court will attempt to give effect to commercial contracts where possible, by construing a reasonable construction of the contract.

Courts may also look to external standards, which are either mentioned explicitly in the contract or implied by common practice in a certain field. In addition, the court may also imply a term; if price is excluded, the court may imply a reasonable price, with the exception of land, and second-hand goods, which are unique.

If there are uncertain or incomplete clauses in the contract, and all options in resolving its true meaning have failed, it may be possible to sever and void just those affected clauses if the contract includes a severability clause. The test of whether a clause is severable is an objective test—whether a reasonable person would see the contract standing even without the clauses.

Contractual Terms

A contractual term is "any provision forming part of a contract". Each term gives rise to a contractual obligation, breach of which can give rise to litigation. Not all terms are stated expressly and some terms carry less legal weight as they are peripheral to the objectives of the contract.

Standard form contracts contain "boilerplate", which is a set of "one size fits all" contract provisions. However, the term may also narrowly refer to conditions at the end of the contract which specify the governing law provision, venue, assignment and delegation, waiver of jury trial, notice, and force majeure. Restrictive provisions in contracts where the consumer has little negotiating power ("contracts of adhesion") attract consumer protection scrutiny.

Classification of Terms

Contractual terms are classified differently depending upon the context or jurisdiction. Terms establish conditions precedent. English (but not necessarily non-English) common law distinguishes between important *conditions* and warranties, with a breach of a condition by one party allowing the other to repudiate and be discharged while a warranty allows for remedies and damages but not complete discharge. Whether or not a term is a *condition* is determined in part by the parties' intent.In a less technical sense, however, a condition is a generic term and a warranty is a promise. Not all language in the contract is determined to be a contractual term. Representations, which are often precontractual, are typically less strictly enforced than terms, and material misrepresentations historically was a cause of action for the tort of deceit. Warranties were enforced regardless of materiality; in modern United States law the distinction is less clear but warranties may be enforced more strictly. Statements of opinion may be viewed as "mere puff".

In specific circumstances these terms are used differently. For example, in English insurance law, violation of a "condition precedent" by an insured is a complete defence against the payment of claims. In general insurance law, a warranty is a promise that must be complied with. In product transactions, warranties promise that the product will continue to function for a certain period of time.

In the United Kingdom the courts determine whether a term is a condition or warranty; for example, an actress' obligation to perform the opening night of a theatrical production is a *condition*, but a singer's obligation to rehearse may be a warranty.Statute may also declare a term or nature of term to be a condition or warranty; for example the Sale of Goods Act 1979s15A provides that terms as to title, description, quality and sample are generally *conditions*. The United Kingdom has also contrived the concept of an "intermediate term" (also called innominate), first established in *Hong Kong Fir Shipping Co Ltd v Kawasaki Kisen Kaisha Ltd* [1962].

Representations Versus Warranties

Statements of fact in a contract or in obtaining the contract are considered to be either warranties or representations. Traditionally, warranties are factual promises which are enforced through a contract legal action, regardless of materiality, intent, or reliance. Representations are traditionally precontractual statements which allow for a tort-based action (such as the tort of deceit) if the misrepresentation is negligent or fraudulent; historically a tort was the only action available, but by 1778, breach of warranty became a separate legal contractual action. In U.S. law, the distinction between the two is somewhat unclear; warranties are viewed as primarily contract-based legal action while negligent or fraudulent misrepresentations are tort-based, but there is a confusing mix of case law in the United States. In modern English law, sellers often avoid using the term 'represents' in order to avoid claims under the Misrepresentation Act 1967, while in America 'warrants and represents' is relatively common. Some modern commentators suggest avoiding the words and substituting 'state' or 'agree', and some model forms do not use the words; however, others disagree.

Statements in a contract may not be upheld if the court finds that the statements are subjective or promotional puffery. English courts may weigh the emphasis or relative knowledge in determining whether a statement is enforceable as part of the contract. In the English case of *Bannerman v. White* the court upheld a rejection by a buyer of hops which had been treated with sulphur since the buyer explicitly expressed the importance of this requirement. The relative knowledge of the parties may also be a factor, as in English case of *Bissett v. Wilkinson* where the court did not find misrepresentation when a seller said that farmland being sold would carry 2000 sheep if worked by one team; the buyer was considered sufficiently knowledgeable to accept or reject the seller's opinion.

Implied Terms

A term may either be express or implied. An express term is stated by the parties during negotiation or written in a contractual document. Implied terms are not stated but nevertheless form a provision of the contract.

Terms Implied in Fact: Terms may be implied due to the factual circumstances or conduct of the parties. In the Australian case of *BP Refinery Westernport v. Shire of Hastings* the UK Privy Council proposed a five stage test to determine situations where the facts of a case may imply terms. The classic tests have been the "business efficacy test" and the "officious bystander test". Under the "business efficacy test" first proposed in *The Moorcock* [1889], the minimum terms necessary to give business efficacy to the contract will be implied. Under the officious bystander test (named in *Southern Foundries (1926) Ltd v Shirlaw* [1940] but actually originating in *Reigate v. Union Manufacturing Co (Ramsbottom) Ltd* [1918]), a term can only be implied in fact if an "officious bystander" listening to the contract negotiations suggested that the term be included the parties would promptly agree. The difference between these tests is questionable.

Terms Implied in Law

Statutes or judicial rulings may create implied contractual terms, particularly in standardized relationships such as employment or shipping contracts. The Uniform Commercial Code of the United States also imposes an implied covenant of good faith and fair dealing in performance and enforcement of contracts covered by the Code. In addition, Australia, Israel and India imply a similar good faith term through laws.

Most countries have statutes which deal directly with sale of goods, lease transactions, and trade practices. In the United States, prominent examples include, in the case of products, an implied warranty of merchantability and fitness for a particular purpose, and in the case of homes an implied warranty of habitability. In the United Kingdom, implied terms are created by the Sale of Goods Act 1979, the Consumer Protection (Distance Selling) Regulations 2000 and the Supply of Goods and Services Act 1982.

Setting Aside the Contract

There can be four different ways in which contracts can be set aside. A contract may be deemed 'void', 'voidable', 'unenforceable'or 'ineffective'. Voidness implies that a contract never came into existence. Voidability implies that one or both parties may declare a contract ineffective at their wish. Unenforceability implies that neither party may have recourse to a court for a remedy. Ineffectiveness implies that the contract terminates by order of a court where a public body has failed to satisfy public procurement law. To rescind is to set aside or unmake a contract.

Misrepresentation

Misrepresentation means a false statement of fact made by one party to another party and has the effect of inducing that party into the contract. For example, under certain circumstances, false statements or promises made by a seller of goods regarding the quality or nature of the product that the seller has may constitute misrepresentation. A finding of misrepresentation allows for a remedy of rescission and sometimes damages depending on the type of misrepresentation.

There are two types of misrepresentation: fraud in the factum and fraud in inducement. Fraud in the factum focuses on whether the party alleging misrepresentation knew they were creating a contract. If the party did not know that they were entering into a contract, there is no meeting of the minds, and the contract is void. Fraud in inducement focuses on misrepresentation attempting to get the party to enter into the contract. Misrepresentation of a material fact (if the party knew the truth, that party would not have entered into the contract) makes a contract voidable.

According to *Gordon v Selico* [1986] it is possible to misrepresent either by words or conduct. Generally, statements of opinion or intention are not statements of fact in the context of misrepresentation. If one party claims specialist knowledge on the topic discussed, then it is more likely for the courts to hold a statement of opinion by that party as a statement of fact.

Mistake

A mistake is an incorrect understanding by one or more parties to a contract and may be used as grounds to invalidate the agreement. Common law has identified three different types of mistake in contract: common mistake, mutual mistake, and unilateral mistake.

- A common mistake occurs when both parties hold the same mistaken belief of the facts. This is demonstrated in the case of *Bell v. Lever Brothers Ltd.*, which established that common mistake can only void a contract if the mistake of the subject-matter was sufficiently fundamental to render its identity different from what was contracted, making the performance of the contract impossible.
- A mutual mistake occurs when both parties of a contract are mistaken as to the terms. Each believes they are contracting to something different. The court usually tries to uphold such a mistake if a reasonable interpretation of the terms can be found. However, a contract based on a mutual mistake in judgement does not cause the contract to be voidable by the party that is adversely affected.
- A unilateral mistake occurs when only one party to a contract is mistaken as to the terms or subject-matter. The courts will uphold such a contract unless it was determined that the non-

mistaken party was aware of the mistake and tried to take advantage of the mistake. It is also possible for a contract to be void if there was a mistake in the identity of the contracting party. An example is in *Lewis v. Avery* where Lord Denning MR held that the contract can only be avoided if the plaintiff can show that, at the time of agreement, the plaintiff believed the other party's identity was of vital importance. A mere mistaken belief as to the credibility of the other party is not sufficient.

Duress and Undue Influence

Duress has been defined as a "threat of harm made to compel a person to do something against his or her will or judgement; esp., a wrongful threat made by one person to compel a manifestation of seeming assent by another person to a transaction without real volition." An example is in *Barton v Armstrong* [1976] in a person was threatened with death if they did not sign the contract. An innocent party wishing to set aside a contract for duress to the person need only to prove that the threat was made and that it was a reason for entry into the contract; the burden of proof then shifts to the other party to prove that the threat had no effect in causing the party to enter into the contract. There can also be duress to goods and sometimes, 'economic duress'.

Undue influence is an equitable doctrine that involves one person taking advantage of a position of power over another person through a special relationship such as between parent and child or solicitor and client. As an equitable doctrine, the court has discretion. When no special relationship exists, the question is whether there was a relationship of such trust and confidence that it should give rise to such a presumption.

Incapacity

Sometimes the capacity of either natural or artificial persons to either enforce contracts, or have contracts enforced against them is restricted. For instance, very small children may not be held to bargains they have made, on the assumption that they lack the maturity to understand what they are doing; errant employees or directors may be prevented from contracting for their company, because they have acted *ultra vires* (beyond their power). Another example might be people who are mentally incapacitated, either by disability or drunkenness. In these cases the contract is either void or voidable.

Illegal Contracts

If based on an illegal purpose or contrary to public policy, a contract is *void*. In the 1996 Canadian case of *Royal Bank of Canada v. Newell*.a woman forged her husband's signature, and her husband signed agreed to assume "all liability and responsibility" for the forged checks. However, the agreement was unenforceable as it was intended to "stifle a criminal prosecution", and the bank was forced to return the payments made by the husband.

In the U.S., one unusual type of unenforceable contract is a personal employment contract to work as a spy or secret agent. This is because the very secrecy of the contract is a condition of the contract (in order to maintain plausible deniability). If the spy subsequently sues the government on the contract over issues like salary or benefits, then the spy has breached the contract by revealing its existence. It is thus unenforceable on that ground, as well as the public policy of maintaining national security (since a disgruntled agent might try to reveal *all* the government's secrets during his/her lawsuit). Other types of unenforceable employment contracts include contracts agreeing to work for less than minimum wage and forfeiting the right to workman's compensation in cases where workman's compensation is due.

Remedies for Breach of Contract

A breach of contract is failure to perform as stated in the contract. There are many ways to remedy a breached contract assuming it has not been waived. Typically, the remedy for breach of contract is an award of money damages. When dealing with unique subject matter, specific performance may be ordered.

As for many governments, it was not possible to sue the Crown in the UK for breach of contract before 1948. However, it was appreciated that contractors might be reluctant to deal on such a basis and claims were entertained under a petition of right that needed to be endorsed by the Home Secretary and Attorney-General. S.1 Crown Proceedings Act 1947 opened the Crown to ordinary contractual claims through the courts as for any other person.

Damages

There are several different types of damages.

- Compensatory damages, which are given to the party which was detrimented by the breach of contract. With compensatory damages, there are two heads of loss, consequential damage and direct damage.

- Liquidated damages are an estimate of loss agreed to in the contract, so that the court avoids calculating compensatory damages and the parties have greater certainty. Liquidated damages clauses may be called "penalty clauses" in ordinary language, but the law distinguishes between liquidated damages (legitimate) and penalties (invalid). A test for determining which category a clause falls into was established by the English House of Lords in *Dunlop Pneumatic Tyre Co. Ltd v. New Garage & Motor Co. Ltd*
- Nominal damages consist of a small cash amount where the court concludes that the defendant is in breach but the plaintiff has suffered no quantifiable pecuniary loss, and may be sought to obtain a legal record of who was at fault.
- Punitive or exemplary damages, which are used to punish the party at fault. These are not usually given regarding contracts but possible in a fraudulent situation. Again, these are not permitted in all jurisdictions, with England & Wales, for instance, prohibiting them.

Compensatory damages compensate the plaintiff for actual losses suffered as accurately as possible. They may be "expectation damages", "reliance damages" or "restitutionary damages". Expectation damages are awarded to put the party in as good of a position as the party would have been in had the contract been performed as promised. Reliance damages are usually awarded where no reasonably reliable estimate of expectation loss can be arrived at or at the option of the plaintiff. Reliance losses cover expense suffered in reliance to the promise. Examples where reliance damages have been awarded because profits are too speculative include the Australian case of *McRae v. Commonwealth Disposals Commission* which concerned a contract for the rights to salvage a ship. In *Anglia Television Ltd v. Reed* the English Court of Appeal awarded the plaintiff expenditures incurred prior to the contract in preparation of performance.

Once a breach has occurred, the non-breaching party has a duty to mitigate damages, which means that damages will not be awarded if the plaintiff could have avoided the losses without undue risk, expense, or humiliation. but Professor Michael Furmston having stated that the rule is that a plaintiff will not recover damages for loss that would not have occurred had he taken reasonable steps to mitigate loss, has warned that "it is wrong to express this rule by stating that the plaintiff is under a duty to mitigate his loss", citing *Sotiros Shipping*

Inc v. Sameiet, The Solholt. If a party provides notice that the contract will not be completed, an anticipatory breach occurs.

Hadley v. Baxendale establishes general and consequential damages. General damages are those damages which naturally flow from a breach of contract. Consequential damages are those damages which, although not naturally flowing from a breach, are naturally supposed by both parties at the time of contract formation. An example would be when someone rents a car to get to a business meeting, but when that person arrives to pick up the car, it is not there. General damages would be the cost of renting a different car. Consequential damages would be the lost business if that person was unable to get to the meeting, if both parties knew the reason the party was renting the car. However, there is still a duty to mitigate the losses the fact that the car was not there does not give the party a right to not attempt to rent another car.

Specific Performance

There may be circumstances in which it would be unjust to permit the defaulting party simply to buy out the injured party with damages. For example where an art collector purchases a rare painting and the vendor refuses to deliver, the collector's damages would be equal to the sum paid.

The court may make an order of what is called "specific performance", requiring that the contract be performed. In some circumstances a court will order a party to perform his or her promise (an order of "specific performance") or issue an order, known as an "injunction," that a party refrain from doing something that would breach the contract. A specific performance is obtainable for the breach of a contract to sell land or real estate on such grounds that the property has a unique value. In the United States by way of the 13th Amendment to the United States Constitution, specific performance in personal service contracts is only legal "*as punishment for a crime whereof the criminal shall be dully convicted.*"

Both an order for specific performance and an injunction are discretionary remedies, originating for the most part in equity. Neither is available as of right and in most jurisdictions and most circumstances a court will not normally order specific performance. A contract for the sale of real property is a notable exception. In most jurisdictions, the sale of real property is enforceable by specific performance. Even in this case the defences to an action in equity (such as laches, the *bona fide* purchaser rule, or unclean hands) may act as a bar to specific performance. Related to orders for specific performance, an injunction may be requested when the contract prohibits a certain action. Action for injunction would prohibit the person from performing the act specified in the contract.

Procedure

In the United States, in order to obtain damages for breach of contract or to obtain specific performance or other equitable relief, the aggrieved injured party may file a civil (non-criminal) lawsuit in state court (unless there is diversity of citizenship giving rise to federal jurisdiction). If the contract contains a valid arbitration clause, the aggrieved party must submit an arbitration claim in accordance with the procedures set forth in the clause.

Many contracts provide that all disputes arising thereunder will be resolved by arbitration, rather than litigated in courts. Customer claims against securities brokers and dealers are almost always resolved by arbitration because securities dealers are required, under the terms of their membership in self-regulatory organizations such as the Financial Industry Regulatory Authority (formerly the NASD) or NYSE to arbitrate disputes with their customers. The firms then began including arbitration agreements in their customer agreements, requiring their customers to arbitrate disputes. On the other hand, certain claims have been held to be non-arbitrable if they implicate a public interest that goes beyond the narrow interests of the parties to the agreement (i.e., claims that a party violated a contract by engaging in illegal anti-competitive conduct or civil rights violations). Arbitration judgements may generally be enforced in the same manner as ordinary court judgements. However, arbitral decisions are generally immune from appeal in the United States unless there is a showing that the arbitrator's decision was irrational or tainted by fraud. Virtually all states have adopted the Uniform Arbitration Act to facilitate the enforcement of arbitrated judgements. Notably, New York State, where a sizable portion of major commercial agreements are executed and performed, has not adopted the Uniform Arbitration Act.

In England and Wales, a contract may be enforced by use of a claim, or in urgent cases by applying for an interim injunction to prevent a breach. Likewise, in the United States, an aggrieved party may apply for injunctive relief to prevent a threatened breach of contract, where such breach would result in irreparable harm that could not be adequately remedied by money damages.

Contract Theory

Contract theory is the body of legal theory that addresses normative and conceptual questions in contract law. One of the most important questions asked in contract theory is why contracts are enforced. One prominent answer to this question focuses on the economic benefits of enforcing bargains. Another approach, associated with Charles Fried, maintains that the purpose of contract law is to enforce promises. This theory is developed in Fried's book, *Contract as Promise.* Other approaches to contract theory are found in the writings of legal realists and critical legal studies theorists.

More generally, writers have propounded Marxist and feminist interpretations of contract. Attempts at overarching understandings of the purpose and nature of contract as a phenomenon have been made, notably relational contract theory originally developed by U.S. contracts scholars Ian Roderick Macneil and Stewart Macaulay, building at least in part on the contract theory work of U.S. scholar Lon L. Fuller, while U.S. scholars have been at the forefront of developing economic theories of contract focussing on questions of transaction cost and so-called 'efficient breach' theory.

Another dimension of the theoretical debate in contract is its place within, and relationship to a wider law of obligations. Obligations have traditionally been divided into contracts, which are voluntarily undertaken and owed to a specific person or persons, and obligations in tort which are based on the wrongful infliction of harm to certain protected interests, primarily imposed by the law, and typically owed to a wider class of persons.

Recently it has been accepted that there is a third category, restitutionary obligations, based on the unjust enrichment of the defendant at the plaintiff's expense. Contractual liability, reflecting the constitutive function of contract, is generally for failing to make things better (by not rendering the expected performance), liability in tort is generally for action (as opposed to omission) making things worse, and liability in restitution is for unjustly taking or retaining the benefit of the plaintiff's money or work.

The common law describes the circumstances under which the law will recognise the existence of rights, privilege or power arising out of a promise.

Contract Awarding

Contract awarding is the method used during a procurement in order to evaluate the proposals (tender offers) taking part and award the relevant contract. Usually at this stage the eligibility of the proposals has been concluded. So it remains to choose the most preferable among the proposed. There are several different methods for this, which are obviously related to the proposition method asked by the procurement management.

Methods

Least Price: This method is the simplest and oldest of all. Under this the procurement contract is awarded to the best price. Some relevant methods are these of examining the overall or in parts and in total discount in a given price list or on a given budget. One of the proposed for Public tenders by the EC.

Most Economically Advantageous

This is applicable to proposals of different quality within the limits set. Under this the proposals are graded according to their price for value and the contract is awarded to the one with the best grade. Similar to this is the grading of the proposals according to time, making the proposals needing less time of implementation seem more valuable. One of the proposed for Public tenders by the EC.

Mean Value

The contract is awarded to a bid closer to the mean value of the proposals. This may apply to procurements where numerous proposals are expected and there is a need for a market-representing value.

Exclusion of the Extremes

Under this method the proposals that are deviating the most from the mass of the proposals are excluded and then the procedure continues with one of the above methods. There are also many variants and/or combinations of these main methods.

Standard Form Contract

A standard form contract (sometimes referred to as an adhesion or boilerplate contract) is a contract between two parties, where the terms and conditions of the contract are set by one of the parties, and the other party has little or no ability to negotiate more favourable terms and is thus placed in a “take it or leave it” position.

Examples of standard form contracts are insurance policies (where the insurer decides what it will and will not insure, and the language of the contract) and contracts with government agencies (where certain clauses must be included by law or regulation).

While these types of contracts are not illegal *per se*, there exists a very real possibility for unconscionability. In addition, in the event of an ambiguity, such ambiguity will be resolved *contra proferentem* against the party drafting the contract language.

Theoretical Issues

There is much debate on a theoretical level whether, and to what extent, courts should enforce standard form contracts.

On one hand, they undeniably fulfill an important role of promoting economic efficiency. Standard form contracting reduces transaction costs substantially by precluding the need for buyers and sellers of goods and services to negotiate the many details of a sale contract each time the product is sold.

On the other hand, there is the potential for inefficient, and even unjust, terms to be accepted by signatories to these contracts. Such terms might be seen as unjust if they allow the seller to avoid all liability or unilaterally modify terms or terminate the contract. These terms often come in the form of, but are not limited to, forum selection clauses and mandatory arbitration clauses, which can limit or foreclose a party's access to the courts; and also liquidated damages clauses, which set a limit to the amount that can be recovered or require a party to pay a specific amount. They might be inefficient if they place the risk of a negative outcome, such as defective manufacturing, on the buyer who is not in the best position to take precautions.

There are a number of reasons why such terms might be accepted:

Standard Form Contracts are Rarely Read: Lengthy boilerplate terms are often in fine print and written in complicated legal language which often seems irrelevant. The prospect of a buyer finding any useful information from reading such terms is correspondingly low. Even if such information is discovered, the consumer is in no position to bargain as the contract is presented on a "take it or leave it" basis. Coupled with the often large amount of time needed to read the terms, the expected payoff from reading the contract is low and few people would be expected to read it.

Access to the Full Terms May be Difficult or Impossible before Acceptance: Often the document being signed is not the full contract; the purchaser is told that the rest of the terms are in another location. This reduces the likelihood of the terms being read and in some situations, such as software license agreements, can only be read after they have been notionally accepted by purchasing the good and opening the box. These contracts are typically not enforced, since common law dictates that *all* terms of a contract must be disclosed *before* the contract is executed.

Boilerplate Terms are Not Salient: The most important terms to purchasers of a good are generally the price and the quality, which are generally understood before the contract of adhesion is signed. Terms relating to events which have very small probabilities of occurring or which refer to particular statutes or legal rules do not seem important to the purchaser. This further lowers the chance of such terms being read and also means they are likely to be ignored even if they are read.

There may be Social Pressure to Sign: Standard form contracts are signed at a point when the main details of the transaction have either been negotiated or explained. Social pressure to conclude the bargain at that point may come from a number of sources. The salesperson may imply that the purchaser is being unreasonable if they read or question the terms, saying that they are "just something the lawyers want us to do" or that they are wasting their time reading them. If the purchaser is at the front of a queue (for example at an airport car rental desk) there is additional pressure to sign quickly. Finally, if there has been negotiation over price or particular details, then concessions given by the salesperson may be seen as a gift which socially obliges the purchaser to respond by being co-operative and concluding the transaction.

Standard form Contracts May Exploit Unequal Power Relations: If the good which is being sold using a contract of adhesion is one which is essential or very important for the purchaser to buy (such as a rental property or a needed medical item) then the purchaser might feel they have no choice but to accept the terms. This problem may be mitigated if there are many suppliers of the good who can potentially offer different terms.

Some contend that in a competitive market, consumers have the ability to shop around for the supplier who offers them the most favourable terms and are consequently able to avoid injustice. However, in the case of credit cards (and other oligopolies), for example, the consumer while having the ability to shop around may still have access to only form contracts with like terms and no opportunity for negotiation. Also, as noted, many people do not read or understand the terms so there might be very little incentive for a firm to offer favourable conditions as they would gain only a small amount of business from doing so. Even if this is the case, it is argued by some that only a small percentage of buyers need to actively read standard form contracts for it to be worthwhile for firms to offer better terms if that group is able to influence a larger number of people by affecting the firm's reputation.

Another factor which might mitigate the effects of competition on the content of contracts of adhesion is that, in practice, standard form contracts are usually drafted by lawyers instructed to construct them so as to minimize the firm's liability, not necessarily to implement managers' competitive decisions. Sometimes the contracts are written by an industry body and distributed to firms in that industry, increasing homogeneity of the contracts and reducing consumer's ability to shop around.

Common Law Status

As a general rule, the common law treats standard form contracts like any other contract. Signature or some other objective manifestation of intent to be legally bound will bind the signor to the contract whether or not they read or understood the terms. The reality of standard form contracting, however, means that many common law jurisdictions have developed special rules with respect to them. In general, in the event of an ambiguity, the courts will interpret standard form contracts *contra proferentem* against the party that drafted the contract, as that party (and only that party) had the ability to draft the contract to remove ambiguity.

United States

Generally: Standard form contracts are generally enforceable in the United States. The Uniform Commercial Code which is followed in most American states has specific provisions relating to standard form contracts for the sale or lease of goods. Furthermore, standard form contracts will be subject to special scrutiny if they are found to be contracts of adhesion.

Contracts of Adhesion

The concept of the contract of adhesion originated in French civil law, but did not enter American jurisprudence until the *Harvard Law Review* published an influential article by Edwin W. Patterson in 1919. It was subsequently adopted by the majority of American courts, especially after the Supreme Court of California endorsed adhesion analysis in 1962.

For a contract to be treated as a contract of adhesion, it must be presented on a standard form on a "take it or leave it" basis, and give one party no ability to negotiate because of their unequal bargaining position. The special scrutiny given to contracts of adhesion can be performed in a number of ways:

- If the term was outside of the reasonable expectations of the person who did not write the contract, and if the parties were contracting on an unequal basis, then it will not be enforceable. The reasonable expectation is assessed objectively, looking at the prominence of the term, the purpose of the term and the circumstances surrounding acceptance of the contract.
- Section 211 of the American Law Institute's Restatement (Second) of Contracts, which has persuasive though non-binding force in courts, provides:

Where the other party has reason to believe that the party manifesting such assent would not do so if he knew that the writing contained a particular term, the term is not part of the agreement.

This is a subjective test focusing on the mind of the seller and has been adopted by only a few state courts.

- The doctrine of unconscionability is a fact-specific doctrine arising from equitable principles. Unconscionability in standard form contracts usually arises where there is an "absence of meaningful choice on the part of one party due to one-sided contract provisions, together with terms which are so oppressive that no reasonable person would make them and no fair and honest person would accept them." (*Fanning v. Fritz's Pontiac-Cadillac-Buick Inc.*)

Shrink Wrap Contracts

Courts in the United States have faced the issue of shrink wrap contracts in two ways. One line of cases follows *ProCD v. Zeidenberg* which held such contracts enforceable (e.g. *Brower v Gateway*), and the other follows *Klocek v. Gateway, Inc*, which found them unenforceable. These decisions are split on the question of assent, with the former holding that only objective manifestation of assent is required while the latter require at least the possibility of subjective assent.

Canada

In Canada, exclusion clauses in a standard form contract cannot be relied on where a seller knows or has reason to know a purchaser is mistaken as to its terms (*Tilden Rent-A-Car Co. v. Clendenning*).

Australia

Standard form contracts have generally received little special treatment under Australian common law. A 2003 New South Wales Court of Appeal case (*Toll (FGCT) Pty Limited v Alphapharm Pty Limited*) gave some support for the position that notice of exceptional terms is required for them to be incorporated. However the defendant successfully appealed to the High Court so currently there is no special treatment of standard form contracts in Australia.

Since 1 January 2011, a new Consumer law has been enacted in Australia at the National level, and due to a Council of Governments Agreement (COAG) this legislation is now part of each jurisdiction's Fair Trading Laws (States and Territories of Australia).

Legislation

In recognition of the consumer protection issues which may arise, many governments have passed specific laws relating to standard form contracts. These are generally enacted on a state level as part of general consumer protection legislation and typically allow consumers to avoid clauses which are found to be unreasonable, though the specific provisions vary greatly. Some laws require notice to be given for these clauses to be effective, others prohibit unfair clauses altogether (e.g. Victorian Fair Trading Act 1999).

United Kingdom

Section 3 of the Unfair Contract Terms Act 1977 limits the ability of the drafter of consumer or standard form contracts to draft clauses which would allow him to perform in a substantially or totally different manner than would be reasonably expected.

Israel

The Standard Form Contract Act 1982 defines a set of depriving conditions that may be canceled by a court of law, including unreasonable exclusion or limitation of liability, unreasonable privileges to unilaterally cancel, suspend or postpone the execution of the contract and to change any fundamental charges or pricing, transfer of liability for the execution of the contract to a third party, unreasonable obligation to use the services of a third party or to limit, in any way, the choice of contracting third parties, denial of legal remedy, unreasonable limitations on contractual remedies or setting unreasonable conditions for the consummation of the remedy, denying or limiting the right for legal procedures, exclusive rights to decide on the location of the trial or arbitration, obligatory arbitration with unilaterally control over the arbitrators or the location of the arbitration and setting the holder of the burden of proof contrary to common law. The act also establishes a Standard Form Contract Court, chaired by a district judge and consists of a maximum of 12 members, appointed by the justice minister, including an acting chairman (also a district judge), civil servants (no more than a third) and, at least, 2 consumer organization representatives. The court holds hearings regarding appeals against standard form contract clauses or approval of a specific standard form contract at the requests of a provider.

Lithuania

Standard conditions in Lithuania shall be such provisions which are prepared in advance for general and repeated use by one contracting party without their content being negotiated with the another party, and which are used in the formation of contracts without negotiation with the other party. Standard conditions prepared by one of the parties shall be binding to the other if the latter was provided with an adequate opportunity of getting acquainted with the said conditions (Article 6.185. Standard conditions of contracts, Lithuanian Civil Code). A consumer shall have the right to claim within the judicial procedure for invalidity of conditions in a consumer contract that are contrary to the criterion of good faith (Article 6.188).

Civil Law Countries

Russia: In July 2013, Russian Dmitry Agarkov won a court case against internet bank *Tinkoff credit systems* after he altered the standard form contract he had received in the mail. The bank, failing to notice the changes, accepted the application and gave him an account based on the amended contract. The judge ruled that the bank was legally bound to the contract it had signed. Agarkov is further suing the bank for failing to comply with the terms he had added to the contract, which it had unwittingly agreed to by signing the contact. Agarkov's lawyer, Dmitry Mihalevich said – "They signed the documents without looking. They said what usually their borrowers say in court: 'We have not read it'."

Joint Contracts Tribunal

The Joint Contracts Tribunal, also known as the JCT, produces standard forms of contract for construction, guidance notes and other standard documentation for use in the construction industry. From its establishment in 1931, JCT has expanded the number of contributing organisations. Following recommendations in the 1994 Latham Report, the current operational structure comprises 8 members who approve and authorise publications. They are the Association of Consulting Engineers, the British Property Federation, the Construction Confederation, the Local Government Association, the National Specialist Contractors Council, the Royal Institute of British Architects, the Royal Institution of Chartered Surveyors and the Scottish Building Contract Committee.

History

The Joint Contracts Tribunal was established in 1931. It initially consisted of the Royal Institute of British Architects (RIBA) and the National Federation of Building Trades Employers (NFBTE). The common purpose was to publish and where necessary amend a standard form of building contract. Its first chairman, from 1931 to 1956 was Sydney Tatchell, followed by Sir Percy Thomas. In 1998 JCT became a limited company.

The JCT published important new editions of the form in 1939, 1963, 1980, 1998, 2005, and 2011.

Suite of Standard Forms

Suite of Standard Forms means a group of all the mutually consistent documents necessary to operate a particular method of procurement and produced to enable them to be used together, including the following where applicable:

- consultant agreements
- a main contract between the employer and the main contractor;
- sub-contracts between the main contractor and its subcontractors (both for sub-contractors selected by the employer and for other sub-contractors);
- a standard form of sub-sub-contract between a subcontractor and such sub-contractor's sub-sub-contractors;
- a design agreement between an employer and a specialist designer;
- forms of tender for issue by an employer to prospective main contractors and for issue by a main contractor to prospective subcontractors and for issue by a subcontractor to prospective sub-sub-contractors;
- a form of contract for the supply of goods;
- forms of bond (including performance bonds) and collateral warranties.

- the Construction Industry Model Arbitration Rules, adapted from those of the Society of Construction Arbitrators

JCT publish guidance on which contract to select.

Main Forms

JCT substantially revises and rewrites the family of forms every decade. The most recent suite, replacing the 1998 version, is the 2005 suite, as is commonly referred to as JCT 05. There are now, however, 2009 amendments published. The 2011 versions will replace 2009 amendments for all contracts signed after October 1st 2011. They are considered to be the most popular construction contracts in use in the UK.

Main Contracts

1. Major Project Form (MP11)
2. Standard Form of Building Contract (SBC11)
3. Intermediate Form of Building Contract (IC11)
4. Minor Works Agreement (MW11)
5. Management Contract (MC11)
6. Design and Build Contract (DB11)
7. Construction Management Documentation

In 2007 JCT published the Constructing Excellence Contract (JCT/CE), a contract designed to support collaborative working, as advocated by the Latham Report, and can trace its roots back to the "collaborative contract" published in 2003 by BE, a joint venture between the Reading Construction Forum and the Design and Build Foundation (and now part of Constructing Excellence).

Smaller Project Contracts

Traditional JCT contracts were seen as too detailed and difficult to use in smaller domestic projects so JCT launched a consumer friendly range of contracts called the "Building Contract for the Home Owner".

- Building Contract for Home Owner/Occupier (where client deals directly with the builder) (HOB)
- Building Contract for Home Owner/Occupier (who has appointed a consultant) (HOC)
- Contract for Home Repairs and Maintenance (HO/RMI)

Key Features

The JCT contracts avoid up front payments from payers to payees. Instead, the payee invoices the payer once work has been certified as completed by an independent third party, the Contract Administrator (often an architect or surveyor). Often interim certificates are issued where itemised components of the work have been completed, or are a verifiable percentage complete. In the 2009 amendments, the payer or payee can issue the certificate if the Contractor Administrator fails to do so.

The JCT encourages Retention of an agreed percentage of the contract sum until Practical Completion and then a percentage until a period after Final Completion. This avoids payment in advance for such things as minor defects or snagging which need to addressed at the end of the project or come to light after the project completes. So the invoice at each point is for a percentage of the value of the work certified complete. The payer can deduct an amount, however under the 2009 amendments the method for calculating the new amount must be stated.

The JCT encourages up front agreement of Liquidated and Ascertained Damages (LAD) as an estimate of the payers weekly losses if the payee fails to reach Practical Completion by the Contractual Completion Date. If delays are for reasons beyond the contractor's control, the contractor can request an Extension of Time: if the Contract Administrator allows this, it in effect extends the period before which the contractor is liable to pay the LAD.

The JCT introduced the concept of Determination, whereby the contract can be terminated for suspension of works, failure to proceed regularly and diligently, failure to remove defective works, failure to execute works in accordance with the contract, and bankruptcy of the contractor. If one party has ceased to perform in the contract (e.g. the contractor has gone past the Contractual Completion Date and has no plan to complete the contract), Determination enables the other party to end their obligations (e.g. to pay the contractor to finish the project). This is in addition to the Common Law remedy of Repudiation.

Reference is made to adjudication as a quick way of resolving disputes which the parties cannot resolve between them. Arbitration or litigation, depending on the preferences of the parties, is also available for the settlement of disputes, but these are never appeals against the decision of an adjudicator; they are the consideration of the dispute or difference as if no decision had been made by an adjudicator. If arbitration is chosen, then the reference is conducted under JCT the amended version of the Construction Industry Model Arbitration Rules published by the Society of Construction Arbitrators.

Criticisms/Alternatives

Lawbuild has proposed a number of amendments to the JCT contract further to protect the client, with the top four being: to ensure the contractor posts a 10% bond to cover the costs of finding a replacement contractor if the contractor goes into liquidation, to ensure the contractor obtains building regulations certificates before Practical Completion, to ensure the contractor must accept design changes, and to ensure the employer can control the identities of the contractor's designers.

One of the most common disputes around building contracts is with regard to the interpretation of failure to proceed regularly and diligently, and whether the contractor is able to make a claim for loss of profits after Determination. In contrast in the US, building contracts can normally be terminated for convenience of the client, only paying for the work already done.

The JCT makes no distinction between work completed by subcontractors and work completed by the contractor. So the client can end up paying the contractor for work certified and yet the contractor may not pay the subcontractor, for example through insolvency. It may then be hard to work with that subcontractor to complete the work. In contrast in some US states, monies due to subcontractors must be held in trust by the contractor.

ICE Conditions, New Engineering Contract, FIDIC, GC/Works/I, Model Form, and IChemE Form are alternative formats for building contracts.

Cost Contingency

When estimating the cost for a project, product or other item or investment, there is always uncertainty as to the precise content of all items in the estimate, how work will be performed, what work conditions will be like when the project is executed and so on. These uncertainties are risks to the project. Some refer to these risks as "known-unknowns" because the estimator is aware of them, and based on past experience, can even estimate their probable costs. The estimated costs of the known-unknowns is referred to by cost estimators as cost contingency.

Contingency "refers to costs that will probably occur based on past experience, but with some uncertainty regarding the amount. The term is not used as a catchall to cover ignorance. It is poor engineering and poor philosophy to make second-rate estimates and then try to satisfy them by using a large contingency account. The contingency allowance is designed to cover items of cost which are not known exactly at the time of the estimate but which will occur on a statistical basis."

The cost contingency which is included in a cost estimate, bid, or budget may be classified as to its general purpose, that is what it is intended to provide for. For a class 1 construction cost estimate, usually needed for a bid estimate, the contingency may be classified as an estimating and contracting contingency. This is intended to provide compensation for "estimating accuracy based on quantities assumed or measured, unanticipated market conditions, scheduling delays and acceleration issues, lack of bidding competition, subcontractor defaults, and interfacing omissions between various work categories." Additional classifications of contingency may be included at various stages of a project's life, including design contingency, or design definition contingency, or design growth contingency, and change order contingency (although these may be more properly called allowances).

AACE International, the Association for the Advancement of Cost Engineering, has defined contingency as "An amount added to an estimate to allow for items, conditions, or events for which the state, occurrence, or effect is uncertain and that experience shows will likely result, in aggregate, in additional costs. Typically estimated using statistical analysis or judgement based on past asset or project experience. Contingency usually excludes:

1. Major scope changes such as changes in end product specification, capacities, building sizes, and location of the asset or project
2. Extraordinary events such as major strikes and natural disasters
3. Management reserves
4. Escalation and currency effects

Some of the items, conditions, or events for which the state, occurrence, and/or effect is uncertain include, but are not limited to, planning and estimating errors and omissions, minor price fluctuations (other than general escalation), design developments and changes within the scope, and variations in market and environmental conditions. Contingency is generally included in most estimates, and is expected to be expended".

A key phrase above is that it is "*expected to be expended*". In other words, it is an item in an estimate like any other, and should be estimated and included in every estimate and every budget. Because management often thinks contingency money is "fat" that is not needed if a project team does its job well, it is a controversial topic.

In general, there are four classes of methods used to estimate contingency. ." These include the following:

1. Expert judgement
2. Predetermined guidelines (with varying degrees of judgement and empiricism used)
3. Simulation analysis (primarily risk analysis judgement incorporated in a simulation such as Monte-Carlo)
4. Parametric Modelling (empirically-based algorithm, usually derived through regression analysis, with varying degrees of judgement used).

While all are valid methods, the method chosen should be consistent with the first principles of risk management in that the method must start with risk identification, and only then are the probable cost of those risks quantified. In best practice, the quantification will be probabilistic in nature (Monte-Carlo is a common method used for quantification).

Typically, the method results in a distribution of possible cost outcomes for the project, product, or other investment. From this distribution, a cost value can be selected that has the desired probability of having a cost underrun or cost overrun. Usually a value is selected with equal chance of over or underrunning. The difference between the cost estimate without contingency, and the selected cost from the distribution is contingency.

Contingency is included in budgets as a control account. As risks occur on a project, and money is needed to pay for them, the contingency can be transferred to the appropriate accounts that need it. The transfer and its reason is recorded. In risk management, risks are continually reassessed during the course of a project, as are the needs for cost contingency.

4

Value Engineering

Value engineering (VE) is a systematic method to improve the "value" of goods or products and services by using an examination of function. Value, as defined, is the ratio of function to cost. Value can therefore be increased by either improving the function or reducing the cost. It is a primary tenet of value engineering that basic functions be preserved and not be reduced as a consequence of pursuing value improvements.

In the United States, value engineering is specifically spelled out in Public Law 104-106, which states "Each executive agency shall establish and maintain cost-effective value engineering procedures and processes."

Value engineering is sometimes taught within the project management or industrial engineering body of knowledge as a technique in which the value of a system's outputs is optimized by crafting a mix of performance (function) and costs. In most cases this practice identifies and removes unnecessary expenditures, thereby increasing the value for the manufacturer and/or their customers.

VE follows a structured thought process that is based exclusively on "function", i.e. what something "does" not what it is. For example a screw driver that is being used to stir a can of paint has a "function" of mixing the contents of a paint can and not the original connotation of securing a screw into a screw-hole. In value engineering "functions" are always described in a two word abridgment consisting of an active verb and measurable noun (what is being done - the verb - and what it is being done to - the noun) and to do so in the most non-prescriptive way possible. In the screw driver and can of paint example, the most basic function would be "blend liquid" which is less prescriptive than "stir paint" which can be seen to limit the action (by stirring) and to limit the application (only considers paint.) This is the basis of what value engineering refers to as "function analysis".

Value engineering uses rational logic (a unique "how" - "why" questioning technique) and the analysis of function to identify relationships that increase value. It is considered a quantitative method similar to the scientific method, which focuses on hypothesis-conclusion approaches to test relationships, and operations research, which uses model building to identify predictive relationships.

Value engineering is also referred to as "value management" or "value methodology" (VM), and "value analysis" (VA). VE is above all a structured problem solving process based on function analysis—understanding something with such clarity that it can be described in two words, the active verb and measurable noun abridgement. For example, the function of a pencil is to "make marks". This then facilitates considering what else can make marks. From a spray can, lipstick, a diamond on glass to a stick in the sand, one can then clearly decide upon which alternative solution is most appropriate.

Origins

Value engineering began at General Electric Co. during World War II. Because of the war, there were shortages of skilled labour, raw materials, and component parts. Lawrence Miles, Jerry Leftow, and Harry Erlicher at G.E. looked for acceptable substitutes. They noticed that these substitutions often reduced costs, improved the product, or both. What started out as an accident of necessity was turned into a systematic process. They called their technique "value analysis".

The Job Plan

Value engineering is often done by systematically following a multi-stage job plan. Larry Miles' original system was a six-step procedure which he called the "value analysis job plan." Others have varied the job plan to fit their constraints. Depending on the application, there may be four, five, six, or more stages. One modern version has the following eight steps:

1. Preparation
2. Information
3. Analysis
4. Creation

5. Evaluation
6. Development
7. Presentation
8. Follow-up

Four basic steps in the job plan are:

- Information gathering - This asks what the requirements are for the object. Function analysis, an important technique in value engineering, is usually done in this initial stage. It tries to determine what functions or performance characteristics are important. It asks questions like; What does the object do? What must it do? What should it do? What could it do? What must it not do?
- Alternative generation (creation) - In this stage value engineers ask; What are the various alternative ways of meeting requirements? What else will perform the desired function?
- Evaluation - In this stage all the alternatives are assessed by evaluating how well they meet the required functions and how great the cost savings will be.
- Presentation - In the final stage, the best alternative will be chosen and presented to the client for final decision.

Understanding the Economics of Tile Drainage

There are more than six million acres of cropland in Iowa where wetness limits productivity. Slightly more than half of the 375 different soils series mapped in Iowa have problems with excess water. The drainage of farmland is obviously important for improving the productivity of Iowa agriculture. Based on the large number of acres susceptible to excessive wetness and the yield response from removing this wetness, farmers and landowners are becoming increasingly interested in drainage.

The two major methods of farmland drainage are surface drainage where standing water is removed using surface ditches and subsurface drainage where excess water is removed through a system of underground drainage tiles. This publication deals only with subsurface tile drainage.

The major soil association areas of Iowa. Although artificial drainage can be utilized anywhere in the state, it is most prevalent in the "prairie-pothole" (Des Moines Lobe) region of the Clarion-Nicollet-Webster soil association of central and northern Iowa.

Designing a Subsurface Drainage System[1]/

The purpose of subsurface drainage is to lower the water table in the soil. The water table is the level at which the soil is entirely saturated with water. The excess water must be removed to a level below the ground surface where it will not interfere with plant root growth and development. Root growth requires air to be present in the soil. Both water and air need to be present in the spaces between the soil particles, often in equal proportions. If water fills all of these spaces (saturated), there is no room for air.

Tile drainage should be designed so the water table between tile lines can be lowered within 24 hours after a rain to a level that will not cause crop injury. Generally, most field crops are not injured if the water table is lowered to at least six inches below the ground surface in the first 24 hours after a rain. During the second day after a rain the water table should be lowered to approximately one foot and on the third day to 1.5 feet below the ground surface.

The soil types in an area to be drained greatly influence the type of system that will be installed and indicate if special problems should be anticipated.

Tile drains are placed at uniform depths where possible. The topography of the land influences the grades available, and it is often possible to orient the drains within the field to obtain a desirable grade. The grades should be sufficient to result in a non-silting velocity yet be flat enough that the maximum allowable velocity rate is not exceeded and the drain is not subjected to excessive pressure flow. Too much flow will cause erosion around the drain.

A subsurface drainage system will function only as well as the outlet for the drainage water. When planning a drainage system, it is essential that suitable outlets are available or there are opportunities to develop outlets. Outlets may be large underground tile mains, open ditches or natural waterways. Outlets may be provided in watersheds where a drainage district has been created. However, many of these outlets may be old and overused. This is especially a problem in the prairie-pothole region of Iowa where there are a lot of small sloughs of standing water and very little slope or access to natural waterways.

Patterns of Subsurface Drainage Systems

Select a drainage pattern that best fits the topography and the groundwater conditions.

The herringbone system (b) consists of parallel tile laterals that enter the main at an angle, usually from both sides. This system is used for long, relatively narrow wet areas such as those next to flat drainageways. The parallel or gridiron system (a) is similar to the herringbone system except that the laterals enter the main from only one side. This system is used on flat, regularly shaped fields with uniform soil types. The double-main system (c) is a modification of the gridiron and herringbone systems. It is used where a depression, which is frequently a natural watercourse, divides the field. A random system (d) is used where the topography is undulating or rolling and contains isolated wet areas.

Investment Analysis

The major reason for installing subsurface drainage is to improve the productivity of the farmland. Higher yields translate into more returns. This is especially true in recent years due to higher grain prices. So the investment decision is based on whether the higher crop returns will justify the investment in subsurface drainage. A secondary benefit is that fields will dry out quicker, allowing planting and harvesting to be completed earlier in the spring and fall.It also provides a larger window of time for a farmer to plant and harvest the crop allowing it to be done in a more efficient manner in terms of time and money. This is especially advantageous for farmers who have large acreages to cover.

Specific advantages of tile drainage are:

1. More consistent yields
    - Allows for more efficient use of resources
    - Reduces financial risk
2. Earlier and more timely planting
3. Improved harvesting conditions
4. Less wear and tear on equipment
5. Less power required for field operations
6. Better plant stand
7. Less plant stress
8. Fewer plant diseases
9. Less soil compaction

Another major advantage of tile drainage is the increase in sale value of the land. If the land will be sold in the future, the advantages listed above will be capitalized into the value of the land.

Subsurface drainage is a long-term investment. The investment is made up-front but the benefits are spread over many future years.

So the investment decision should be made with the time-lag in mind. The most difficult part of computing a tile investment analysis is estimating the yield response from the improved drainage. The size of the expected yield improvement dramatically impacts the economic feasibility of installing tile drainage, as shown in the example below.

Example

A 10 bushel per acre yield response from corn and a 4 bushel per acre yield response from soybeans will provide an average annual return of $35 for corn at a price of $3.50 price ($3.50 x 10 bu. = $35) and $36 for soybeans at a price of $9 ($9 x 4 bu. = $36). If the yield responses are 20 bushels for corn and 8 bushels for soybeans, the returns are double.

There are additional annual costs associated with these higher yield levels. For example, more fertilizer may be required to support these higher yields. Also, more hauling, drying and storage is required. In addition, there may be costs associated with the maintenance of the drainage system. So these additional costs need to be deducted from the returns listed above to compute a "net" return per year from installing drainage.

Estimating Future Returns

In the analysis above we assumed that the annual income stream will stay constant throughout the entire life of the tile. However, this may not be the case. Corn and soybean yields have increased over recent decades. Corn yields have increased by 2.4 percent and soybean yields by 1.8 percent per year since 1980. Most experts expect this trend to continue, if not increase. The impact of trend yield increases over the life of the tile drainage can be substantial. The yield response to tile drainage can be estimated by comparing the area to be drained to portions of the field with similar soil types that are already adequately drained or don't need drainage.

Investment Analysis Methods

Below are two ways of computing the economic returns from investing in subsurface drainage.

1) Payback Period – This is a relatively simple analysis. It is computed as the number of years required to repay the original investment in tile drainage.

Example:

If the cost of installing tile drainage is $500 per acre and the expected annual net cash return in crop returns from tile drainage is

$100 per acre, the payback period is 5 years ($500 / $100 = 5 years). The payback period does not take into account the "time value of money" from the time the tile is purchased until the returns are received (interest on the money). If money is borrowed to install the tile, the debt payment (interest and principle) is subtracted from the annual cash return and only the equity portion of the investment is used to compute the payback period.

2) Internal Rate of Return (IRR) – The IRR is based on future cash flows rather than future profits (ROI).

Example

The $100 additional cash return over the lifetime of the tile is compared to the $500 tile investment and results in an IRR of 20 percent.

If money is borrowed to install the tile, the debt payment (interest and principle) is subtracted from the annual cash return and only the equity portion of the investment is used in the computation. The IRR takes into account the time period between the time of the investment and the future years in which the annual returns are received. The IRR is based on the concept of "time value of money" which states that money received now is of more value than money received at some point in the future.

Income Tax Implications

The methods outlined above do not take income taxes into account, so it is a "before tax" analysis. However, income taxes have a significant impact on the returns that can be expected from an investment in tile drainage. Combining your marginal tax rates for federal and state income taxes, along with self-employment tax (when appropriate), provides an estimate of the how much of your returns will be paid to the government.

In general, the additional revenue (e.g. grain sales from additional production) generated from tile drainage is taxable income and the added costs (added fertilizer, tile maintenance, etc.) are tax deductible. So the added "net" return is taxable income. In addition, the annual depreciation of the tile investment is tax deductible. The government allows land owners to depreciate tile over a period of 16 years on a fixed schedule. In situations where the investor is activity involved in the farming operation (e.g. farmers owner/operator), much of the investment may be deducted in the year of installation through an IRS provision called Section 179. After taxes have been taken into account in determining annual net returns, the resulting returns are considered to be "after tax."

Typical Tile Investment Strategies

A variety of investment strategies have emerged for the installation of tile drainage. Some of these are based on installations over a period of time. Others are investment arrangements between tenants and landlords on rented land.

Investment Timing Strategies

1) Install subsurface drainage on the entire field With this strategy, the decision is made to install drainage tile on the entire field or farm. Bids and designs are obtained from various tilers, and the decision is made to move forward with tiling the entire field or farm.
2) Design the entire drainage system but install over a period of years – This is similar to the strategy above in that the drainage system for the entire field or farm is designed up-front. However, the actual investment and installation of tile drainage is spread over a period of years, often as income becomes available.
3) Invest a fixed amount of money in drainage With this strategy, the investment decision is based on spending a fixed amount of money on drainage. The system is then designed to get the most drainage benefit from the limited amount of money. Although this may optimize the benefit from the investment, it often leads to a "patchwork" system as subsequent investments are made over a period of years and does not provide for the best overall drainage system.

Landlord/tenant Strategies

1) Landlord Investment Strategy – The traditional landlord/tenant investment strategy is for the landlord to make the tiling investment and charge the tenant a higher cash rental rate. The higher cash rental rate is due to higher yields achieved from the drainage and provides the landlord with a return on his/her tiling investment.
   - The additional cash rent can be computed from the estimated increase in net return from tile installation. For example, if the cash rental rate is currently based on the typical rate in the local community, the new rate will be

the typical rate plus the additional net return from the estimated increase in net returns from drainage.

- The additional cash rent can be computed based on a fixed rate of return from the tile investment. For example, if the tiling investment is $500 per acre and a rate of return of 8 percent is desired, the additional cash rent is $40 per acre ($500 x 8% = $40). If the cash rental rate is currently based on the typical rate in the local community, the new rate will reflect this typical rate plus $40.

2) Tenant Investment Strategy – The tenant makes the tile investment on the landlord's farm. Because the landlord makes none of the investment, the cash rental rate does not increase due to the increase in productivity. The additional net returns go to the tenant as compensation for the tiling investment.

A major concern for the tenant is whether he/she will have access to the land for a long enough period of time to justify the capital investment. One approach is to enter into a long-term lease between the two parties. However, individuals often do not want to lock themselves into a lease for this length of time. In Iowa, farm leases of five or more years in length must be recorded and multiple-year leases may not exceed 20 years.

Another option is to continue with one year leases but execute an ancillary contract dealing specifically with the tiling. Under this contract the tenant receives a pro-rata buyout of the tiling investment from the landowner if he/she ceases to rent the farm during the lifetime of the tile.

For example, assume the tiling investment is $400 per acre and the life of the investment is 20 years. If the tenant ceases to rent the land after five years, he/she receives a payment of $300 per acre. Leaving after 15 years results in a payment of $100 per acre and after 20 years there is no payment.

The length of the buyout period is negotiable between tenant and landlord. The buyout payment can be made by the landlord. An alternative is for the new tenant to make the buyout payment to the tenant that is leaving and take over the remaining life of the contract.

3) Shared Investment Strategy – The landlord and tenant share the tiling investment and use a crop-share lease. The investment is shared in the same proportion as the crop is shared in the leasing arrangement (e.g. 50/50). With this arrangement, each party receives the additional net returns in the same proportion

as the investment. An arrangement is made where the tenant will receive a prorated buyout if he/she leaves the farm before the useful life of the tile is expended. An alternative is for the landlord to make the investment and modify the crop share lease provisions to reflect the change in contribution.

Getting Started

If the tiling will be performed by an outside contractor, get bids from a variety of tile contractors. Have them prepare the tile layout for your farm and then provide a bid for doing the job. You need to compare both the bid and the layout when choosing among contractors.

Prepare a Plan

The person doing the drainage design should prepare a plan and construction notes for the contractor. The plan should be corrected for any modifications during construction. The plans should include a map showing the locations, sizes and grades of all lines and appurtenances. Contractors with GPS equipment can provide detailed tile maps. Profiles or construction notes of all mains and sub-mains should be included. One or more copies of the final plan and notes, along with construction modifications, should be given to the landowner. The owner should keep two copies. File one copy with your legal papers of the land and keep a working copy with your farm records. If plans, notes and maps are lost or misplaced, it will cause considerable confusion and difficulty in the future when the drainage system needs to be repaired or rebuilt.

Contact USDA

You need to get approval from the United State Department of Agriculture (USDA) for any farmland that will be installed with tile drainage. Start the process by contacting your county Farm Service Agency (FSA) office and provide them with a description of the exact acreage on which you are planning to install tile drainage. This information will be provided to the Natural Resource Conservation Service (NRCS) to make a determination if any "wetlands" are included in the drainage area. Land areas considered to be "wetlands" by USDA cannot be tile drained. After its investigation, NRCS will provide you with a Certified Wetland Determination.

Tile Drainage Inspection and Maintenance

You should inspect your tile drainage system regularly and conduct maintenance when required. Prompt repair of any drain failure will keep the system in working order and prevent permanent damage to the entire system.

1) Inspection – Subsurface drainage systems do not require extensive maintenance, but the maintenance that is required is extremely important. If subsurface drains are working, water will stand in the field for only a short time after a heavy rain. If water stands for a few days, the drain may be partly or completely blocked.
2) Cleaning outlet ditches – Many subsurface drainage systems fail because outlet ditches are blocked. If the outlet ditch is filled with sediment, a survey should be conducted to determine the extent of the cleanout work.
3) Cleaning surface inlets – Poorly constructed surface inlets are subject to severe damage and require frequent repair. Inlet covers often become sealed with trash and should be checked frequently. Clean the covers after a heavy rain and replace them carefully.
4) Repair blowouts – Holes that have developed over subsurface drains should be repaired at once. Otherwise, large amounts of soil may wash into the line and block the entire system.
5) Remove sediment – Sediment traps can be used for subsurface drains laid in fine sand or silty soils. If cleaned regularly, traps keep soil from filling the lines.
6) Protect drain outlets – Gullies commonly form at unprotected outlets of subsurface drains. Gullies may damage the field, silt up the drainage ditch and reduce the flow of water from the subsurface drain.
7) Control rodents – A flap gate or fixed pin guard can be used to prevent rodents and other small animals from entering and blocking outlets.
8) Control tree roots – Trees such as willow, elm, soft maple, cottonwood and other water-loving trees within approximately 100 feet of the drain should be removed. A clearance of 50 feet should be maintained from other species of trees.
9) Ochre accumulations in the drain – Ochre, which is an iron oxide, may block the drain when iron in solution moves from the soil to the drain and accumulates.

Iowa Drainage Guide, Iowa State University Extension, Special Report 13, revised June 2008.

Additional information available on the drainage of Iowa farmland

Iowa Drainage Guide (a $25 purchase) includes 1) Iowa drainage laws, 2) drainage guidelines for Iowa soils, 3) subsurface drainage, 4) surface drainage, 5) open channels, 6) pump drainage. Iowa Drainage Law Manual

Adjudication

Adjudication is a contractual or statutory procedure for swift interim dispute resolution. Adjudication is provided by a third party adjudicator selected by the parties to the dispute. Adjuducation is often is subject to a strict timetable and may be based purely on documentary submissions.

Adjudicators can adopt an inquisitorial role which may involve taking the initiative in ascertaining facts and law.

Adjudication decisions are binding unless and until they are revised by arbitration or litigation. There is no right of appeal and limited right to resist enforcement. Award of legal costs is at the discretion of the adjudicator unless this is excluded by the terms of the contract.

If parties to a construction contract do not agree an adjudication procedure, then one is imposed by statute.Contractualadjudication procedures must comply with Section 108 of the Housing Grants, Construction and Regeneration Act.

The adjudicator is either named in the contract, agreed by the parties or appointed by a nominating body, usually named in the contract (see for example, the Technology and Construction Solicitors Association (TeSCA) which has developed its own Adjudication Rules (now version 3.1). If the parties do not agree procedural rules which comply with the Housing Grants, Construction and Regeneration Act then the Act imposes the rules set out in the Scheme for Construction Contracts.

Alternative Dispute Resolution

Construction contracts usually provide for disputes to be dealt with by agreed dispute resolution procedures involving mediation, adjudication and arbitration. Often a combination of all three.

The construction sector is also subject to statutory schemes which impose adjudication procedures in the absence of contractual agreement (such as the Housing Grants, Construction and Regeneration Act 1996 and the Local Democracy, Economic Development and Construction Act 2009).

Many contracts for large and complex projects now have, in addition to the dispute resolution procedures set out above, tiered dispute resolution procedures with obligations to negotiate in good faith, dispute resolution boards, steering committees and partnering meetings under the nomenclature of 'Partnering Obligations'.

Contractdisputes are a complex area of law and the choice of procedure is one which requires careful consideration.

Definitions

A very wide range of Alternative Dispute Resolution techniques are available.

A consultative document, 'Alternative Dispute Resolution – A Discussion Paper', produced by the Lord Chancellor's Department (LCD) in 1999 provides a helpful summary of the wide range of Alternative Dispute Resolution (ADR) techniques and these are reproduced below:

- Arbitration is a procedure whereby both sides to a dispute agree to let a third party, the arbitrator, decide. In some instances, there may be a panel. The arbitrator may be a lawyer, or may be an expert in the field of the dispute. They will make a decision according to the law. The arbitrator's decision, known as an award, is legally binding and can be enforced through the courts.
- Court-annexed non-binding arbitration is widely used in the United States. The finding of the arbitrator becomes a binding order of the court if neither party seeks a rehearing by a judge.
- Court settlement process – this is a combination of early neutral evaluation and mediation, which was recently introduced by the Technology and Construction Court (TCC) on a trial basis in 2006. It has been produced for use in those situations where, following a request from the parties, a case managing judge feels that the parties should be able to achieve an amicable settlement. In those circumstances, the case managing judge would then be at liberty to offer a court settlement process to the parties and, if accepted by all relevant parties to the case, that judge or another TCC judge would make a court settlement order embodying the parties' agreement and fixing a date for a court settlement conference, with an estimated duration proportionate to the issues in the case. The judge would then conduct the court settlement process and if a settlement were not reached, then the case would proceed with another case

management judge: the judge conducting the court settlement process (the settlement judge) would take no further part in the litigation.

- Early neutral evaluation is a process in which a neutral professional, commonly a lawyer, hears a summary of each party's case and gives a non-binding assessment of the merits. This can then be used as a basis for settlement or for further negotiation.
- Expert determination is a process in which an independent third party who is an expert in the subject matter is appointed to decide the dispute. The expert's decision is binding on the parties.
- Mediation is a way of settling disputes in which a third party, known as a mediator, helps both sides to come to an agreement that each considers acceptable. Mediation can be 'evaluative', where the mediator gives an assessment of the legal strength of a case, or 'facilitative', where the mediator concentrates on assisting the parties to define the issues. When a mediation is successful and an agreement is reached, it is written down and forms a legally binding contract, unless the parties state otherwise.
- Conciliation is a procedure like mediation but in which the third party, the conciliator, takes a more interventionist role in bringing the two parties together and in suggesting possible solutions to help achieve an agreed settlement. The term 'conciliation' is gradually falling into disuse and the process is regarded as a form of mediation. It remains, however, a specific process available under various Institution of Civil Engineers' contracts.
- Med-arbitration (med-arb) is a combination of mediation and arbitration. The parties agree to a mediation initially but, if that fails to achieve a settlement, the mediator takes on the role of arbitrator, with powers to make a legally binding award. The same person may act as mediator and arbitrator in this type of arrangement.
- Neutral fact finding is a non-binding procedure used in cases involving complex technical issues. A neutral expert in the subject matter is appointed to investigate the facts of the dispute and make an evaluation of the merits of the case. This can form the basis of a settlement or a starting point for further negotiation.

- Ombudsmen are independent office holders who investigate and rule on complaints from members of the public about maladministration in Government and in particular services in both the public and private sectors. Some ombudsmen use mediation as part of their dispute resolution procedures. The powers of ombudsmen vary. Most ombudsmen are able to make recommendations; only a few can make decisions that are enforceable through the courts.
- Utility regulators are watchdogs appointed to oversee the privatised utilities such as water or gas. They handle complaints from customers who are dissatisfied by the way a complaint has been dealt with by their supplier.

In addition to those listed above by the LCD, the following may be added:

- Mini-trial, also known as executive tribunal, in which each party, often through its legal advisers, makes a presentation of its case to a 'mini-trial panel'. An abbreviated version of the discovery process may have taken place in advance of the mini-trial. The panel generally consists of three members – a management executive from each party (with sufficient authority to reach a settlement), and a third party neutral who may act as a mediator or adviser. The executive members usually have not been involved in the particular dispute. After the submissions have been made, the executives seek to negotiate a settlement. The role of the third party neutral may vary. They may act as a mediator or may act as an adviser, assessing objectively both the facts and the merits of the case and advising on the most appropriate solution.
- Construction adjudication is a statutory right introduced into UKconstruction contracts by the Housing Grants, Construction and Regeneration Act 1996, applicable to all relevant contracts entered into after 1 May 1998. It provides a temporarily binding decision which must be complied with by the parties until overturned or varied by the courts, arbitration or agreement.
- Dispute board (also known as dispute review board or dispute resolution board (DRB) and disputeadjudication board (DAB)) is a procedure where a panel, normally of three independent and well-established individuals, is appointed at the commencement of a large construction project and considers project issues and recommends resolutions of disputes. Normally

the employer and contractor each appoint one member and the third member is chosen by the first two. The recommendations are normally non-binding.

- Judicial appraisal is a procedure where the parties appoint a judge to receive written representations from each side and make an appraisal of the likely result if the case goes to court. The parties must agree the form and extent of the submissions and whether the appraisal is to be binding or not.
- Med-adjudication (med-ad) is a process in which the appointed neutral begins conducting the process as if they were an adjudicator, but after meeting the parties' key professionals and expert witnesses together, gives a preliminary view on the matter in dispute. If the parties settle, this is recorded in writing, but if no settlement is reached within a fixed period of time the neutral proceeds to make a decision in which they are not bound by their preliminary view.
- Michigan mediation is an interesting variation on the theme and, as the name suggests, is used in the US state of Michigan. In any civil case where the primary relief sought is monetary, the assigned judge may refer the case to process. The term 'mediation' is, however, something of a misnomer: it is more properly described as a 'case valuation' process. After disclosure has been completed, the parties meet with a panel of three neutrals who are all attorneys. They hear 15-minute presentations by each party and give a non-binding evaluation of the case.
- Project neutral is effectively a one-person dispute board.
- Summary jury trial is a non-binding, abbreviated mock trial using a panel of actual jurors. The normal rules of evidence and procedure are normally modified to expedite the process, and negotiations generally follow the trial. It is used so far only in the United States.

The above processes can be divided into two broad categories which the LCD has described as:

- alternative adjudication, which comprises those processes whereby a neutral third party makes a decision, such as arbitration, construction adjudication, expert determination, ombudsmen and industry regulators;
- assisted settlement, which comprises those processes whereby a neutral third party offers an opinion and/or seeks to bring

the parties to an agreement, such as mediation, conciliation and early neutral evaluation.

Selection of Technique

Whether or not a particular form of ADR is suitable depends upon a number of factors including the nature and value of the dispute, the attitude and financial resources of the parties, the desired outcome, and the balance of representation.

Both (or all) parties must be willing to submit their dispute to a form of alternativeadjudication, or willing to try a form of assisted settlement as clearly, if both parties are not willing, there can be problems in enforcing an apparently contractual agreement to try mediation or conciliation.

Litigation is, of course, the only option where one party needs to set a legal precedent or obtain an injunction, or where one party is refusing to acknowledge the problem or engage in negotiations. Any form of ADR will be worth considering where the cost of court proceedings is likely to equal or exceed the amount of money at issue.

Where parties wish to preserve an existing relationship, mediation or conciliation may be helpful. A great advantage of mediation is that the mediator is not bound merely to consider the obvious disputes between the parties but can bring in other matters, perhaps unrelated to the particular dispute, provided they may help the parties towards settlement.

Arbitration may be suitable in cases where there is no relationship to preserve and a rapid decision is needed.

Where available, trade association arbitration schemes, utility regulators and ombudsmen can provide a cheaper alternative for an individual seeking redress against a company or large organisation, but they may be limited in the redress they can provide.

Early neutral evaluation might be applicable in cases where there is a dispute over a point of law, or where one party appears to have an unrealistic view of their chances of success at trial.

Where there is a technical dispute with a great deal of factual evidence, mediation or determination by an expert in that area might be best. In addition, parties involved in a commercial dispute may prefer to use a form of ADR to keep sensitive commercial information private.

In many apparently intractable, large-scale and complex multi-party cases, mediation has achieved settlement. Where there is a significant imbalance of power, however, mediation might not be appropriate. Mediation is also now the preferred method of settlement of family disputes, such as divorce. Part III of the Family Law Act 1996 allows for the provision of publicly funded mediation in family proceedings. There has been a wide take-up of this service and the statistics for the six full years of operation are as shown in the following table:

Financial year	***Number of mediations started***
1997/98	406
1998/99	1,349
1999/00	6,333
2000/01	9,308
2001/02	12,335
2002/03	13,841

Section 29 of the Act, which requires those seeking legal aid for representation in family proceedings to attend a meeting with a mediator to consider whether mediation might be suitable in their case, has now been implemented in over 60% of the country and was intended to be in force across England and Wales in 2000.

Figures for 2005 produced by the Legal Services Commission show that over 14,000 family mediations took place which were either wholly or partly publicly funded. The UK College of Family Mediation reports that for the same year some 4,000 privately funded family mediations took place, making a total of some 18,000 for that year.

Mediation is also frequently used in neighbour disputes. Not all disputes between neighbours are necessarily suited to mediation, however, particularly where there are issues of harassment or mental health problems. MediationUK reports that, between 2004 and 2005, more than 40,000 people were involved in community mediation.

Arbitration

Arbitration is a private, contractual form of dispute resolution. It provides for the determination of disputes by a third party arbitrator or arbitration panel, selected by the parties to the dispute. Disputes are resolved on the basis of material facts, documents and relevant principles of law.

The arbitration process is administered by an appointed arbitrator subject to any relevant contractual rules and subject to the statutory regulatory framework applied by the domestic courts. There are only limited rights of appeal and legal costs are usually awarded to the successful party.

English law does not insist on any formal requirements for an arbitration agreement (for example it can be verbal), however if the agreement is not in writing it will be outside the supervisory regime of the courts established by the Arbitration Act. In addition, construction projects with complex disputes require properly constituted arbitration procedures in order for them to be effective.

Arbitration clauses are traditionally found in all standard form contracts used in the UK, often with related adjudication clauses (for example JCT 05, and ICE 7th Edition (now withdrawn in favour of NEC3)). In the last few years there has been a tendency to set the dispute resolution default at litigation rather than arbitration, leaving the parties to specifically agree to arbitration (for example JCT 05 Section 9 and NEC3 option W2). Arbitration remains the favoured method of dispute resolution for international projects (for example FIDIC contracts) and UNCITRAL are widely accepted in international commerce.

Arbitration commences with a notice to concur which provides for agreement on the appointment of an arbitrator, failing which an arbitrator may be appointed by a nominating body (which should be named in the contract). Arbitration is now usually combined with adjudication and mediation in tiered dispute resolution procedures.

Bill of Quantities

The bill of quantities (sometimes referred to as 'BoQ') is a document prepared by the cost consultant (often a quantity surveyor) that provides project specific measured quantities of the items of work identified by the drawings and specifications in the tender documentation. The quantities may be measured in number, length, area, volume, weight or time. Preparing a bill of quantities requires that the design is complete and a specification has been prepared.

The bill of quantities is issued to tenderers for them to prepare a price for carrying out the works. The bill of quantities assists tenderers in the calculation of construction costs for their tender, and, as it means all tenderingcontractors will be pricing the same quantities (rather than taking-off quantities from the drawings and specifications themselves), it also provides a fair and accurate system for tendering.

The contractortenders against the bill of quantities, stating their price for each item. This priced bill of quantities constitutes the tenderer's offer. As the offer is built up of prescribed items, it is possible to compare both the overall price and individual items directly with other tenderers' offers, allowing a detailed assessment of which aspects of a tender may offer good or poor value. This information can assist with tender negotiations.

The priced bill of quantities will also:

- Assist with the agreement of the contract sum with the successful tenderer.
- Provide a schedule of rates assisting with the valuation of variations.
- Provide a basis for the valuation of interim payments.
- Provide a basis for the preparation of the final account.

Preparing Bills of Quantities

It is very important that bills of quantities are prepared according to a standard, widely recognised methodology. This helps avoid any ambiguities or misunderstandings and so helps avoid disputes arising through different interpretations of what has been priced. In the UK, bills of quantities for general construction works will most commonly be prepared in accordance with the Standard Method of Measurement, currently in its 7th Edition (SMM7).

Other methods of measurement are used for civil engineering works (Civil Engingineering Method of Measurement) currently in its 3rd Edition (CESMM).

SMM7 adopts the Common Arrangement of Work Sections (CAWS), a standard method for categorising the works:

- A - Preliminaries and general conditions.
- B - Complete buildings, structures and units.
- C - Existing site, buildings and services.
- D - Groundwork.
- E - In situ concrete and large precast concrete.
- F - Masonry.
- G - Structural carcassing, metal and timber.
- H - Cladding and covering.
- J - Waterproofing.
- K - Linings, sheathing and dry partitioning.
- L - Windows, doors and stairs.

- M - Surface finishes.
- N - Furniture and equipment.
- P - Building fabric sundries.
- Q - Paving, planting, fencing and site furniture.
- R - Disposal systems.
- S - Piped supply systems.
- T - Mechanical heating, cooling and refrigeration systems.
- U - Ventilation and air conditioning systems.
- V - Electrical systems.
- W - Communications, security, safety and protection systems.
- X - Transport systems.
- Y - General engineering services.
- Z - Building fabric reference specification.

Each section offers detailed information, additional classification tables and supplementary rules.

NB This system is currently undergoing considerable change, with CAWS being incorporated into Uniclass, Uniclass being replaced with Uniclass2 and SMM7 being superceded by the New Rules of Measurement (NRM). SMM7 is likely to be replaced by NRM in July 2013.

Bills of quantities can be prepared elementally or in works packages, and are most useful to the contractor when they are prepared in work sections that reflect likely sub-contractpackages. This makes it easier for the contractor to obtain prices from sub-contractors and is more likely to result in an accurate and competitive price.

The bill of quantities should identify the different kinds of work required, but should not specify them as this can lead to confusion between information in the bill of quantities and information in the specification itself.

Disputes can occur where there is discrepancy between the bill of quantities and the rest of the tender documents (for example where an item is included in the drawings and specification but not in the bill of quantities), or where there has been an arithmetical error. Generally the priced bill of quantities will take precedent, and the client will be responsible for their own errors or omissions, which may be classified as relevant events (or compensation events) giving rise to claims for an extension of time and loss and expense. However if an ambiguity or error is noticed by the contractor during the tender process, it is best practice for them to tell the client, even if there may be some commercial advantage to them not doing so.

Increasingly, software packages are available to assist in the preparation of preparation of bills of quantities, and building information modelling systems can be used to produce bills of quantities from information already contained within the model.

Bills of quantities are normally only prepared on larger projects. On smaller projects, or for alteration work the contractor can be expected to measure their own quantities from drawings and schedules of work. Schedules of work are 'without quantities' instructional lists that allow the contractor to identify significant work and materials that will be needed to complete the works and to calculate the quantities that will be required.

Approximate Bill of Quantities

An approximate bill of quantities (or notional bill of quantities) can be used on projects where it is not possible to prepare a firm bill of quantities at the time of tendering, for example if the design is relatively complete, but exact quantities are not yet known. However this will tend to result in more variations during construction and so less price certainty when the investment decision is made.

Some contracts allows for re-measurement of approximate quantities (for example, this is common on cut and fill on roadworks). Here, quantities are simply revised and payments made accordingly without the need to instruct a variation.

If an approximate quantity turns out not to have been a realistic estimate of the quantity actually required, this may constitute a relevant event giving rise to claims for an extension of time and loss and expense.

Approximate bills of quantities can also be used during the design process as a tool for controlling design. They are then sometimes included in the tender documents as a guide with a caveat stating that responsibility for measuring quantities lies with the contractor, and drawings and specifications take priority over any description in the approximate bills.

Bonds in Construction Contracts

Bonds are a means of protection against the non-performance of the contractor. They are an undertaking by a bondsman or surety to make a payment to the client in the event of non-performance of the contractor. The cost of the bond is usually borne by the contractor, albeit, this is likely to be reflected in the contractor's tender price.

Bonds can be 'on demand' or 'conditional', with conditional bonds requiring that the client provides evidence that the contractor has not performed their obligations under the contract and that they have suffered a loss as a consequence.

Performance Bond

A performance bond is commonly used as a means of insuring a client against the risk of a contractor failing to fulfil contractual obligations to the client, although they can also be required from other parties.

Performance bonds are typically set at 10% of the Contractvalue. This compensation can enable the client to overcome difficulties that have been caused by non-performance of the contractor, such as, finding a new Contractor to complete the works.

Advance Paymentbond

If the client agrees to make an advance payment to the contractor, (for example where the contractor incurs significant start up and procurement costs before construction begins), a bond may be required to secure the payment against default by the contractor.

This will normally be an on-demand bond.

Off-site Materialsbond

It can sometimes be appropriate for the client to pay for items even though they remain 'off-site', for example, where a contractor has made a large payment for plant or materials that have yet to be delivered to site, or if the client wishes to 'reserve' key items in order to protect the programme.

This is similar to the situation where an advanced payment is made in that a bond secures the payment against default by the contractor and is likely to be an on-demand bond. The bond might be up to the value of the off-site items, with the value of the bond reducing as deliveries to site are made.

Bid Bond (or Tenderbond)

Bid bonds are rare in the UK, but can be a requirement of an international tender process. They are usually on-demand bonds submitted with a tender to secure the tender's commitment to commence the contract. The bond is partially or fully forfeited if the winning tender fails to execute the contract or meet other specified conditions.

Bid bonds can be open to abuse by the client and may prevent smaller companies from tendering.

Retentionbond

Retention is a percentage (often 5%) of the amount certified as due to the contractor on an interim certificate that is retained by the client. The purpose of retention is to ensure the contractor properly completes the activities required of them under the contract. Half of the amount retained is released on certification of practical completion and the remainder is released upon certification of making good defects.

An alternative to retention is a retentionbond, where the client agrees to pay the amounts which would otherwise have been held as retention, but instead a bond is provided to secure the amount that would have been retained. As with retention, the value of the bond will usually reduce after practical completion has been certified.

Defects Liability Bond (or Defects Liability Demand Guarantee)

The defects liability period (now called the 'rectification period' in Joint Contracts Tribunal (JCT) contracts) begins upon certification of practical completion and typically lasts six to twelve months. During this time, it is the contractor's responsibility to rectify any defects that become apparent in the works.

A defects liability bond can be used to ensure that the contractor continues to provide services, rectifying defects that become apparent after practical completion has been certified. This is generally an on-demand bond that may be required on projects where there are no remaining payments to be made, or other security such as retention, after practical completion.

Adjudicationbond

Adjudication is a contractual or statutory procedure for swift dispute resolution. Adjudication is provided by a third party adjudicator selected by the parties to the dispute.

Adjudicationbonds are conditional bonds that have emerged on PFI/PPP projects and are payable on an adjudicators decision. Adjudicationbonds are most suitable when the adjudicator's decision is final and binding. If this is not the case, (ie the adjudicator's decision is an interim one) complex procedures are necessary ot balance payments if subsequent dispute resolution procedures reach different decisions.

Bonds v Guarantees

What is in a name? Never is that question more relevant than in response to whether a document is a bond or guarantee. Does it matter and what is the difference between them?

These are all pertinent questions for contractors and consultants in these tough times when faced with the decision between giving either bonds or guarantees, or both.

Increasingly in the current economic climate, employers, whether domestic or international, are demanding protection against default from contractors and consultants. Seldom were consultants ever required to give such protection to employers, but now particularly for international and public sector clientsbonds and guarantees are featuring commonly in the menu of project requirements.

The first thing to bear in mind is that the name of the document can be misleading and does not necessarily accurately describe the nature of document. It is the content of the document that is key. Bonds and guarantees are forms of security that accompany contractual obligations (either building contracts or consultancy agreements) and are based on either primary or secondary obligations.

Examples of primary obligation bonds are simple or on-demand bonds or demand guarantees, where the bondsman pays an amount of money set out in the bond immediately on demand in writing without any preconditions, including the contractor's liability. On demand bonds tend to be common in international projects but are rarely seen in the UK. They are generally resisted where possible because of their draconian nature.

Secondary obligation instruments normally comprise guarantees, including parent company guarantees (PCG), or conditional bonds and the bondsman is only liable where a breach of contract has occurred, for example, the contractor is in breach of contract. Due to their nature they are more common in the domestic construction market, and contractors are more likely to provide such forms of security than the on-demand variety.

For employers deciding between the two, various considerations must be assessed including the cost of procuring them, where a bond has a direct impact on the tender price, but a parent company guarantee may not.

Recent cases have assisted in distinguishing between the two forms of security, but of course there are no guarantees the bondsman (or the surety) will meets its liability under the bond should it be called in. The Court of Appeal case of *Aviva Insurance Limited v Hackney Empire Limited [2012] EWCA Civ 1716* provided useful guidance on the court's approach to circumstances where a bondsman's liability under the bond might be discharged.

In this case Hackney Empire ('Hackney') had engaged a contractor under a JCT 1998 traditional building contract to undertake renovation works to the old Hackney Empire. The contractor obtained a performance bond from Aviva in favour of Hackney for £1.1m. The contractor fell into delay claiming extensions of time and loss and expense and Hackney faced with the dilemma as to whether to leave the contractor to struggle with financial difficulties and late completion, made advance payments to aid its cash flow and enable prompt completion. These payments were made under a separate side agreement between Hackney and the contractor. Unfortunately, the contractor went into administration and Hackney called in the bond. Aviva resisted payment due to Hackney's advance payments to the contractor which it claimed discharged it from liability under the bond. The matter reached the Court of Appeal where it was decided that Aviva's liability as bondsman was not discharged by the advance payments and it remained liable to Hackney for the full amount of the bond. Interesting findings arose from the court's decision as to circumstances where a surety may be discharged:

- Where parties to a contract have varied the terms of that contract without the surety's consent.
- Advance payments of the contract price paid by an employer to a contractor*may* discharge the surety, but additional payments (e.g. a gift/loan) to the contractor falling outside the terms of the original contract do not discharge the surety's liability.
- The surety is not released from liability arising from contractualvariations or advance payments if (a) he specifically consented to what was done or (b) the contract contained an indulgence clause.

The court's reasoning fell within (ii) above in that the advance payments made to the contractor were outside the terms of the original contact and for extraneous reasons; the payments were not part of the original contract sum nor were they certified as due by the architect. Aviva's liability as surety only related to the original building contract.

Practically, the safe course may be to ensure explicit consent is obtained from a surety if advance payments are considered and an appropriately drafted indulgence clause in the contract. Such clauses recognise potential variations to the contract and maintain the surety's liability in these instances. Alternatively, advance payments made via side agreements outside the contract could be considered, as any variation to the original contract itself could still discharge the surety.

5

Breach of Contract

If the one of the parties to a contract fails to perform as required by the contract, this may constitute a breach of contract. A breach of contract may entitle the innocent party to make a claim for damages for the losses it has suffered.

If the breach of contract is serious (a material breach), then the innocent party may also consider that it is discharged from any further obligations under the contract.

If the breach is less serious, (a non-material breach, sometimes referred to as a default) the innocent party may make a claim for damages, but may not consider it is discharged from any further obligations under the contract. This prevents the innocent party from excusing their performance because of a minor breach of just one part of the contract.

This is generally the position on construction contracts, where some works are likely to have been carried out, but one or more may remain undone, incomplete or defective. As building contracts are usually divided up in to parts (divisible), and include a series of separate payments, this sort of partial failure would not allow the innocent party to excuse their performance, ie a failure in one part will generally only mean that the client is not liable to pay for that part. Furthermore, if the works have been substantially performed, then the client must pay for them subject to a claim for the parts that have not been performed.

On construction contracts, it is generally in the interests of both parties for the contract to continue and for the works to proceed irrespective of minor problems. Whilst damages for breach of contract may seek to put the innocent party in the position it would have been in had there not been a breach of contract, the delay and disruption caused, for example, by having to appoint a new contractor can far outweigh the difficulties of proceeding, albeit under difficult circumstances.

Construction contracts generally make provisions for the contract to be varied without there being a breach. Variations, extensions of time, claims for loss and expense, liquidated damages, and the defects liability period all provide for the contract to be varied or for problems to be rectified.

Where one party behaves in such a way that it indicates it no longer intends to accept its obligations under the contract, this is considered to be a repudiatory beach (or fundamental breach) allowing the innocent party to terminate the contract and to sue for damages. Generally the contract will set out what those breaches are, but they might include:

- Refusal to carry out work.
- Abandoning the site.
- Removing plant from the site.
- Failure to make payments.
- Employing others to carry out the work.
- Failure to allow access to the site.
- Failure to proceed regularly and diligently.
- Failure to remove or rectify defective works.

Where repudiation is considered to have occurred, the innocent party can either affirm that the contract will continue or accept the repudiation and so terminate the contract. In either case, they will have the right to claim damages. Either way, it is important that there is some sort of response, as inaction may be considered to be an affirmation of the contract.

Assessing the seriousness of breaches of contract depends on the particular circumstances and terms of the contract. For example, if a contractor failed to carry out the work to an agreed timetable, this might be considered a relatively minor issue on some projects, whilst on others it could be an extremely serious breach. The innocent party must be careful therefore to establish that there has actually been a material breach before considering that the contract is terminated, otherwise they might find themselves in breach of contract.

This can lead to disputes, where for example, the client refuses to make payment, claiming that the contractor has failed to perform, whereas the contractor contends that they are not performing because the client has refused to make payment.

An anticipatory breach (or anticipatory repudiation) occurs when one of the parties to the contract declares to the other that they do not intend to perform their obligations under the contract.

The contract may also allow termination under other circumstances, such as frustration or insolvency. It may also allow termination for 'convenience', but this may leave the terminating party open to significant claims by the other party.

Rescission is a process of returning both parties to the position they would have been in had they not entered into a contract, that might be appropriate for example if there is a serious error in the contract.

NB The term irremediable breach refers to a situation where there is a defect in the works for which the cost of rectification is unreasonable relative to the nature of the defect. Under these circumstances the contract administrator may issue a certificate of making good defects, with a deduction relative to the amount by with the value of the works has been reduced by the defect.

NB The Construction Act now gives contractors the right to suspend performance for non-payment.

Certificate of Making Good Defects

The certificate of making good defects is now referred to as the 'certificate of making good' in the new JCT '05 suite of contracts.

The Purpose of the Certificate of Making Good Defects

Once practical completion has been certified, the defects liability period begins (now called the 'rectification period' in Joint Contracts Tribunal (JCT) contracts). Typically, the defects liability period is six to twelve months.

During this period, the client reports any defects that arise in the works to the contract administrator who decides whether they are in fact defects (i.e. works that are not in accordance with the contract), or whether they are maintenance issues. If the contract administrator considers that they are defects, then they may issue instructions to the contractor to make good the defects within a reasonable time.

At the end of the defects liability period, the contract administrator prepares a schedule of defects, listing those defects that have not yet been rectified, and agrees with the contractor the date by which they will be rectified. Defects must be made good within a 'reasonable time', and at the contractor's cost. NB. It is the contractor's responsibility to identify and rectify defects, not the client's or the contract administrator's, so if they do bring defects to the contractor's notice, they should make clear that this is not a comprehensive list of all defects.

When the contract administrator considers that all items on the schedule of defects have been made good, they issue a certificate of making good defects. This has the effect of releasing the remainder of any retention and brings about issuing of the final certificate.

Particular Circumstances Relating to the Certificate of Making Good Defects.

If the contractor, having been given the opportunity to rectify defects, fails to do so within a reasonable time, they may be in breach of contract. In this situation others may be employed to rectify the defects, and the cost of such works deducted from the contractor's retention.

In particular circumstances where the cost of rectifying a defect is disproportionate relative to the impact of the defect on the works, the client may agree to have the certificate of making good defects issued anyway, but only on agreement that the contract sum is reduced by an amount that reflects the reduction in the value of the works as a consequence of the defect.

If a defect becomes apparent after the certificate of making good defects has been issued, but before the final certificate has been issued, the contractor may be given the opportunity to rectify the defect anyway, but the final certificate should not be issued until this has been done.

On construction management projects and management contract projects, a separate certificate of practical completion is issued for each trade contract (or works contract). This means that defects liability periods may be at different times for each trade contract (or works contract).

Where sectional completion (or phased completion) occurs, a separate certificate of making good defects may be issued for each section and then for the whole of the works. This may also be the case where the client arranges for partial possession of part of the works. NB The Housing Grants Construction and Regeneration Act disallows 'pay when paid' clauses, this means that it is not longer acceptable for a contractor to withhold the release of retention to a subcontractor simply because they themselves have not had their retention released.

What are Defects?

Defects are works that have not been carried out in accordance with the contract. Defects which are discoverable before the end of the defects liability period are described as 'patent defects'. Defects which could not have been discovered during the defects liability period are known as 'latent defects' (for example, a problem with foundations which have been covered up and does not become apparent until several years later when settlement causes cracks to appear).

Patent defects should be rectified as an ongoing process, and certainly, before the certificate of practical completion is issued, then before the certificate of making good defects is issued and ultimately before the final certificate is issued.

Latent defects can result in liability for damages for up to 15 years. The Limitation Act 1980 governs time limits for bringing different types of legal claims.

Latent defects can be highly problematic and very expensive to repair. If there is a suspicion of latent defects, it is sensible to have investigations carried out before the end of the defects liability period.

Difficulties Surrounding Practical Completion

It is important to note that the defects liability period is not a chance to correct problems apparent at practical completion, it is a period during which the contractor may be recalled to rectify defects which appear. If there are defects apparent before practical completion, then these should be rectified before a certificate of practical completion is issued.

This can put the contract administrator in a difficult position, where both the contractor and the client are keen to issue the certificate (so that the building can be handed over) and yet defects (more than a de minimis) are apparent in the works. Issuing the certificate however could render the contract administrator liable for problems that this causes, for example in the calculation of liquidated damages.

If the contract administrator is pressured to certify practical completion even though the works are not complete, they might consider informing the client in writing of the potential problems of doing so, obtaining written consent from the client to certify practical completion and obtaining agreement from the contractor that they will complete the works and rectify any defects. It might also be possible to prepare a qualified practical completion certificate however care must be taken to use the correct wording. If the contract administrator is not confident about the potential problems surrounding practical completion, they might advise the client to seek legal advice.

Certificate of Non Completion

The date for completion of construction works (or dates for completion of sections of the works) is generally set out in the contract particulars. However, it is not uncommon for delays to cause the completion date to be missed, that is, the works are not complete, and so a certificate of practical completion cannot issued by the date for completion.

Where the client is responsible for the delay, an extension of time may be granted, the completion date adjusted, and the contractor may be entitled to claim loss and expense.

Where the contractor is responsible for the delay, the client may be entitled to claim liquidated and ascertained damages (at a rate set out in the contract particulars).

Some contracts (such as the JCT Standard Form of Building Contract) require that the contract administrator issues the contractor with a certificate of non-completion (sometimes referred to as a 'non-completion certificate' or 'non-completion notice') as a pre-requisite to claiming liquidated and ascertained damages. The certificate of non-completion gives formal written notice to the contractor that they have failed to complete the works described in the contract by the completion date that was last agreed (the original completion date may have been adjusted during the course of the works).

The contract administrator must give due consideration to any applications for extension of time before issuing a certificate of non-completion, and if there are subsequent extensions of time that result in the completion date being adjusted, and the contractor then fails to meet this adjusted date, a new certificate of non-completion must be issued.

Where the contract provides for sectional completion of the works, separate certificates of non-completion must be issued for each section that is not completed by the required date.

The client may then deduct liquidated and ascertained damages from payments otherwise due to the contractor, providing that an appropriate notice has been issued (a pay less notice) setting out the basis of the calculation. Contractors may challenge claims for liquidated and ascertained damages if the procedures and the notice periods set out in the contract have not been followed.

Some contracts (such as the JCT Minor Works Building Contract) do not require that a certificate of non-completion is issued, although it may be considered best practice to issue one anyway.

Contract claims

Contractors

Contractors and subcontractors should avoid unmerited and exaggerated claims which in extreme cases can lead to personal prosecution on charges of criminal fraud. Claims must be properly constituted and documented:

- Proper legal entitlement must be established.
- Cause and effect must be clearly demonstrated by contemporaneous records.
- Additional costs must be backed up by full supporting documents.

Claimants should avoid unnecessary optimism when reporting settlement figures to managers and should be willing to accept a reasonable offer of settlement without recourse to expensive legal action, which occupies management resources that would be better utilised elsewhere.

There is no guarantee of success in court.

Clients and Their Agents

The client should keep mind:

- The desirability of avoiding claims.
- Their obligation to resolve proper claim entitlements in an efficient and professional way.
- Investing in front end surveys, particularly ground investigation and topographical surveys, can help reduce the likelihood of claims. A National Economic Development Office (NEDO) report on 5000 industrial buildings, 8000 commercial buildings and 200 roads and bridges established that over 60% of claims arose from delays due to ground problems.
- It is important to ensure that all geotechnical data is made available to all parties in the bidding process.

- It is important to pick the most suitable method of procurement in relation to risk allocation and appropriate contract conditions. This includes deciding which elements of a project are to be designed by the contractor or subcontractors.
- Avoid drafting changes to standard forms of contract, which while attempting to re-allocate risk, can lead to ambiguity and uncertainty. The balance of marginal judgement will favour the party that had no hand in drafting the contract. The 'contra proferentum' rule may be applied against the interpretation of ambiguities.
- Usually the earlier a dispute is settled, the cheaper the settlement. In addition, there are considerable advantages to reducing the period of antagonism between parties to the contract.

Tender Documentation

A number of strategies can be used in the preparation of tender documentation to help avoid claims:

- Avoid dealing with items post tender. Statements such as 'to be agreed' can lead to dispute without the leverage of competition.
- Phrases such as 'to suit the contractor's programme' are open ended.
- Setting a conditional date such as, 'in accordance with the architect's instruction' creates uncertainty for tendering contractors. It is not possible to enforce an 'agreement to agree'.
- Avoid ambiguity in design responsibility, such as, 'the contractor shall complete any design required after the consultants have finalised the drawings provided for tender purposes'.
- Ensure that programmes, resource charts and method statements supplied by contractors with their tenders are provided for tender assessment only and are not adopted as contract documents or as the basis for variations.
- If possible avoid 'letters of intent' as they encourage arguments over details in the contract not covered in the letter of intent. There are many cases where disputes have gone to Court with no signed contract in place. At the very least a letter of intent should limit activity to pre-construction activity, such as engineering design and pre-ordering of long-delivery items of manufacture. It is also beneficial to define payment terms in a

letter of intent as this can be one of the most contentious matters of legal disputes. There is no exact legal definition of Quantum Merruit, and so a letter of intent should describe how overheads, profit and indirect costs are to be treated.

Design

Many claims are based on delays resulting from design consultants issuing schedules, drawings and specifications after construction has begun. Conflict can then arise due to arguable deficiencies in that information:

- Missing, or not produced.
- Late.
- Incorrect.
- Insufficient to order or build.
- Impractical.
- Unclear or conflicting.
- Inconsistent with pricing information.
- Inappropriate or not fit for purpose.
- Uncoordinated with other information.

Some flexibility is allowed by standard traditional contracts for the design team to issue further drawings and details reasonably necessary either to explain or amplify the contract drawings.

There can be an onus on the contractor to raise any queries on newly received information within 28 days of its receipt or forfeit their right to additional payment.

Contractor's Master Programme

Many contracts require the contractor to draw up a contractor's master programme after the execution of the contract. The contract documents should specify the level of detail required by the contractor's master programme, however, the contractor should make allowance for the following:

- Realistic time for carrying out each section of the work, with proper consultation and agreement with the major subcontractors involved.
- Sensible periods for specialist design and manufacture, including approval periods for checking conformity and co-ordination with other specialist input.

- Providing consultants with an even workload for the approval of specialist drawings.
- A stated system for recording progress against programme and future updating to reflect enforced changes.

Upon receipt of the contractor's master programme, the client's team should examine and challenge any aspects of the programme that cannot be justified. This programme is most likely to be the basis upon which all future claims for delay, extensions of time, disruption and loss and expense are based and judgements made. Challenging the contractor's master programme at a later date when claims are submitted is arguing from a position of weakness.

The client should not 'approve' the contractor's master programme, as approval might be considered to relieve the contractor of liability for programming the works in such a way as to achieve the completion date.

NB. As it is produced after the execution of the contract, the contractor's master programme does not impose any obligation on the contractor beyond those imposed by the contract documents.

Cause and Effect

Global claims, made by lumping together many different causes of delay to make a case for continuous disruption and cumulative effect, has not always found favour with the courts. This method of 'death by a thousand cuts' can be fairly easily counter-challenged by the client's team, citing all the contractor's deficiencies such as; labour shortages, poor management, plant breakdowns and subcontractor non-performance. This all leads to the argument of parallel, concurrent or contemporaneous delay.

It is better to be specific rather than generic. This is a more painstaking exercise requiring more intellectual rigour, as the claimant lists each alleged default, linking it against the consequential delay and its knock-on effect, backed by contemporary records. This approach is obviously a more precise way of establishing quantum and will lead to a more factually based judgement. In other words, to succeed, a claimant needs to establish a discernible nexus between the breaches pleaded and the consequential delay and/or associated costs.

Notice and Particulars

Under UK commercial law and under all forms of building contract any party has to give the other notice as soon as a breach is apparent so that it can be remedied or its consequences mitigated. Failure to do this expunges the right to additional payment for loss or expense. The delay or loss and expense notice should:

- Identify the specifics of the breach and legal entitlement clauses in the contract.
- Disclose as full information as possible, including the effect of the delay.
- Identify relevant dates and periods of delay involved.
- State any criticality and effect on the completion date.

The client team should immediately check the factual basis of such a notification and comment on any content that appears to be subjective.

Concurrent Delay

Concurrent delay is a situation where several causes of delay are running in parallel. An example might be where consultants details were issued late, but an industrial dispute delayed progress of critical work at the same time. In more recent judgements the courts have disregarded arguments about which was the dominant delay and judgement has been made on the basis that the loss should lie where it falls.

In the above example the contractor may be entitled to an extension of time and relief from damages but not entitled to loss and expense.

Quantifying Claims

Quantifying claims may involve a number of considerations:

Costs: Actual cost is the proper basis for evaluating claims. It is a popular misconception that the contractor is bound by its tender rates as its full entitlement. Costs may include allowance for inflation resulting from delay.

Preliminaries

Preliminaries include set-up costs, running costs and dismantling costs. Thus extensions of time should not include set-up or dismantling costs but merely running cost at the time of the breach and its associated period of delay.

Disruption

Disruption describes loss due to inefficient productivity. It is extremely difficult to assess. Often the most effective approach is to localise the claim to a specific area of breach. Then compare individuals productivity prior to and after the disruption occurred against the productivity during the period of disruption. Generic claims based on statements such as 'this was the tender price and this is the outturn cost' are unlikely to succeed.

Head Office or Factory Overheads

Hudson's formula appears to be the one most readily accepted by the courts:

(HO Profit % / 100) X (contract sum / contract period (weeks)) X (delay (weeks))

In applying the above formula the following should be subtracted:

- Credit for staff time included in the project costs as visiting supervision.
- Any additional overhead recovered within the final account, such as the variation account.
- Credit where resources were re-deployed due to delay.

Loss of Profit / opportunity Costs

This is only valid when the claimant can prove breaches of contract directly prevented it making a profit elsewhere. Deductions must be made for additional profit that has been paid on the project as a result of extra work instructed and priced within the final account.

Finance Charges and Interest

Finance charges and interest on extra capital required to fund costs arising from breaches in the contract are recoverable providing:

- Interest rates are proven and reasonable (eg market rates prevailing during the period of breach).
- If financed within the corporate group, the rate will be that received from monies it has placed on deposit.

Compensation Event

The NEC Engineering and Construction Contract 3rd Edition (NEC3) was published in June 2005. It has been adopted as the contract of choice by the government who no longer update the GC Works contracts, and has been endorsed by the ICE whose own suite of contracts will no longer be updated.

Compensation events are referred to in NEC3, and are similar to relevant events referred to in other forms of contract such as JC Tcontracts.

If events occur during the course of the works that cause the completion of the works to be delayed then these may be compensation events. Compensation events will normally result in additional payment being made to the contractor and may result in adjustment of the completion date or key dates.

The contract limits compensation events to those, and only those, identified in the contract. If an event is not identified in the contract as being a compensation event then no claim should be submitted whether or not there has been a delay. The contract prevents the parties circumventing the contract by making a claim for damages at common law.

Events that normally constitute compensation events are set out in clause 60.1. There is also provision for the parties to add additional compensation events, but great care must be taken here as to how such events are defined.

Very broadly, compensation events tend to be those events that impact on the completion date, but are not the contractor's fault. This might include events that are caused by the client, or neutral events such as exceptionally adverse weather. However, NEC3 does not treat compensation events as an allocation of blame, but rather an allocation of risk. Any risk that is not specifically identified as being attributed to the client is borne by the contractor.

Specific identified compensation events include:

- Instructions to change the service (unless this results from accepting a defect, or from a change requested by the contractor).
- Failure to provide access.
- Failure of the client to provide equipment, plant or materials.
- An instruction to halt, or delay the works.
- Work done by others.
- Conditions that could not reasonably have been foreseen.
- Exceptionally adverse weather (beyond one in ten year frequency).
- Force majeure (such as an epidemic or an 'act of God').

If an event occurs that the contractor considers to be a compensation event, they must notify the project manager within 8 weeks of becoming aware of the event (unless the project manager should have given notification). This is a condition precedent to making a claim, and compensation events cannot be considered if the 8 week deadline is missed. However the phrase 'becoming aware of' leaves some scope for dispute.

The project manager then has one week to agree whether they consider that it is a compensation event. The contractor then has up to three weeks to provide quotation, and the project manager a further two weeks to respond. When agreement has been reached, any changes to the contract are implemented.

NB The contract also makes provision for early warning procedures. Both parties must give early warning of anything that may delay the works, or increase costs. They should then hold an early warning meeting to discuss how to avoid or mitigate impacts on the project. In the case of a compensation event, if the contractor fails to give early warning of a possible delay to the works, or increase in costs, they will only be compensated for effects that would have remained anyway even if they had given early warning.

Consequential Loss

In the event that there are problems with a development, it is possible that losses will be incurred by the injured party. For example, the cost of repairs, loss of rent, loss of profit and so on. The party that suffers the loss may then try to recover it from the party that caused it. Under the common law of negligence, losses that are purely economic (such as loss of profit) are generally not recoverable, but under contract law they may be, depending on the wording of the contract.

The general position regarding losses resulting from a breach of contract was established by the case of Hadley v Baxendale (1854) where the court held that the injured party could recover losses that could be reasonably considered to arise naturally from the breach of contract in the usual course of things (direct losses), or losses that whilst they may not arise naturally from the breach, could have been reasonably contemplated by the parties to the contract at the time that they entered into that contract (indirect or consequential losses).

Losses that are unusual, special or unlikely are generally considered too 'remote' to be recoverable unless the special circumstances were known at the time that the contract was entered into, whether or not they were caused by the breach. If this were not the case, an almost unlimited liability could arise for losses that were entirely unforeseeable.

This position however remains fairly open-ended and leaves a great deal of uncertainty as to whether a loss could have been 'reasonably contemplated' at the time that a contract was entered into. As a result, in order that both parties can understand specifically those losses that will be recoverable, it is very important that they are set out explicitly and very clearly in the contract. Very broadly, contracts often allow direct losses to be recovered (such as the cost of repairs), but may exclude indirect or consequential losses (such as loss of profit).

However, it is not always this straight forward. For example, profit can be held by the courts to be a direct loss (British Sugar plc v NEI Power Projects Ltd and Another (1997)) or it may be considered that some component of profit is a direct loss. It cannot be assumed therefore that profit is excluded just because consequential losses are excluded.

The exact wording of the contract must be studied and requires very careful drafting. The FIDIC form of contract for example allows overheads, preliminaries, loss of productivity, interest and finance charges and claims preparation, but excludes profit, inflation or exchange rate fluctuations and lost commercial operation.

It is generally in the interest of the client that recoverable losses are unlimited, but for the contractor (or consultant) to try to restrict recoverable losses by excluding indirect or consequential losses.

This is also the case with regards liability to third parties, and so a similar situation is found within collateral warranties.

Contractors and consultants are likely to wish to restrict recoverable losses in collateral warranties to the cost of repairs. Clients on the other hand (or purchasers or tenants) may argue that contractors and consultants should be able to anticipate the consequences of a breach of contract and so should allow recovery of consequential losses. A compromise position is likely, for example the BPF form of collateral warranty allows consequential losses, but includes a requirement for the injured party to mitigate those losses and sets a cap for liability in respect of each breach.

It can be worth assessing what losses might occur before drafting a contract, and also defining clearly within the contract what constitutes a breach.

NB The Unfair Contract Terms Act can apply under certain circumstances and so any contractual provisions should be 'reasonable'.

Construction Industry Scheme

The Construction Industry Scheme (CIS) sets out a series of rules for how contractors should make payments to sub-contractors.

The scheme was introduced in order to try and prevent the loss of revenue to the Exchequer arising from payments between contractors not being properly accounted for for tax purposes. For all contractors and sub - contractors who fall within scope, the obligation to account properly for tax and to apply deductions from payments made is clear and severe penalties automatically arise if the provisions of the scheme are not followed rigorously.

The definition of 'contractor' for the purposes of the scheme includes not just organisation traditionally considered to be contractors, but any organisation that spends more than an average of £1 million a year on construction operations over a three year period (for example local authorities).

Qualifying contractors are required to register under the Construction Industry Scheme with HM Revenue & Customs (HMRC) and to inform them of changes to their business.

Sub-contractors are also required to register with HMRC and to inform them of changes to their business.

Contractors then have certain obligations, including;

- Checking with HMRC that sub-contractors are registered under the Construction Industry Scheme (this can be done on the HMRC website).
- Paying sub-contractors in accordance with procedures laid down by HMRC once the sub-contractor has been verified. These include procedures for making deductions and for issuing payment and deduction statements.
- Submitting monthly Construction Industry Scheme returns to HMRC giving details of payments made to sub-contractors under the scheme.

Contract Sum

The contract sum is the price agreed with the contractor and entered into the contract. The contract sum should be calculated and checked very carefully as errors are deemed to have been accepted by both parties.

The contract sum may be subject to adjustment under the terms of the contract for example:

- Variations.
- Fluctuations.
- Prime cost sums.
- Provisional sums.
- Payments to nominated sub-contractors or nominated suppliers.
- Statutory fees.

- Payments relating to opening-up and testing the works.
- Loss and expense.

When the contract sum is adjusted, this adjustment should be taken into account in the valuation of subsequent interim certificates.

Preparing the final account is the process of calculating and agreeing any adjustments to the contract sum at the end of the defects liability period so that the amount of the final paymentto the contractor can be determined. The amount of the final payment is then set out in the final certificate (or final statement). NB it is possible for the final certificate to show that money is owed to the client, rather than due to the contractor.

Construction contracts may in fact not require the preparation of a final account, although they generally do require the contractor to provide all documents necessary for the adjustment of the contract sum within a specified time, and set out the time scale for, and consequences of, issuing the final certificate.

On measurement contracts, the contract sum may not be known when the contract is entered into, but instead is calculated as the works progress based on some agreed method of measurement.

Dayworks in Construction

Daywork is a means by which a contractor is paid for specifically instructed work on the basis of the cost of labour, materials and plant plus a mark up for overheads and profit. It is generally used when work cannot be priced in the normal way.

Examples of when daywork may be applied are when unforeseen obstructions are encountered during ground works or when work is instructed for which there are no comparative rates in a bill of quantities.

It is usual for most contracts to contain clauses that provide a method of evaluating variations, additional work and instructions by using existing contract rates and prices. NEC contracts favour pre-agreed sums based on acceptance of a contractor's quotation.

There are two basic options as to how daywork rates can be priced:

Option A – a percentage addition

- Prime cost to which a percentage is added for overheads, profit and incidental costs.

Option B – all inclusive rates

- All inclusive rates are quoted at tender and incorporated in the contract documents. These include an allowance for overheads and profit, either fixed for the period of the contract, or, in the case of contract conditions that are index linked, subject to an inflation allowance.

Default Payment Notice

The Housing Grants, Construction and Regeneration Act 1996 (also known as the Construction Act) include provisions to ensure that payments are made promptly throughout the supply chain.

These provisions include:

- The right to be paid in interim, periodic or stage payments.
- The right to suspend (or part suspend) performance for non-payment and to claim costs and expenses incurred and extension of time resulting from the suspension.
- Pay when certified clauses are not allowed, and the release of retention cannot be prevented by conditions within another contract.

In addition, there are specific provisions in relation to the procedures for making payments.

- The client must issue a payment notice within five days of the date for payment, even if no amount is due. Alternatively, if the contract allows, the contractor may make an application for payment, which is treated as if it is the payment notice.
- The client must issue a pay less notice if they intend to pay less than the amount set out in the payment notice, setting out the basis for its calculation.
- The notified sum is payable by the final date for payment.
- If the client (or specified person) fails to issue a payment notice, the contractor may issue a default payment notice. The final date for payment is extended by the period between when the client should have issued a payment notice and when the contractor issued the default payment notice. If the client does not issue a pay less notice, they must pay the amount in the default payment notice.

Deferment of Possession

Contracts generally grant the contractor exclusive possession of the site until practical completion when a handover meeting takes place and possession reverts to the client. The contract may state the date for possession of the site by the contractor (sometimes called the 'commencement date'), or, if not, then the site must be handed over to the contractor within a reasonable time after signing of the contract.

Some contracts (such as the JCT Standard Form of Building Contract) will entitle the client to defer giving the contractorpossession of the site for a period of up to six weeks unless a shorter period was stipulated in the contract particulars (it is probably unwise to reduce the period). This provision enables the client to defer possession without being in breach of contract.

It is considered that deferment of possession is a positive activity which the employer should signal by giving written notice although that is not expressly stated.

Deferment of possession can be considered a relevant event, giving rise to the possibility of the contractor claiming an extension of time or loss and expense. However, for such a claim to succeed, the deferment must have a material effect on the regular progress of the works. Obviously, deferment will have an immediate effect on progress, however, it does not extend the contract period, it simply moves it in time with dates for possession and completion which continue to have the same relationship to each other.

If the contractor is given early notice of deferment, they are likely to incur far fewer costs than if the deferment is only notified a few days before start on site. Issues that might be considered include:

- Plant hire.
- The possibility of using operatives elsewhere.
- Delivery dates
- Key dates for sub-contractors
- The possibility of increased costs and interest charges.

Direct Loss

In the event that there are problems with a development, it is possible that losses will be incurred by the injured party. For example, the cost of repairs, loss of rent, loss of profit and so on. The party that suffers the loss may then try to recover it from the party that caused it. Under the common law of negligence, losses that are purely economic (such as loss of profit) are generally not recoverable, but under contract law they may be, depending on the wording of the contract.

The general position regarding losses resulting from a breach of contract was established by the case of Hadley v Baxendale (1854) where the court held that the injured party could recover losses that could be reasonably considered to arise naturally from the breach of contract in the usual course of things (direct losses), or losses that whilst they may not arise naturally from the breach, could have been reasonably contemplated by the parties to the contract at the time that they entered into that contract (indirect or consequential losses).

Losses that are unusual, special or unlikely are generally considered too 'remote' to be recoverable unless the special circumstances were known at the time that the contract was entered into, whether or not they were caused by the breach. If this were not the case, an almost unlimited liability could arise for losses that were entirely unforseeable.

This position however remains fairly open-ended and leaves a great deal of uncertainty as to whether a loss could have been 'reasonably contemplated' at the time that a contract was entered into. As a result, in order that both parties can understand specifically those losses that will be recoverable, it is very important that they are set out explicitly and very clearly in the contract.

Very broadly, contracts often allow direct losses to be recovered (such as the cost of repairs), but may exclude indirect or consequential losses (such as loss of profit).

However, it is not always this straight forward. For example, profit can be held by the courts to be a direct loss (British Sugar plc v NEI Power Projects Ltd and Another (1997)) or it may be considered that some component of profit is a direct loss. It cannot be assumed therefore that profit is excluded just because consequential losses are excluded.

The exact wording of the contract must be studied and requires very careful drafting. The FIDIC form of contract for example allows overheads, preliminaries, loss of productivity, interest and finance charges and claims preparation, but excludes profit, inflation or exchange rate fluctuations and lost commercial operation.

It is generally in the interest of the client that recoverable losses are unlimited, but for the contractor (or consultant) to try to restrict recoverable losses by excluding indirect or consequential losses.

This is also the case with regards liability to third parties, and so a similar situation is found within collateral warranties.

Contractors and consultants are likely to wish to restrict recoverable losses in collateral warranties to the cost of repairs. Clients on the other hand (or purchasers or tenants) may argue that contractors and consultants should be able to anticipate the consequences of a breach of contract and so should allow recovery of consequential losses. A compromise position is likely, for example the BPF form of collateral warranty allows consequential losses, but includes a requirement for the injured party to mitigate those losses and sets a cap for liability in respect of each breach.

It can be worth assessing what losses might occur before drafting a contract, and also defining clearly within the contract what constitutes a breach.

NB The Unfair Contract Terms Act can apply under certain circumstances and so any contractual provisions should be 'reasonable'.

Earned Value

Earned value analysis is a technique used to assess project progress by comparing the amount and cost of work that was planned to have been done by a particular stage with the amount that has actually been done and what it has actually cost. This gives a good indication of how the project is progressing compared to what was planned and enables forecasts to be made about the eventual cost and time that will be required to complete the project.

Typically earned value analysis is carried out for each of the packages that make up the project. Actual outputs are measured against planned outputs (often on a weekly basis) using the units that individual companies use to price and measure work. This provides an opportunity to investigate discrepancies and take remedial action where necessary. It also provides a fairly accurate insight into the financial wellbeing of packagecontractors and provides early warning of a shortage of resources or of an inefficient use of resources.

The key is to measure actual resource against planned resource using the production units by which estimates have been produced in order to price a tender. This can be:

- Hours worked per week.
- Number of workers per week.
- Volume of say concrete per week per person.
- Units fixed per week per person.

These items can be plotted weekly to alert the user to trends and allow them to investigate causes. Furthermore it provides an overall general picture of labour productivity for each monitored operation.

Carrying out this sort of analysis requires that project planning is broken down into packages and that tender documentation is drafted to require contractors to supply the information required.

Fair Payment Practices

The Housing Grants, Construction and Regeneration Act 1996 (also known as the Construction Act) include provisions to ensure that payments are made promptly throughout the supply chain. These provisions include:

- The right to be paid in interim, periodic or stage payments.
- The right to suspend (or part suspend) performance for non-payment and to claim costs and expenses incurred and extension of time resulting from the suspension.
- The client must issue a payment notice within five days of the date for payment, even if no amount is due. Alternatively, if the contract allows, the contractor may make an application for payment, which is treated as if it is the payment notice.
- The client must issue a pay less notice if they intend to pay less than the amount set out in the payment notice, setting out the basis for its calculation.
- The notified sum is payable by the final date for payment.
- If the client (or specified person) fails to issue a payment notice, the contractor may issue a default payment notice. The final date for payment is extended by the period between when the client should have issued a payment notice and when the contractor issued the default payment notice. If the client does not issue a pay less notice, they must pay the amount in the default payment notice.
- Pay when certified clauses are not allowed, and the release of retention cannot be prevented by conditions within another contract.

Interestingly, the HGCRA does not stipulate payment periods, simply providing that parties are free to agree what payments are due and when, ie, the contract must set out an adequate mechanism for determining these matters. In default the Scheme for Construction Contracts applies providing a payment period of 17 days from the due date to the final date for payment.

The Late Payment of Commercial Debts (Interest) Act provides for simple interest to be payable on outstanding debts at a penal rate of 8% above the Bank of England base rate. Additional penalties can also be levied.

Introduced in 2013, The Late Payment of Commercial Debts Regulationsbolster the provisions of the Late Payment of Commercial Debts (Interest) Act. The Regulations amend the Act by imposing limits on payment periods of:

- 30 calendar days when the purchaser of goods/services is a public authority;
- 60 calendar days when the purchaser is another business, but this can be extended if expressly agreed in the contract and provided it is not grossly unfair to the supplier.

The Regulations also:

- impose a limit of not more than 30 calendar days (before the payment period begins) for the purchaser to verify the conformity of goods/services are in accordance with the contract - but this period can be exceeded by agreement and provided it is not grossly unfair to the supplier.
- allow the supplier compensation for its reasonable costs of debt recovery *above* the fixed costs currently recoverable under the Act (£40 for debts of under £1,000, £70 for debts of under £10,000 and £100 for debts over £10,000).

On public sector projects, the OGCGuide to best fair payment practices (endorsed by the Public Sector Construction Clients' Forum which recommends adoption of its principals by public sector clients) sets out additional procedures for public sector projects. The procedures are intended to ensure transparent, and proper payments are made to the main supply chain members within 30 days. They can been integrated into JCT (The Joint Contracts Tribunal) contracts by making amendments set out in the JCT Public sector supplement.

The recommendations in the OGC Guide to best fair payment practices include:

- The drafting of a fair payment charter that is signed up to by the client and the main supply chain members.
- Transparency regarding payment procedures throughout the supply chain, and the provision of information relating to payments works (for example information about a particular work package that appears on certificates for the main contract) so that it is clear what sub-contractors and sub-sub-contractors can expect to be paid and when.

- Any amount to be withheld should be justified (also now required by the Construction Act).
- All contracts (including sub-contracts and sub-sub-contracts) should be valued on the same day, the 'common valuation date'.
- All payments should be made no more than 30 days from the date when the payment was first valued, the 'common valuation date'. This may involve paying main contractors before the 30 days has expired, so that subsequent payments to sub-contractors and sub-sub-contractors can all be made within 30 days. The JCT Public sector supplement proposes payment under the main contract within 19 days and payment to sub-contractors within 23 days, allowing payment to sub-sub-contractors within 30 days. NB if the valuation date is before the due date (certification generally precedes the due date on construction contracts), then payment should be made within 30 days of the valuation date, not the due date.
- Provisions in relation to protection in the event of insolvency.

NB The Office of Government Commerce (OGC) has now been absorbed into the Efficiency and Reform Group (ERG) within the Cabinet Office. OGC guidance has been archived, however, it is cited in the Government Construction Strategy and the Common Minimum Standards, and links are provided to OGC documents from government websites such as the Major Projects Authority.

Final Account

Construction contracts generally provide some mechanism for the final payment to be made to the contractor on completion of the works described in the contract. Generally this payment will be made at the end of the defects liability period providing that all patent defects have been rectified.

Preparing the final account is the process of calculating and agreeing any adjustments to the contract sum (the amount originally set out in the contract to be paid to the contractor for completion of the works) so that the amount of the final payment can be determined. The amount of the final payment is then set out in the final certificate (or final statement). It is possible for the final certificate to show that money is owed to the client, rather than due to the contractor.

Construction contracts may in fact not require the preparation of a final account, although they generally do require the contractor to provide all documents necessary for the adjustment of the contract sum within a specified time, and set out the time scale for and consequences of issuing the final certificate.

The contract sum may need to be adjusted for a number of reasons, including:

- Variations.
- Fluctuations.
- Prime cost sums.
- Provisional sums.
- Payments to nominated sub-contractors or nominated suppliers.
- Statutory fees.
- Payments relating to the opening-up and testing of the works.
- Loss and expense.
- Liquidated and ascertained damages.
- Contra claims imposed as a result of the contractor's operations (such as a third-party claim resulting from contractornegligence or contractual breach, for example, flooding a neighbour's property).
- The release of any remaining retention.

Agreeing the final account can be a complicated, time consuming and adversarial process, often resulting in disputes. The process can be made easier if adjustments to the contract sum are agreed as the project progresses rather than saving them up for the end. It is also beneficial if the client'squantity surveyor and the contractor's quantity surveyor work together on drafts of the final account before agreement it sought. It is preferable that a draft copy of the final account is signed off by the contractor as an 'in full and final settlement' prior to issue.

Agreement of the final account will allow the contract administrator to issue the final certificate. The final certificate is conclusive that all patent defects have been remedied, all adjustments to the contract sum have been agreed and all claims settled. Latent defects may still become apparent after completion of the contract and these may give rise to action for damages, for breach of contract or negligence.

Where proceedings have begun in relation to a dispute, the conclusiveness of the final certificate is subject to the findings of those proceedings.

In addition, the final certificate itself can be disputed (usually within 28 days). Adjudication, arbitration or other dispute resolution procedures may then be necessary to resolve the dispute. The final certificate is then only conclusive in relation to matters that are not disputed.

If the client intends to pay a different amount from that shown on the certificate, they must give notice to the contractor of the amount they intend to pay and the basis for its calculation.

Final Certificate

The final certificate is certification by the contract administrator that the contract has been fully completed. It is issued at the end of the defects liability period and has the effect of releasing all remaining money due to the contractor, including any remaining retention.

The value of the final certificate will be based on the final account agreed by the cost consultant and the contractor. This means that all defects must have been remedied, all adjustments to the contract sum must have been agreed and all claims settled.

Where proceedings have been commenced in relation to a dispute, the conclusiveness of the final certificate is subject to the findings of those proceedings. In addition, the final certificate itself can be disputed (usually within 28 days). Adjudication, arbitration or other proceedings may then be necessary to resolve the dispute. The final certificate is then only conclusive in relation to matters that are not disputed.

If the client intends to pay a different amount from that shown on the certificate, then they must give notice to the contractor of the amount they intend to pay and the basis for its calculation.

6

Alternative Procedures

In design and build contracts (such as Joint Contracts Tribunal (JCT) DB 05) the final certificate may be described as the final statement.

In construction managementcontracts, where there are many trade contracts, final statements are issued for each trade contract. Once final statements have been issued for each trade contract, the construction manager co-ordinates preparation of the final report and issues the final certificate for the whole project.

There is a similar procedure on management contracts, where final certificates are issued by the management contractor for each individual works contract, and then once all works contracts have received a final certificate, the management contractor provides the client'scontract administrator (or cost consultant) with information allowing them to calculate the prime cost (the cost of the works contracts) and a final certificate is issued to the management contractor.

Fluctuations

Fluctuations are a way of dealing with inflation on large projects that may last for several years. On smaller projects, the contractor will be considered to have taken into account inflation when calculating their price (a firm price). However, on the larger projects, the contractor may be asked to tender based on current prices and then the contract makes provisions for the contractor to be reimbursed for price changes over the duration of the project (a fluctuating price).

Fluctuation clauses in contracts may allow for:

- Changes in taxation.

- Changes in the cost of labour, transport and materials.
- Increases in head office or administrative costs.

Generally the contractor is not entitled to fluctuations after the completion date.

The amount of fluctuations may be calculated from nationally published price indices (for example Joint Contracts Tribunal (JCT) bulletins) rather that calculating actual cost increases which would be very time consuming.

Payment calculations are then based on a project programme for activity and a payment chart against the programme resulting in a cash flow projection. Quarterly percentage assessments of inflation for labour and materials are then added to the projected figures thus allowing for price fluctuation. If industry negotiated labour rates are known in advance or a particular commodity such as steel is subject to spiralling price rises, additional allowances may come into play.

Guaranteed Maximum Price

A guaranteed maximum price (GMP) is a form of agreement with a contractor in which it is agreed that the contract sum will not exceed an specified maximum.

Typically this is a mechanism used on design and build contracts where the contractor has responsibility for completing the client's design and for carrying out the construction works, so they are in a good position to control costs.

If the actual cost of the works is higher than the guaranteed maximum price, then the contractor must bear the additional cost. If the cost is lower than the guaranteed maximum price, then the contract should set out whether the savings made go to the client, to the contractor or are shared. This can create a 'pain / gain', or a target cost agreement, where the contractor is incentivised to make savings, but the client has the security of a cost cap.

Effectively, this sort of contract transfers risks for delivering the project from the client to the contractor. So for example, if events such as exceptionally adverse weather or strikes occur, or if items that might otherwise have been the subject of provisional sums (such as complex groundworks, the nature of which cannot be determined until the ground is opened up), which on other forms of contract might have resulted in a claim by the contractor for loss and expense, on a guaranteed maximum pricecontract, the contractor has to bear any additional costs.

As a consequence the contractor is likely to tender a higher price. Effectively they price the risks that they are taking on. This may be acceptable to the client if their priority is certainty rather than the lowest possible cost, for example, if the client has fixed funding available that cannot be exceeded.

However, a guaranteed maximum price is not a panacea, and the price is not necessarily fixed. If the client requests 'extras', for example, if the scope of the works increases, then the contract must provide for the price to be increased. Similarly, if work is omitted, then the price should be reduced. There is obviously scope here for disagreement about what constitutes a change that should result in a price adjustment, and there is the potential for the contractor to use the valuation of changes to recover costs they have incurred elsewhere. This can cause tension in a form of contract that was selected to provide certainty.

In deciding whether to seek a guaranteed maximum price, the client should assess the nature of the project, the likely risks and whether it is sensible to expect the contractor to bear those risks. If risks are priced by the contractor, but then do not transpire, the client will have paid for nothing, whilst if serious unforeseen problems are encountered, the contractor may attempt to find a way out of their obligation, or may be at risk of insolvency.

Whilst a simple project on a green field site might be suitable for a guaranteed maximum price, works to existing, older properties, or complex projects with inherent uncertainty (in particular in relation to ground works) might not. To assess these risks, it is important to ensure that proper investigations are undertaken and a fair apportionment of risks made. It is also important to ensure the client's requirements have been clearly defined to avoid potential dispute about the nature of the works. A guaranteed maximum price is not an excuse to leap into the unknown and hope for the best.

Guaranteed maximum pricecontracts tend to be either bespoke (on small projects, often written by the contractor, and so potentially including hidden get-out clauses), or modified standard form contracts – which themselves have potential risks. It is important that these contracts have unambiguous wording, particularly where there are pain / gain provisions. Despite the name 'guaranteed maximum price' the client should still ensure that they have an adequate contingency.

Interim Certificate

Interim certificates provide a mechanism for the client to make payments to the contractor before the works are complete. The Housing

Grants, Construction and Regeneration Act, states that a party to a construction contract in excess of 45 days is entitled to interim or stage payments.

Interim payments can be agreed in advance and paid at particular milestones, but they are more commonly regular payments the value of which is based on the value of work that has been completed (this is the actual value of the work completed, taking into account variations etc). The amount of these payments is entered onto an interim certificate (generally valued by the cost consultant, perhaps having taken advice from the lead designer) and the client must honour the certificate within the period stipulated by the contract.

If the client intends to pay a different amount from that shown on the interim certificate, then they must give notice to the contractor of the amount they intend to pay and the basis for its calculation.

The value of interim certificates is the value of the work completed, less any amounts already paid, less retention. Half of this retention will be released on certification of practical completion and the other half upon issue of the certificate of making good defects.

Interim certificates should make clear the amount of retention and a statement should also be prepared showing retention for nominated sub-contractors if there are any. The contract may require that retention is kept in a separate bank account and that this is certified. In this case, the client will generally keep any interest paid on the account.

There may be particular provision to include the value of particularly costly materials that the contractor has not yet delivered to site. This allows the contractor to order items in good time, without incurring unnecessary long-term expense, but does put the client at some risk if the contractor becomes insolvent.

On design and build projects, the amounts certified as payable may be based on a contract sum analysis.

Interim Valuation

Interim valuation is a pre-cursor to the issue of an interim certificate (which in turn allows an interim payment to be made). It is a detailed breakdown, generally prepared by a contractor, that constitutes an application for part payment of work undertaken since the last valuation. It is checked and signed off by the client'scontract administrator who often delegates the task to a cost consultant.

Interim payments are generally used on larger projects to ease the contractor's cash flow, on the premise that project finance is cheaper for the client than it is for individual contractors.

The basis of the contractor's interim valuation (application for payment) will vary depending on the type of contract being used. Calculations can be based on:

- Activity schedules assessed in terms of percentage achieved or completion of the activity.
- Milestones reached on a pre-agreed programme.
- Measurement against a bill of quantities.
- Stage payments against calendar dates.

Or a Combination of the Above.

The detailed build up of the valuation will show all work and entitlement up to the date of the interim valuation and will comprise:

- Works packages.
- Variations. These elements should only be paid after the work has been undertaken based on additional costs actually incurred, avoiding duplicate payment of concurrent costs or resources.
- Extension of time (EOT) and / or loss and expense. Payment entitlement is only due upon delay that is solely caused by the client or items of risk that fall to the client. Concurrent delay where the contractor has part liability may lead to an extension of time and relief of liquidated and ascertained damages but not entitle the contractor to additional payment.
- Preliminaries. Set up and dismantling costs (only incurred once) and running costs such as insurance and electrical consumption (that will occur regularly), as well as staff and management costs, overhead and profit (which can amount to 50% of the overall cost of preliminaries).
- Special payments for off-site goods and materials. Such payments might apply on large items of manufacture prior to site installation but only when such payment has been pre-agreed. Such items might include transformers, chillers, lifts, prefabricated units or expensive cladding systems. The application must be accompanied by evidential proof (sometimes photographic), or a factory visit by the client's representative, a certificate of client ownership and appropriate identification labelling on the items of completed manufacture, stored separately in the factory from other materials.

- Acceleration costs. Sometimes acceleration agreements can be negotiated as an addendum to the contract in lieu of extensions of time caused by elements constituting client's risk. Such agreements will stipulate the payment provisions.
- Provisional sums. These are the substitution of agreed costs for any items in the contract documents that were provisional and therefore subject to negotiation and resolution after further and better particulars were available upon which to fix a price.

Certain deductions might be made by the contract administrator when certifying the contractor's application for payment, such as:

- Retention. As set out in the contract.
- Liquidated and ascertained damages. These can only be levied after the completion date has expired.
- Set off costs. The client's right to deduct costs it has incurred through the contractor's negligence such as a successful claim by an adjacent property owner for subsidence due to failure of temporary bracing of a party wall.
- Substandard or rejected work. Occasionally a client might agree a reduction in payment to reflect diminution of value rather than insisting on replacement.

The interim valuation is for all work completed, not for the work completed in that period. This means that the certified interim payment is calculated by subtracting the previous valuation from the current valuation, less any deductions. The resulting total and retention figure are then included in the interim certificate issued to the client for payment by the contract administrator.

Under management contracts the works package contracts will be administered and valued by the management contractor or the construction manager to which the management staff costs and fee will be added prior to onward transmission to the client after sign off by the client's certifying authority.

NB the Housing Grants Construction and Regeneration Act sets out statutory procedures for making and withholding payments on construction contracts.

Key Performance Indicators

Key performance indicators can be used to:

- Monitor costs.
- Track progress.

- Assess client satisfaction.
- Identify strengths & weaknesses.
- Compare performance across and between projects.
- Assess specific areas of a project such as sustainability, safety, waste management etc.

It is important that key performance indicators are identified in tender documentation and that the regular provision of the information required to assesskey performance indicators is a requirement of the contract. This may require the provision of sub-contractor information where performance on specific packages is to be monitored.

Key performance indicators may be of particular importance where the contract stipulates that the contractor will be rewarded or penalised based on their performance relative to certain indicators.

Examples of key performance indicators that can be used on construction projects include:

- Cost vs budget.
- Project progress relative to milestones.
- Number of complaints.
- Number of incidents / accidents.
- The number of working hours spent on different aspects of the works.
- The use of materials (for example the amount of concrete poured).
- The number of defects.
- The amount of waste generated and the amount of recycling.
- The number of variations.

Only genuinely important performance indicators should be monitored so that it does not simply become a time consuming paper exercise.

Key performance indicators can also be used more broadly as part of a bench-marking exercise to assess the performance of one project relative to another, to assess businesses compared to others within the industry and to assess the performance of the industry as a whole relative to the rest of the economy.

Liquidated Damages

Contracts generally include a provision for the contractor to pay liquidated damages (or liquidated and ascertained damages, sometimes referred to as LAD's) to the client in the event that the contract is breached. In building contracts, liquidated damages usually relate to the contractor failing to achieve practical completion (ie completing the works so they can handover the site to the client) by the completion date set out in the contract.

Liquidated damages are not penalties, they are pre-determined damages set at the time that a contract is entered into, based on a calculation of the actual loss the client is likely to incur if the contractor fails to meet the completion date. They might include, rent on temporary accommodation, removal costs, extra running costs and so on. They are generally set as a fixed daily or weekly sum. There may be a more complicated formulae where the works are phased, or where there will be partial possession. It is important that the method of calculation is formally documented.

If the contract prevents the client claiming liquidated damages, or if actual losses are significantly different to those that were estimated at the time the contract was entered into, then the client may pursue a claim for unliquidated (i.e. actual) damages through the courts. This would require them to prove that an actual loss had been incurred and that loss was not too 'remote'.

As liquidated damages are not a penalty, they must have been based on a genuine calculation of damages when they were set. If they are not genuine, they may be considered a penalty by the courts and so will be unenforceable. Under these circumstances, the client would still be able to pursue a claim for breach of contract.

If the project is delayed by an event that impacts on the completion date, but is not the fault of the contractor, then this may constitute a 'relevant event' for which the contractor may be granted an extension of time (ie the completion date in the contract is adjusted), and the contractor may be able to make a claim for loss and expense. A relevant event might be a delay that is caused by the client, or a neutral event such as exceptionally adverse weather.

Mechanisms allowing extensions of time are not simply for the contractor's benefit. If there was no such mechanism and a delay occurred which was not the contractor's fault, then the contractor could no longer be required to complete the works by the completion date and would only have to complete the works in a 'reasonable' time. With no enforceable completion date, the client would lose any ability to claim liquidated damages.

NB Some contracts require that a certificate of non-completion is issued before a claim is made for liquidated damages.

NB On construction management projects, trade contracts (such as the Joint Contracts Tribunal (JCT) CM/TC 2011) may not include provisions for liquidated damages, instead the trade contractor indemnifies the client's direct loss and/or expense for lateness.

Loss and Expense

Construction contracts will generally provide for the contractor to claim direct loss and / or expense as a result of the progress of the works being materially affected by relevant matters for which the client is responsible, such as:

- Failure to give the contractorpossession of the site.
- Failure to give the contractor access to and from the site.
- Delays in receiving instructions.
- Opening up works or testing works that then prove to have been carried out in accordance with the contract.
- Discrepancies in the contract documents.
- Disruption caused by works being carried out by the client.
- Failure by the client to supply goods or materials.
- Instructions relating to variations and expenditure of provisional sums.
- Inaccurate forecasting of works described by approximate quantities.
- Issues relating to CDM.

The contractor must give written notice of a claim as soon as it becomes reasonably apparent that the regular progress of the works is being materially affected. This need not necessarily result in a delay to the completion date, and so claims for loss and expense and claims for extensions of time do not necessarily always run together.

Claims are restricted to 'direct' loss and expense and so 'consequential' losses (such as lost production, or profits) are generally excluded. Direct losses are those that 'flow naturally' from the breach of contract. There is disparity between contract types about whether items such as head office overheads can be included in claims for loss and expense, and some court rulings have allowed such claims. If there are specific consequential losses which the parties to the contract wish to exclude, it may be prudent therefore to state these explicitly within the contract.

NB The New Engineering Contract (NEC3) contains provision for the contractor to claim payment for 'compensation events' rather than loss and expense.

Lump Sum Contract

A lump sum contract is the traditional means of procuring construction, and still the most common form of construction contract. Under a lump sum contract, a single 'lump sum' price for all of the works is agreed before the works begin.

It is generally appropriate where the project is already well defined when tenders are sought and changes are unlikely. This means that the contractor is able to accurately price the risk they are being asked to accept.

Lump sum contracts might be less appropriate where speed is important, or where the nature of the works is not well defined. Other forms of contract that might be more appropriate include measurement contracts (used where the works can be described in reasonable detail, but the amount cannot), cost reimbursement contracts (used where the nature of the works cannot be properly defined at the outset, often used where an immediate start on site is required), target cost contracts and so on.

Lump sum contracts apportion more risk to the contractor that some other forms of contract and give the client some certainty about the likely cost of the works. The tender process will tend to be slower than for other forms of contract and preparing a tender may be more expensive for the contractor.

A lump sum contract does not give all the project risk to the contractor, and it is not a fixed price, or even a guaranteed maximum price. The price of a lump sum contract can change.

Mechanisms for varying the contract sum on a lump sum contract include:

- Variations: These are changes in the nature of the works. Most contracts will contain provision for the architect or contract administrator to issue instructions to vary the design, quantities, quality, sequence or working conditions.
- Relevant events: A relevant event may be caused by the client (for example failure to supply goods or instructions), or may be a neutral event (such as exceptionally adverse weather) and may result in a claim for loss and expense by the contractor.

- Provisional sums: An allowance for a specific element of the works that is not defined in enough detail for tenderers to price.
- Fluctuations: A mechanism for dealing with inflation on projects that may last for several years where the contractortenders based on current prices and then the contract makes provisions for the contractor to be reimbursed for price changes over the duration of the project.
- Payments to nominated sub-contractors or nominated suppliers.
- Statutory fees.
- Payments relating to opening-up and testing the works.

The better defined the works are when the contract is agreed, the less likely it is that the contract sum will change.

A truly 'fixed' price contract would not necessarily be in the interests of the client as it would require that the contractor price risks over which they may have no control, and which might not arise.

Off Site Materials

It can sometimes be appropriate for the client to pay for items even though they remain 'off-site', for example, where a contractor has themselves made a large payment for plant or materials that have yet to be delivered to site, or if the client wishes to 'reserve' key items in order to protect the programme.

Such items should be agreed in advance and listed in an annex to the contract bills.

Paying for off-site goods or materials can be useful, however, it does put the client at risk, for example if the contractor becomes insolvent and the items are then not delivered, even though payment has been made.

Several mechanisms are available to protect the client:

- The client should check the financial status of the contractor to assess the likelihood of insolvency.
- The client should require proof that the property in the items is vested in the contractor before payment is made. This may include a vesting certificate (certifying that property has passed to the contractor and that the materials will be properly identified, stored and insured), and checking that the suppliers terms and conditions do not include a retention of title clause.
- The items should be set aside, and clearly marked with the client's details.

- The materials should be "ready for incorporation".
- The client should require proof that the materials are insured against specified perils for the period they remain off site.
- If the contractor is part of a larger group, then a guarantee might be required from the holding company.
- An on-demand bond might be required up to the value of the off-site items, with the value of the bond reducing as deliveries to site are made.
- The client might enter into a contract direct with the supplier.

However, none of these methods is fool proof. For example, a vesting certificate may be of limited value in practice, as it is difficult to sue an insolvent contractor. Furthermore, despite best endeavours, items may simply be removed or disappear in the event of insolvency, or if there is a rumour that insolvency might occur. This is particularly true for items that have yet to be fabricated, items that have still to be worked on, or items that are abroad.

In a perfect world, items would be delivered to the site and affixed to the property before payment is made, but where this is not possible, a judgement is necessary to assess the risk to the project, or the potential loss to the client versus the cost of ensuring absolute certainty in relation to off-site goods.

Contract Sum Analysis

There are very many different names given to cost planning documents. Cost plans are generally prepared by cost consultants (often quantity surveyors). They evolve through the life of the project, developing in detail and accuracy as more information becomes available about the nature of the design, and then actual prices are provided by specialist contractors, contractors and suppliers. They range from very early initial cost appraisals through to tender pricing documents and the final account.

As a consequence there area a great number of names that can be used for key cost planning information. On Designing Buildings Wiki we have standardised these as follows:

- Initial cost appraisals (studies of options prepared during the feasibility study stage).
- Elemental cost plan (prepared during the project brief stage and carried through to detailed design).
- Approximate quantities cost plan (from the end of detailed design through to tender).

- Pre-tender estimate (prepared alongside tender documentation).
- Tender pricing document (strictly speaking this is not a priced document, but is part of the tender documentation issued to the contractor for pricing).
- Contract sum (agreed with the contractor during the tender period and adjusted during the construction period).
- Contract sum analysis (a break down of the contract sum prepared by the contractor on design and build projects).
- Final account (agreed during the defects liability period).

Other than initial cost appraisals, these all relate to the construction cost of the project (rather than wider project costs that the client might incur, which could include; fees, equipment costs, furniture, the cost of moving staff, contracts outside of the main works and so on). It is important that the client makes clear what costs should be monitored by the cost consultant and what will remain within the control of the client organisation.

A contract sum analysis is generally prepared by a contractor as part of their tender on design and build projects. It breaks down the contractor's price into a form allowing the client to analyse it and to compare it to other tenders, and may then be used as a basis for calculating payments due to the contractor as the works progress. A contract sum analysis is necessary as there is unlikely to be a bill of quantities on a design and build project when the contract is entered into, and so an alternative means of assessing tenders and valuing payments is necessary.

The contract sum analysis might be re-visited and expanded before construction commences to ensure that it still properly reflects the nature of the project and to ensure that it is a suitable basis for payment (contractors may be tempted to front-load the contract sum analysis so that they receive more payment at the beginning of the construction process).

Cost Control in Building Design and Construction

A development budget study is undertaken to determine the total costs and returns expected from the project. A cost plan is prepared to include all construction costs, all other items of project cost including professional fees and contingency. All costs included in the cost plan will also be included in the development budget in addition to the developer's returns and other extraneous items such as project insurance, surveys and agent's or other specialist advisers' fees.

The purpose of the cost plan is to allocate the budget to the main elements of the project to provide a basis for cost control. The terms budget and cost plan are often regarded as synonymous. However, the difference is that the budget is the limit of expenditure defined for the project, whereas the cost plan is the definition of what the money will be spent on and when. The cost plan should, therefore, include the best possible estimate of the cash flow for the project and should also set targets for future running costs. The cost plan should cover all stages of the project and will be the essential reference against which the project costs are managed.

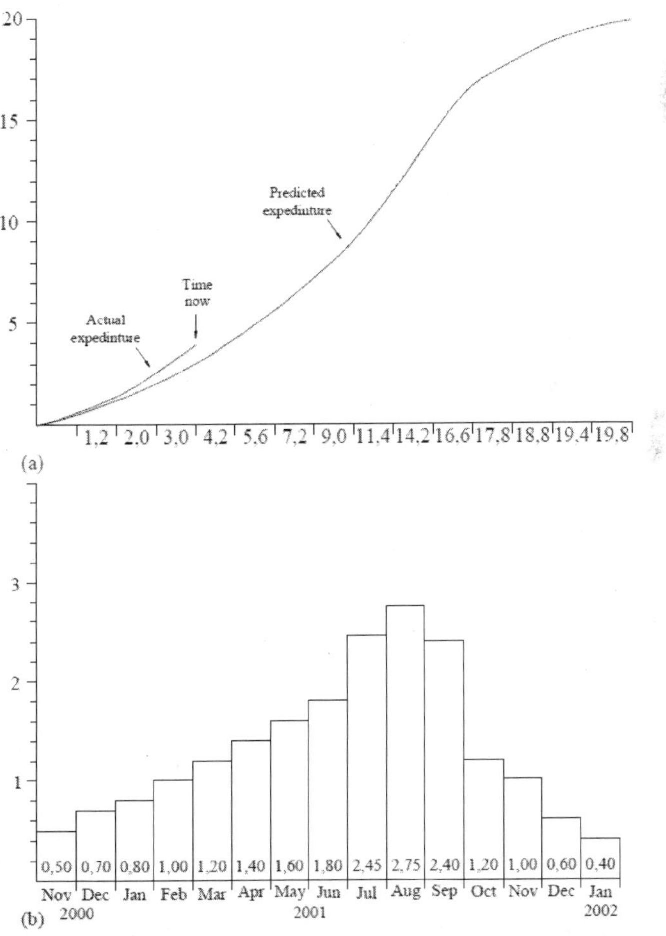

Figure: *Examples of a construction expenditure graph and cash flow histogram.*

The method used to determine the budget will vary at different stages of the project, although the degree of certainty should increase as project elements become better defined. The budget should be based on the client's business case and should change only if the business case changes. The aim of cost control is to produce the best possible building within the budget

The cost plan provides the basis for a cash flow plan, allocating expenditure and income to each period of the client's financial year. The expenditures should be given at a stated base-date level and at out-turn levels based upon a stated forecast of inflation.

The objective of cost control is to manage the delivery of the project within the approved budget. Regular cost reporting will facilitate, at all times, the best possible estimate of:

- Established project cost to date.
- Anticipated final cost of the project.
- Future cash flow.

In addition cost reporting may include assessments of:

- Ongoing risks to costs.
- Costs in the use of the completed facility.
- Potential savings.

Monitoring expenditure to any particular date does not exert any control over future expenditure and, therefore, the final cost of the project. Effective cost control is achieved when the whole of the project team adopts the correct attitude to cost.

Effective cost control will require the following actions to be taken:

- Establishing that all decisions taken during design and construction are based on a forecast of the cost implications of the alternatives being considered, and that no decisions are taken whose cost implications would cause the total budget to be exceeded.
- Encouraging the project team to design within the cost plan at all stages and follow the variation/change and design development control procedures for the project. It is generally acknowledged that 80% of cost is determined by design and 20% by construction. It is important that the project team is aware that no member of the team has the authority to increase costs on its section or element of the work. Increased costs on one item must always be balanced by savings on another.
- Regularly updating and reissuing the cost plan and variation orders causing any alterations to the brief.

- Adjusting the cash flow plan to reflect alterations in the target cost, the master schedule or the forecast of inflation.
- Developing the cost plan in liaison with the project team as design and construction progress. At all times it should comprise the best possible estimate of the final cost of the project and of the future cash flow. Adherence to design freezes will aid cost control. Developing the cost pan also involves adding detail as more information about the work is assembled, replacing cost forecasts with more accurate forecasts or actual costs whenever better information can be obtained.
- Reviewing contingency and risk allowances at intervals and reporting the assessments is an essential part of risk management procedures. Developing the cost plan should not involve increasing the total cost.
- Checking that the agreed change management process is strictly followed at all stages of the project. The procedure should only be carried out retrospectively, and then only during the construction phase of the project, when it can be demonstrated that otherwise significant delay, cost or danger would have been incurred by awaiting responses.
- Arranging for the contractor to be given the correct information at the correct time in order to minimise claims. Any anticipated or expected claims should be reported to the client and included in the regular cost reports.
- Contingency provisions are based on a thorough evaluation of the risks and are available to pay for events which are unforeseen and unforeseeable. It should not be used to cover; changes in the specification, changes in the client's requirements or variations resulting from errors or omissions. Should the consultants consider that there is no alternative but to exceed the budget, a written request must be submitted to the client and the correct authorisation received. This must include the following:

1. Details of variations leading to the request.
2. Confirmation that the variations are essential.
3. Confirmation that compensating savings are not possible without having an unacceptable effect on the quality or function of the completed project.

   - Submitting regular, up-to-date and accurate cost reports to keep the client well informed of the current budgetary and cost situation.

- Ensuring that all parties are clear about the meaning of each entry in the cost report. No data should be incorrectly entered into the budget report or any incorrect deductions made from it.
- Ensuring that the project costs are always reported back against the original approved budget. Any subsequent variations to the budget must be clearly indicated in the cost reports.
- Plotting actual expenditure against predicted to give an indication of the project's progress.

Change Control Procedure

Changes to a project may have impacts on time, cost or quality. Broadly, the later in the development of the project that changes occur, the greater those impacts are likely to be.

At certain stages in the design process, a complete package of information will be provided for the client to approve. Once this approval has been given, a change control procedure may be introduced to ensure that the approved information is not changed without the express permission of the client.

Examples of stages where change control procedures might be introduced include:

- At the end of the concept design stage if the project is tendered at this stage (for example on a design and build project)
- At the end of the concept design stage if the project brief if this is frozen.
- During the detailed design stage when the detailed design, technical design and specification are finalised.
- During the tender stage when the tender documentation has been prepared.
- When the contractor is appointed and any further changes may qualify as variations.

It is important that the need for changes is minimised. This can be done by:

- Undertaking thorough site investigations and condition surveys.
- Ensuring that the project brief is comprehensive and is supported by stakeholders.
- Ensuring that legislative requirements are properly integrated into the project.

- Ensuring that risks are properly identified.
- Ensuring that designs are properly co-ordinated before tender.

It is common for the cost consultant to report on the estimated cost of changes and for the client to prioritise which changes are acceptable. The client may decide to fund additional costs from a design contingency. A change control procedure should clearly define the process by which changes are requested and approved and who is responsible for those processes, including:

- The reasons for the change.
- Who is requesting the change.
- The consequences of the change, including health and safety, time, quality, cost (and who will bear the cost).
- Proposals for mitigation of any consequences.
- The risks associated with the change.
- Alternatives to the proposed change.
- Time by which the change must be instructed.

There may then be:

- Client evaluation of whether the impact of the change is acceptable and whether the proposal provides value for money.
- Clientinstructions to the consultant team.
- Contract administratorinstructions to the contractor.

The client may have to consider a number of requests for changes and may therefore need the appropriate information to be able to prioritise them relative to one another.

Any approved changes should be properly documented, and implementation of the changes properly controlled.

Cost Plans

There are very many different names given to cost planning documents.

Cost plans are generally prepared by cost consultants (often quantity surveyors). They evolve through the life of the project, developing in detail and accuracy as more information becomes available about the nature of the design, and then actual prices are provided by specialist contractors, contractors and suppliers. They range from very early initial cost appraisals through to tender pricing documents and the final account.

As a consequence there area a great number of names that can be used for key cost planning information. On Designing Buildings Wiki we have standardised these as follows:

- Initial cost appraisals (studies of options prepared during the feasibility study stage).
- Elemental cost plan (prepared during the project brief stage and carried through to detailed design).
- Approximate quantities cost plan (from the end of detailed design through to tender).
- Pre-tender estimate (prepared alongside tender documentation).
- Tender pricing document (strictly speaking this is not a priced document, but is part of the tender documentation issued to the contractor for pricing).
- Contract sum (agreed with the contractor during the tender period and adjusted during the construction period).
- Contract sum analysis (a break down of the contract sum prepared by the contractor on design and build projects).
- Final account (agreed during the defects liability period).

Other than initial cost appraisals, these all relate to the construction cost of the project (rather than wider project costs that the client might incur, which could include; fees, equipment costs, furniture, the cost of moving staff, contracts outside of the main works and so on). It is important that the client makes clear what costs should be monitored by the cost consultant and what will remain within the control of the client organisation.

Initial cost appraisals are carried out without the benefit of a design for the project. They include client costs that may not feature in later cost plans and as a result will almost certainly need input from the client's finance director or financial advisers. Once the initial cost appraisal is completed, the client will decide the scope of costs that will in future be monitored by the cost consultant and those that will be monitored and controlled by the client organisation.

Elemental Cost Plan

There are very many different names given to cost planning documents. Cost plans are generally prepared by cost consultants (often quantity surveyors). They evolve through the life of the project, developing in detail and accuracy as more information becomes available about the nature of the design, and then actual prices are provided by specialist contractors, contractors and suppliers. They range from very early initial cost appraisals through to tender pricing documents and the final account.

As a consequence there area a great number of names that can be used for key cost planning information. On Designing Buildings Wiki we have standardised these as follows:

- Initial cost appraisals (studies of options prepared during the feasibility study stage).
- Elemental cost plan (prepared during the project brief stage and carried through to detailed design).
- Approximate quantities cost plan (from the end of detailed design through to tender).
- Pre-tender estimate (prepared alongside tender documentation).
- Tender pricing document (strictly speaking this is not a priced document, but is part of the tender documentation issued to the contractor for pricing).
- Contract sum (agreed with the contractor during the tender period and adjusted during the construction period).
- Contract sum analysis (a break down of the contract sum prepared by the contractor on design and build projects).
- Final account (agreed during the defects liability period).

Other than initial cost appraisals, these all relate to the construction cost of the project (rather than wider project costs that the client might incur, which could include; fees, equipment costs, furniture, the cost of moving staff, contracts outside of the main works and so on). It is important that the client makes clear what costs should be monitored by the cost consultant and what will remain within the control of the client organisation.

The elemental cost plan is a detailed cost plan which is broken down into a series of elements. Initially, the elemental cost plan will simply be the total construction cost for the project divided into elements on a percentage basis. As the design becomes more detailed however, the elemental cost plan will be 'measured', based on the actual quantities of work and materials that will be required to construct the project.

The Common Arrangement of Work Sections (CAWS) offers a standard method for categorising the works.

- A - Preliminaries / general conditions .
- B - Complete buildings / structures / units.

- C - Existing site / buildings/services.
- D - Groundwork.
- E - In situ concrete / large precast concrete.
- F - Masonry.
- G - Structural / carcassing metal/timber.
- H - Cladding / covering.
- J - Waterproofing.
- K - Linings / sheathing / dry partitioning.
- L - Windows / doors / stairs.
- M - Surface finishes.
- N - Furniture / equipment.
- P - Building fabric sundries.
- Q - Paving / planting / fencing /site furniture.
- R - Disposal systems.
- S - Piped supply systems.
- T - Mechanical heating, cooling and refrigeration systems.
- U - Ventilation and air conditioning systems.
- V - Electrical systems.
- W - Communications, security, safety and protection systems.
- X - Transport systems.
- Y - General engineering services.
- Z - Building fabric reference specification.

NB This system is currently undergoing considerable change, with CAWS being incorporated into Uniclass, Uniclass being replaced with Uniclass2 and SMM7 being superceded by the New Rules of Measurement (NRM).

The elemental cost plan should identify any exclusions agreed with the client and should present an outline assessment of whole life costs. It might also include a list of abnormal or non-standard items, to help inform any value management exercises.

The elemental cost plan will be monitored by the cost consultant. The client's project cost plan is monitored by the client's finance officer and is calculated by adding to the elemental cost plan:

- Inflation.
- Professional fees.

- VAT.
- Clientcontingency.
- Statutory fees.
- Exclusions.

Appointing the Construction Manager

Construction management is a procurement route in which the works are constructed by a number of different trade contractors who are managed by a construction manager but are contracted to the client. The construction manager is generally appointed early in the design process so their experience can be used to improve the cost and buildability of proposals as they develop as well as to advise on packaging and the selection of trade contractors. Within this plan we suggest the construction manager is appointed on completion of concept design. Earlier or later appointment might result in some activities being re-allocated between the consultant team and the construction manager (for example the role of cost consultant).

The construction manager might be an individual with limited responsibilities, or could be a large organisation taking full responsibility for cost planning, packaging and tendering trade contracts as well as managing construction. For a description of the services a construction manager might offer.

Identifying the need to appoint a construction manager.

1. The client identifies the need to appoint a construction manager (perhaps with advice from the consultant team).
2. The client may decide that they require advice from independent client advisers or member of the consultant team to help them make the appointment. If this requires a new appointment, go to the work stage: Construction management: appointment .
3. The client determines the selection procedure that will be adopted. This might be a process of recommendation, research and interview, open competition, selective competition, or an existing relationship such as a framework agreement. The client may have to follow a pre-determined procedure if; there are in-house rules governing appointments, if they are a local authority or other public body, or if the project will be publicly funded. Such procedures may include assessing whether OJEU procurement rules are likely to apply which can cause significant delays unless implemented early in the project as the procedures that must be followed are quite lengthy.

Agreeing the exact nature of appointments required.

1. The client should agree the wording of any adverts that are required (such as OJEU adverts) and if appropriate prepare a pre-qualification questionnaire.
2. The client should prepare documents describing the nature of the development (if the construction manager is appointed very early in the project, this might simply be the strategic brief, whereas if they are appointed later, it could include the project brief and concept design).
3. The client should define the schedule of services that will be required (pre-construction and construction services), selection criteria, form of agreement and contract terms for the appointment. Construction managers are likely to be paid based on reimbursable costs (such as site facilities, staff costs, statutory fees, offices and so on) and a management fee, comprising pre-construction and construction fees, which may be fixed, or calculated based on an agreed formula. It is important to establish what is included in the construction manager's price (for example insurance requirements or payment of statutory fees) and to agree the limit of the construction managers delegated authority in issuing instructions which affect the cost of the project. As construction managers tend to be appointed early in the project, their appointment is unlikely to include a completion date. Construction managers may be required to hold professional indemnity insurance and to provide collateral warranties for tenants, purchasers or funders. There is merit in incentivising the construction manager to achieve key performance objectives set by the client. Any such mechanism should be clearly set out in the appointment contract.
4. The client should agree the form of proposal that will be requested from candidates.
5. The client prepares the construction management appointment documents. These are likely to include: the construction manager's appointment; the trade contract; the construction manager's warranties (eg purchasers, tenants or funders) and the trade contractor's warranties (eg purchasers, tenants or funders).
6. The client prepares a formal request for proposals.

Preparing a list of possible candidates.

1. The client prepares a long list of possible candidates, either from recommendations, existing relationships or expressions of interest received in response to adverts.
2. The candidates may be required to complete a pre-qualification questionnaire, or there may be some other assessment procedure (such as interviews) that results in the preparation of a short list that will be invited to submit proposals. Such assessments may include assessing experience and capability, checking professional indemnity insurance, assessing CDM competence, checking references and so on.
3. The client should put in place procedures for responding to queries from candidates.
4. Short-listed candidates are invited to submit proposals in response to the client's request for proposals.

Selecting the preferred candidate and making the appointment.

1. The client collates responses to queries from candidates and issues these responses to all candidates.
2. The client receives and opens the candidates' proposals and makes a record of the fee proposals of each candidate. In some circumstances, fee proposals may be submitted in a sealed envelope and opened separately from the rest of the proposals so that the assessment procedure is not initially prejudiced by the fee (which it may be possible to negotiate down).
3. The client assesses the candidates' proposals (including the personnel the construction manager will use on the project). The client may seek advice from existing consultants or independent client advisers.
4. The client invites the candidates to interview.
5. The client identifies the preferred candidate(s).
6. The client opens negotiations with the preferred candidate(s).
7. The client appoints the selected candidate and arranges a start-up meeting with the construction manager and the consultant team.
8. The client informs other candidates that they have been unsuccessful. It is best practice to give clearly thought-out, specific feedback to unsuccessful candidates as they have take the time to prepare proposals often for no fee. Candidates greatly

appreciate this feedback and will be more likely to express interest in future projects.

Public Project: Feasibility Studies

The feasibility studies stage considers the options for satisfying the client's needs, enabling the client to prepare a business case for the preferred option and deciding whether to proceed with the project. It is possible to make an outline planning application during this stage if the risk to the project of not receiving planning permission is very high, or if delays in receiving planning permission would be problematic.

The Government Construction Strategy proposes that publicly-funded projects adopt either a design and build, private finance initiative (PFI) or prime contract procurement route. These routes involve contracting an integrated supply team to design, construct and sometimes finance, operate and maintain the development. Traditional procurement routes that separate design and construction should not be used unless it can be demonstrated that they offer better value.

Depending on how experienced the client is, they may appoint external consultants such as independent client advisers or a project manager to assist them. This means that some of the tasks attributed to the client below might actually be carried out by independent client advisers or a project manager and vice versa.

Publicly-funded projects are expected to commission independent peer reviews at key points. This project plan follows the OGC (Office of Government Commerce) Gateway Review procedure. The OGC has now been absorbed into the Efficiency and Reform Group and its guidance archived, however, the OGC Gateway Review procedure is still cited by the Government Construction Strategy and remains the only complete reviewing system.

A. Updating the project documents.
    1. The client updates the preliminary business case and strategic brief to reflect comments made at the end of the previous stage (public project: business justification).
    2. The client collates site information ready to issue to the independent client advisers.

B. Appointing independent client advisers.
    1. The client appoints independent client advisers and if necessary a project manager and CDM co-ordinator. Go to work stage: Public project: appointment. NB The role of project manager can be performed by in-house personnel,

or may be taken on by the project sponsor if they have the relevant experience.

2. The client chairs a start-up meeting to issue information to new appointments (such as the strategic brief and site information). This meeting is also an opportunity to establish collaborative practices and agree a programme.
3. The CDM co-ordinator (if appointed) confirms that the client is are aware of their duties under the CDM regulations.

C. Developing the strategic brief so that feasibility studies can be carried out and preferred options selected.

1. The independent client advisers work with the client to help them develop the strategic brief sufficiently for feasibility studies and options appraisals to be carried out.
2. The independent client advisers assess the site information issued to them by the client and undertake site appraisals.
3. The independent client advisers obtain any further information about the site that might be required to undertake feasibility studies, such as; site surveys, information about site services, site access conditions, legislative constraints, existing planning consents etc. Where necessary, approval should be sought from the client (for example site surveys requiring additional expenditure).
4. The independent client advisers co-ordinate the preparation of feasibility studies to establish whether the project is viable, and to identify feasible options.
5. The client considers the feasibility studies, and agrees which options the independent client advisers should develop.

D. Preparing an options review report.

1. The independent client advisers co-ordinate the identification of any further site surveys or site information required in order to carry out options appraisals and where appropriate seek approval from the client.
2. The independent client advisers prepare options studies with a view to drafting an options review report.
3. The CDM co-ordinator (if appointed at this stage) assesses the risks of the options in relation to the CDM regulations.
4. The independent client advisers and the client prepare for and enter into consultations with the local authority and

other statutory authorities and assess possible planning permission requirements and other statutory requirements (such as the need for an environmental impact assessment for the options).

5. The independent client advisers prepare initial cost appraisals of the options.
6. The independent client advisers co-ordinate the preparation of a draft options review report.
7. The client considers the draft options review report and either selects a preferred option or instructs the independent client advisers to revise the options review report.

E. Preparing a business case and project execution plan for the preferred option.

1. The independent client advisers co-ordinate further assessment of the preferred option to assist the client in preparing the business case and project execution plan.
2. The independent client advisers establish the requirements for statutory approvals and other regulations with which the preferred option must comply.
3. The independent client advisers enter into consultations with utility providers.
4. The independent client advisers assess the need for additional specialist advice and advise the client.
5. With the benefit of assessments carried out by the independent client advisers, the client develops a business case and project execution plan for the preferred option.
6. The client considers, and if appropriate approves the business case and project execution plan for the preferred option and gives instructions to proceed to the next stage along with any other instructions that may be necessary.
7. Once it has been decided that the project will progress to the next stage, the client places (or arrange to have placed) all necessary OJEU or other advertisements.
8. At this stage, the client and the independent client advisers may consider whether it would be appropriate to make an outline planning application for the proposed development. It can be important that the planning parameters for the project and, where appropriate, outline planning consent

are obtained prior to tender, as any changes to the project resulting from the planning permission process after the integrated supply team has been appointed may prove expensive for the client and can cause significant delays. If an outline planning application is required, go to the work stage: Public project: planning permission.

Site Surveys

Site surveys are detailed studies carried out to supplement site information provided by the client and site appraisals carried out by the consultant team.

Site surveys might be carried out by the consultant team if they have the required skills, or might be commissioned from specialists. The consultant team should assess what surveys are required (generally after initial feasibility studies have been carried out) and request approval from the client to commission those surveys or carry them out themselves.

Site surveys might include:

- Existing buildings (including valuation, measured surveys, structural surveys, structural investigations, condition surveys and demolition surveys).
- Geological and geotechnical.
- Topographical.
- Contamination.
- Ecological.
- Archaeological.
- Traffic and transport.
- Local climate.
- Flood risk.
- Air quality.
- Acoustic.
- Photographic.
- Historic use.
- Boundary surveys.
- Structural surveys (including retained structures, underground structures and obstructions).
- Unexploded bomb survey.

- Railway and tunnel search.
- Asbestos and other hazardous materials surveys and registers.
- Fire hydrants.
- Telecommunications.
- Wireless networks and satellite reception.
- Electrical infrastructure and capacity.
- Gas network infrastructure and capacity.
- Foul sewers and drains infrastructure and capacity.
- Existing water supply infrastructure and capacity.

Land Value

Size

The ideal developable piece of land is of an adequate size to maximise its potential. For example, think about a site that is too big for 2 houses, but not big enough for 3. Simply building bigger houses, might not solve this problem, as the size of a dwelling is not the only characteristic affecting its price (for example, in some areas the market expects houses of a particular size).

Proportion

The ideal site for a specific project will be of a certain proportion. For example, a 1000 m sq site at 50m x 20m. is likely to be a well-proportioned site. However, a 1000 m sq that is 200m x 5m may not be very suitable for development.

Frontage

As with size, depending on the nature of a project, the proportion of the site that fronts a road is important when assessing its value. In the worst case, where a site is land locked and has no direct access to a public highway, the purchaser will need to buy a second piece of land in order to create access.

Shape

As with proportion, shape is one of the most influential factors on value, especially in smaller sites. Consider for example a one acre square compared to a one acre triangle. The amount of wasted space due to the sites shape pushes down the overall value of the land.

Development Potential

It is generally not feasible to build a 20 storey apartment block in a country village or a warehouse in a city centre. Development potential is defined by the permissions that can gained and what can be marketed in a particular area.

Time Constraints

What time pressures is the project under? The vendor can ultimately define the price based on whether or not they require a quick sale. It is important when carrying out this sort of time-based assessment to take into account costs of interest repayments on any loans.

Location

Where is the site? For example, edge of town sites offer more freedom than city centre sites, but may have less of a premium.

Where is the project's target demographic? What sort of people are likely to use the development? Where are they based? How will they get to the site?

Use Class.

If a site has been classed as A1 Retail, it may be difficult to have this changed to C3 Dwellings (although this is very dependent on local policy).

Assessing Value

There are a number of ways that a quick assessment of land value can be made:

- Research what other sites of similar type and location are selling for (for example Zoopla, area stats for UK)
- Advertise the site, asking for offers.
- Many commercial estate agents will offer a free initial review of land.
- Seek advice, from a professional such as a surveyor.

Sustainability in Building Design and Construction

Sustainability is a broad term describing a desire to carry out activities without depleting resources or having harmful impacts, defined by the Brundtland Commission as '*meeting the needs of the present without compromising the ability of future generations to meet their own needs.*' (Brundtland Commission, Our Common Future, 1987). Some broader descriptions include social and economic welfare although these can confuse the basic issue of the depletion of resources.

Sustainability in building developments is a vast and complex subject that must be considered from the very earliest stages.

Once it has been decided to build a new building, as opposed to say changing working practices or refurbishing an existing building, a very significant commitment to consume resources has already been made. Designers and contractors may be able to help limit that consumption, but they cannot change the overall commitment.

This consumption of resources can be even more significant if the client makes a decision to relocate, with the impact this has on their staff, requiring that they either move house or change their travel plans. Decisions such as this which are often made outside of any environmental assessment process can have a far greater impact on sustainability than decisions that designers are able to influence such as the form of the building and selection of materials. Key decisions may be picked up by an environmental impact assessment on larger projects, but even then, this can be a post-rationalisation process used to justify decisions to the local planning authority, rather than a genuine decision making process.

Clients may wish therefore to appoint an independent client adviser with specialist knowledge of sustainability during the very early stages of their project (before the consultant team has been appointed) to help them address these high level decisions.

Clients may have an existing environmental policy, that sets out an overall sustainability vision, as well as detailed objectives and targets. They may also have environmental accreditation such as ISO 14000 (a series of standards which provides a framework for environmental management). Other standards may be imposed by funders, the building regulations, and planning legislation (including the possible need for an environmental impact assessment). It is wise however to write a specific environmental plan for the development being considered, as building projects involve many detailed issues that go beyond the scope of an existing corporate plan.

A project-specific environmental plan could form part of the brief, or on larger projects might be a stand-alone document. It might include an overall vision, objectives and and specific targets in relation to:

- Business planning: the need for a new building as opposed to doing nothing, refurbishment or changes in working practices.
- Selection of consultants: contractual requirements in relation to the selection of materials, monitoring and reporting, track record, environmental accreditation and qualifications of staff.

- Selection of location: availability of transport, the selection of a greenfield or brownfield site, the local availability of resources and services, the local infrastructure and local ecology.
- Project brief: procurement route, travel plan, working methods, standards, ecology and landscape, energy use and energy source, flexibility and durability, waste management, water management, material selection and pollution.
- Design: energy use and energy source, embodied energy, use of harmful materials, material sources, ecology and landscape, flexibility and durability, waste management, water management, disposal, travel plan and pollution.
- Tender: contractual requirements such as monitoring and reporting, working practices, track record, environmental accreditation and qualifications of staff.
- Construction: transport, embodied energy, use of harmful materials, material sources, working methods, site waste management plan, recycling, pollution, wheel washing, dust generation and noise nuisance.
- Operation: energy source, energy use, water management, maintenance, resource management, waste management, flexibility, durability, landscape and ecology, pollution, evaluation and feedback.
- Resilience to climate change.
- Disposal: dismantling and demolition, re-use, re-sale and recycling, landscape and ecology, hazardous materials and pollution.

The environmental plan should:

- Set specific, measurable targets.
- Set standards that must be adhered to.
- Establish risks and mitigation measur es.
- Establish procedures for communication and training.
- Establish procedures for monitoring and reporting.
- Establish procedures for revision and updating.

Environmental plans require policing, and on a large project this can be a full-time job for a specialist. At the client level, a senior champion should be appointed to take responsibility for environmental matters.

Predicting the likely environmental performance of a development during the design phase is becoming more important as regulations become increasing strict. As well as the building regulations, and government targets for low carbon construction the National Planning Policy Framework makes clear that there should be a presumption in favour of granting planning permission for sustainable development, this might include low-carbon developments, and developments with resilience to climate change. This should be reflected in design and access statements for outline planning applications.

There are a number of assessment tools and standards available to help assess environmental performance:

- BREEAM.
- Passivhaus.
- SAP the Government's Standard Assessment Procedure for energy rating of dwellings.
- Leadership in Energy and Environmental Design (LEED), an international green building certification system.
- The code for sustainable homes.

These assessment techniques are beginning to allow whole-life costing to form a fundamental part of the design process as it becomes possible to demonstrate that higher initial costs can sometimes result in lower long-term impacts and greater long-term benefits. Demonstration of actual performance in use may be necessary through requirements for a Energy Performance Certificates (EPC's) or Display Energy Certificates (DEC's)

Appointments should make clear the extent and standard of environmental performance and assessment that is required.

Construction

A. Starting the work stage.
   1. The construction manager arranges a handover meeting to take possession of the site.
   2. Before work on site proceeds, the CDM co-ordinator confirms that suitable welfare facilities have been provided.
   3. Before work on site proceeds, the client and construction manager (in their role as as principal contractor) confirm that a suitable site waste management plan is in place.
   4. Before work on site proceeds, the CDM co-ordinator confirms that a suitable initial construction phase plan has been prepared by the principal contractor.

5. When appropriate, the construction manager issues notices for each trade contractor to commence work on site along with instructions regarding phasing and sequencing of the works . NB the construction manager should keep trade contractors informed about the progress of the project so that they are able to plan their works in advance of receiving a notice to commence work.

B. Construction.

1. The construction manager manages, schedules, supervises, organises and co-ordinates the trade contractors and preliminaries packages on a day-to-day basis. The construction manager is generally the principal contractor under the CDM regulations as well as having overall responsibility for the site management, and is responsible for welfare provisions, site clearance, waste disposal, site security and trade union issues.
2. The lead designer co-ordinates the preparation of any additional information required by the trade contractors for construction.
3. The construction manager co-ordinates the issue of any additional information required by the trade contractors and co-ordinates the review of design information prepared by the trade contractors.
4. The CDM co-ordinator assesses and gives advice about any additional design information that is prepared by the consultant team or trade contractors (including temporary works) and the construction manager (in their role as principal contractor) updates the construction phase plan and re-issues it as required.
5. Where there are any proposed variations, procedures for their valuation should be implemented (as described in the contract). Where variations exceed the delegated authority of the construction manager, approval should be requested from the client.
6. The construction manager assesses any claims for extension of time or loss and/or expense with advice where appropriate from the consultant team.
7. The construction manager co-ordinates site inspections and issues instructions as required.

8. The construction manager issues regular payment notices to each trade contractor. The notices must be issued within five days of the dates for payment set out in the contract. If they intend that the trade contractors should be paid a different amount, they must issue a pay less notice giving the basis for the calculation of the amount that will be paid.
9. The client makes payments to the trade contractors by the final date for payment.
10. On large projects the construction manager holds a daily logistic meeting on site with trade contractor foremen to organise, schedule and co-ordinate on-site shared services such as deliveries and offloading, hoists and craneage, scaffolding and safety issues, rubbish clearance etc.
11. The construction manager performs weekly checks on trade contractor earned value and takes action if necessary
12. The construction manager holds regular construction progress meetings with trade contractors (and on large projects, with the construction manager's package manager) to discuss on and off-site progress against the programme and to co-ordinate the release of information. It may sometimes be appropriate for these meetings to take place at the trade contractors premises.
13. Construction progress reports are prepared for the client.
14. The construction manager holds regular construction progress meetings with the client and consultant team.

C. Preparing for occupation.

1. The client begins preparations for occupation of the development, including the preparation of an operational policy and migration strategy setting out how they will manage the transition into and the operation of the new facility.
2. The client may have an 'occupation services contract' for delivering and installing equipment , fixtures and furniture (sometimes from other premises). This contract may also pick up small building changes that they consider would be costly if instructed under the main contract.
3. The client should ensure they have sufficient funds to release 50% of the retention (where the contract provides for retention) upon certification of practical completion for each trade contract.

D. Inspections, commissioning and testing.

   1. The construction manager agrees procedures for inspections, commissioning, testing and client training with the consultant team and client (representatives of the facilities management department).
   2. If it has not already been done, the client appoints an in-house or outsourced engineering team to witness testing and commissioning and to take over the running of the services as soon as project (or sectional) completion is certified. Go to work stage: Construction management: appointment.
   3. The services engineer co-ordinates procedures for inspections, commissioning, testing and client training in relation to building services.
   4. The construction manager co-ordinates procedures for inspections, commissioning, testing and client training in relation to other aspects of the building.
   5. The trade contractors rectify any defects that become apparent during commissioning, testing and inspection procedures.

E. Practical completion.

1. The construction manager prepares a draft building owner's manual (with information supplied by the trade contractors, designers, suppliers and the CDM co-ordinator) and if required a building user's guide.
2. The CDM co-ordinator completes the health and safety file.
3. The lead designer co-ordinates the preparation of the building log book.
4. The trade contractors confirm to the construction manager that their works are complete.
5. The construction manager issues a certificate of practical completion and payment notice for each trade contract as it is completed. If they intend that the trade contractors should be paid a different amount, they must issue a pay less notice giving the basis for the calculation of the amount that will be paid.
6. The client pays the amount due by the final date for payment (this may include the release of half of the retention if provided for in the contract).

7. The construction manager should take steps to protect completed work from any ongoing work.
8. Once all of the trade contracts are complete (or all of the trade contracts in a section of the works) the construction manager arranges for final inspection of the works by the building control inspector (or approved inspector) and arranges for the issue of a building regulations completion certificate. NB Within 5 days of the completion of the building, the construction manager must notify building control that the works have been carried out in accordance with the specification submitted with the building emission rate (BER) calculations, or the changes that have been made.
9. The construction manager arranges a handover meeting to confirm that the works are complete and to handover the site to the client.
10. Once all of the trade contracts are complete (or all of the trade contracts in a section of the works), the construction manager issues a certificate of project completion (or sectional completion).
11. The construction manager prepares and submits a construction stage report for the client.
12. The client assesses the construction stage report, and gives instructions as necessary.

Civil Engineering

Civil engineering is a professional engineering discipline that deals with the design, construction, and maintenance of the physical and naturally built environment, including works like roads, bridges, canals, dams, and buildings. Civil engineering is the oldest engineering discipline after military engineering, and it was defined to distinguish non-military engineering from military engineering. It is traditionally broken into several sub-disciplines including environmental engineering, geotechnical engineering, geophysics, geodesy, control engineering, structural engineering, transportation engineering, earth science, atmospheric sciences, forensic engineering, municipal or urban engineering, water resources engineering, materials engineering, offshore engineering, quantity surveying, coastal engineering, surveying, and construction engineering. Civil engineering takes place on all levels: in the public sector from municipal through to national governments, and in the private sector from individual homeowners through to international companies.

History of Civil Engineering

Civil engineering is the application of physical and scientific principles for solving the problems of society, and its history is intricately linked to advances in understanding of physics and mathematics throughout history. Because civil engineering is a wide ranging profession, including several separate specialized sub-disciplines, its history is linked to knowledge of structures, materials science, geography, geology, soils, hydrology, environment, mechanics and other fields. Throughout ancient and medieval history most architectural design and construction was carried out by artisans, such as stonemasons and carpenters, rising to the role of master builder. Knowledge was retained in guilds and seldom supplanted by advances. Structures, roads and infrastructure that existed were repetitive, and increases in scale were incremental.

One of the earliest examples of a scientific approach to physical and mathematical problems applicable to civil engineering is the work of Archimedes in the 3rd century BC, including Archimedes Principle, which underpins our understanding of buoyancy, and practical solutions such as Archimedes' screw. Brahmagupta, an Indian mathematician, used arithmetic in the 7th century AD, based on Hindu-Arabic numerals, for excavation (volume) computations.

Sub-disciplines

In general, civil engineering is concerned with the overall interface of human created fixed projects with the greater world. General civil engineers work closely with surveyors and specialized civil engineers to fit and serve fixed projects within their given site, community and terrain by designing grading, drainage, pavement, water supply, sewer service, electric and communications supply, and land divisions. General engineers spend much of their time visiting project sites, developing community consensus, and preparing construction plans. General civil engineering is also referred to as site engineering, a branch of civil engineering that primarily focuses on converting a tract of land from one usage to another. Civil engineers typically apply the principles of geotechnical engineering, structural engineering, environmental engineering, transportation engineering and construction engineering to residential, commercial, industrial and public works projects of all sizes and levels of construction.

Coastal Management

In some jurisdictions the terms sea defence and coastal protection are used to mean, respectively, defence against flooding and erosion.

The term *coastal defence* is the more traditional term, but *coastal management* has become more popular as the field has expanded to include techniques that allow erosion to claim land.

Historical Background

Coastal engineering, as it relates to harbours, starts with the development of ancient civilizations together with the origin of maritime traffic, perhaps before 3500 B.C.

Docks, breakwaters, and other harbour works were built by hand and often in a grand scale. Basic source of modern literature on coastal engineering is the "European Code of Conduct for Coastal Zones" issued by the European Council in 1999. This document was prepared by the Group of Specialists on Coastal Protection and should be used 'as a source of inspiration for national legislation and practice' by decision makers.

The Group of Specialists on Coastal Protection (PE-S-CO), set up in 1995, pursuant to a decision by the Committee of Ministers of the Council of Europe, met for the first time on 6 and 7 June 1996. It noted that a great deal of technical and scientific research had been carried out in the field of coastal protection and that various principles and legal texts had been drawn up. It also noted that all of the work undertaken highlighted the need for integrated management and planning of coastal areas, but that, despite all the efforts already made, the situation of coastal areas continued to deteriorate. The Group had acknowledged that this was due to difficulties in implementing the concept of "integrated management", and that it was becoming necessary to provide instruments which would make it easier to apply the principles of integrated coastal management and planning, which had to be pursued to ensure sustainable management of coastal areas. The Group therefore proposed that the Council of Europe, in close co-operation with the European Union for Coastal Conservation (EUCC) and United Nations Environment Programme (UNEP). The final version of the Code as well of the a MODEL LAW to be used as a guide for modefying local and national legislation, can be free downloaded from the web.

Ancient harbour works are still visible in a few of the harbours that exist today, while others have recently been explored by underwater archaeologists. Most of the grander ancient harbor works have disappeared following the fall of the Roman Empire.

Most ancient coastal efforts were directed to port structures, with the exception of a few places where life depended on coastline protection.

Venice and its lagoon is one such case. Protection of the shore in Italy, England and the Netherlands can be traced back at least to the 6th century. The ancients understood such phenomena as the Mediterranean currents and wind patterns and the wind-wave cause-effect link.

The Romans introduced many revolutionary innovations in harbor design. They learned to build walls underwater and managed to construct solid breakwaters to protect fully exposed harbors. In some cases wave reflection may have been used to prevent silting. They also used low, water-surface breakwaters to trip the waves before they reached the main breakwater. They became the first dredgers in the Netherlands to maintain the harbour at Velsen. Silting problems here were solved when the previously sealed solid piers were replaced with new "open"-piled jetties.

Middle Ages

The threat of attack from the sea caused many coastal towns and their harbours to be abandoned. Other harbours were lost due to natural causes such as rapid silting, shoreline advance or retreat, etc. The Venetian Lagoon was one of the few populated coastal areas with continuous prosperity and development where written reports document the evolution of coastal protection works.

Engineering and scientific skills remained alive in the east, in Byzantium, where the Eastern Roman Empire survived for six hundred years while Western Rome decayed.

Modern Age

Although great strides were made in the general scientific arena, little improvement was done beyond the Roman approach to harbour construction after the Renaissance. In the early 19th century, the advent of the steam engine, the search for new lands and trade routes, the expansion of the British Empire through her colonies, and other influences, all contributed to the revitalization of sea trade and a renewed interest in port works.

Twentieth Century

Evolution of shore protection and the shift from structures to beach nourishment. Prior to the 1950s, the general practice was to use hard structures to protect against beach erosion or storm damages. These structures were usually coastal armoring such as seawalls and revetments or sand-trapping structures such as groynes. During the 1920s and '30s, private or local community interests protected many areas of the shore using these techniques in a rather ad hoc manner. In certain resort areas, structures had proliferated to such an extent that the protection actually impeded the recreational use of the beaches. Erosion of the sand continued, but the fixed back-beach line remained, resulting in a loss of beach area.

The obtrusiveness and cost of these structures led in the late 1940s and early 1950s, to move toward a new, more dynamic, method. Projects no longer relied solely on hard coastal defence structures, as techniques were developed which replicated the protective characteristics of natural beach and dune systems. The resultant use of artificial beaches and stabilized dunes as an engineering approach was an economically viable and more environmentally friendly means for dissipating wave energy and protecting coastal developments.

Over the past hundred years the limited knowledge of coastal sediment transport processes at the local authorities level has often resulted in inappropriate measures of coastal erosion mitigation. In many cases, measures may have solved coastal erosion locally but have exacerbated coastal erosion problems at other locations -up to tens of kilometers away- or have generated other environmental problems.

Current Challenges in Coastal Management

The coastal zone is a dynamic equilibrium area of natural change and of increasing human use. They occupy less than 15% of the Earth's land surface; yet accommodate more than 40% of the world population (it is estimated that 3.1 billion people live within 200 kilometres from the sea). With three-quarters of the world population expected to reside in the coastal zone by 2025, human activities originating from this small land area will impose an inordinate amount of pressures on the global system. Coastal zones contain rich resources to produce goods and services and are home to most commercial and industrial activities. In the European Union, almost half of the population now lives within 50 kilometres of the sea and coastal zone resources produce much of the Union's economic wealth. The fishing, shipping and tourism industries all compete for vital space along Europe's estimated 89 000 kilometres of coastline, and coastal zones contain some of Europe's most fragile and valuable natural habitats. Shore protection consists up to the 50's of interposing a static structure between the sea and the land to prevent erosion and or flooding, and it has a long history. From that period new technical or friendly policies have been developed to preserve the environment when possible. Is already important where there are extensive low-lying areas that require protection. For instance: Venice, New Orleans, Nagara river in Japan, the Netherlands, Caspian Sea Protection against the sea level rise in the 21st century will be especially important, as sea level rise is currently accelerating. This will be a challenge to coastal management, since seawalls and breakwaters are generally expensive to construct, and the costs to build protection in the face of sea-level rise would be enormous.

Changes on sea level have a direct adaptative response from beaches and coastal systems, as we can see in the succession of a lowering sea level. When the sea level rises, coastal sediments are in part pushed up by wave and tide energy, so sea-level rise processes have a component of sediment transport landwards. This results in a dynamic model of rise effects with a continuous sediment displacement that is not compatible with static models where coastline change is only based on topographic data.

Planning Approaches

There are five generic strategies for coastal defence:

- inaction leading to eventual abandonment
- Managed retreat or realignment, which plans for retreat and adopts engineering solutions that recognise natural processes of adjustment, and identifies a new line of defence where to construct new defences
- Hold the line, shoreline protection, whereby seawalls are constructed around the coastlines
- Move seawards, this happens by constructing new defences seaward the original ones
- Limited intervention, accommodation, by which adjustments are made to be able to cope with inundation, raising coastal land and buildings vertically

The decision to choose a strategy is site-specific, depending on pattern of relative sea-level change, geomorphological setting, sediment availability and erosion, as well a series of social, economic and political factors.

Alternatively, integrated coastal zone management approaches may be used to prevent development in erosion- or flood-prone areas to begin with. Growth management can be a challenge for coastal local authorities who often struggle to provide the infrastructure required by new residents seeking seachange lifestyles. Sustainable transport investment to reduce the average footprint of coastal visitors is often a good way out of coastal gridlock. Examples include Dongtan and the

Gold Coast Oceanway. The 'Managed Retreat' option, involving no protection, is cheap and expedient. The coast takes care of itself and coastal facilities are abandoned to coastal erosion, with either gradual landward retreat or evacuation and resettlement elsewhere. This is the usual response when land of little value will be lost. The only pollution produced is from the resettlement process. Where endangered property has high value, it is less often applied.

Managed Retreat

Managed retreat is an alternative to constructing or maintaining coastal structures. Managed retreat allows an area to become flooded. This process is usually in low lying estuarine or deltaic areas and floods land that has at some point in the past been reclaimed from the sea. Managed retreat is often a response to a change in sediment budget or to sea level rise. The technique is used when the land adjacent to the sea is low in value. A decision is made to allow the land to erode and flood, creating new shoreline habitats. This process may continue over many years and natural stabilization will occur.

The earliest managed retreat in the UK was an area of 0.8 ha at Northey Island in Essex, that was flooded in 1991. This was followed by Tollesbury and Orplands in Essex, where the sea walls were breached in 1995. In the Ebro delta (Spain) coastal authorities have planned a managed retreat in response to coastal erosion (MMA 2005, Sitges, Meeting on Coastal Engineering; EUROSION project).

Cost – The main cost is generally the purchase of land to be flooded. Compensation for relocation of residents may be needed. Any other human made structure which will be engulfed by the sea may need to be safely dismantled to prevent sea pollution. In some cases, a retaining wall or bund must be constructed inland in order to protect land beyond the area to be flooded, although such structures can generally be lower than would be needed on the existing coast. Monitoring of the evolution of the flooded area is another cost. Costs may be lowest if existing defences are left to fail naturally, but often the realignment project will be more actively managed, for example by creating an artificial breach in existing defences to allow the sea in at a particular place in a controlled fashion, or by pre-forming drainage channels for created salt-marsh.

Hold the Line

Human strategies on the coast have been heavily based on a static engineered response, whereas the coast is in, or strives towards, a dynamic equilibrium (Schembri, 2009). Solid coastal structures are built and persist because they protect expensive properties or infrastructures, but they often relocate the problem downdrift or to another part of the coast. Soft options like beach nourishment, while also being temporary and needing regular replenishment, appear more acceptable, and go some way to restore the natural dynamism of the shoreline. However in many cases there is a legacy of decisions that were made in the past which have given rise to the present threats to coastal infrastructure and which necessitate immediate shore protection. For instance, the seawall and promenade of many coastal cities in Europe represents a highly engineered use of prime seafront space, which might be preferably designated as public open space, parkland and amenities if it were available today. Such open space might also allow greater flexibility in terms of future land-use change, for instance through managed retreat, in the face of threats of erosion or inundation as a result of sea-level rise. Foredunes areas represent a natural reserve which can be called upon in the face of extreme events; building on these areas leaves little option but to undertake costly protective measures when extreme events (whether amplified by gradual global change or not) threaten. Managed retreat can comprise 'setbacks', rolling easements and other planning tools including building within a particular design life. Maintenance of those structures or soft techniques can arrive at a critical point (economically or environmental) to change adopted strategy.

- Structural or hard engineering techniques, i.e. using permanent concrete and rock constructions to "fix" the coastline and protect the assets locate behind. These techniques—seawalls, groynes, detached breakwaters, and revetments—represent a significant share of protected shoreline in Europe (more than 70%).
- Soft engineering techniques (e.g. sand nourishments), building with natural processes and relying on natural elements such as sands, dunes and vegetation to prevent erosive forces from reaching the backshore. These techniques include beach nourishment and sand dune stabilization.

Move Seaward

The futility of trying to predict future scenarios where there is a large human influence is apparent. Even future climate is to a certain extent a function of what humans choose to make of it, for example by restricting greenhouse gas emissions to control climate change. In some cases - where new areas are needed for new economic or ecological development - a move seaward strategy can be adopted. Examples from erosion include: Koge Bay (Dk) Western Scheldt estuary (NI), Chatelaillon (F), Ebro delta (E)

There is an obvious downside to this strategy. Coastal erosion is already widespread, and there are many coasts where exceptional high tides or storm surges result in encroachment on the shore, impinging on human activity. If the sea rises, many coasts that are developed with infrastructure along or close to the shoreline will be unable to accommodate erosion. They will experience a so-called "coastal squeeze" whereby the ecological or geomorphological zones that would normally retreat landwards encounter solid structures and are squeezed out. Wetlands, salt marshes, mangroves and adjacent fresh water wetlands are particularly likely to suffer from this squeeze.

An upside to the strategy is that moving seaward (and upward) can create land of high value which can bring the investment required to cope with climate change.

Limited Intervention

Limited intervention is an action taken whereby the management only solves the problem to some extent, usually in areas of low economic significance. Measures taken using limited intervention often encourage the succession of haloseres, including salt marshes and sand dunes. This will normally result in the land behind the halosere being more sufficiently protected, as wave energy will be dissipated by the accumulated sediment and additional vegetation residing in the newly formed habitat. Although the new halosere is not strictly man-made, as many natural processes will contribute to the succession of the halosere, anthropogenic factors are partially responsible for the formation as an initial factor was needed to help start the process of succession. This must not be confused with 'accommodate' which is about property e.g. effective insurance, early warning systems and not about habitat.

Construction techniques

The following is a catalogue of relevant techniques that could be employed as coastal management techniques. *The costs given are very rough estimates made during 2005, based on UK Pound sterling.*

Hard Engineering Methods

Groynes: Groynes are barriers or walls perpendicular to the sea often made of greenhart, concrete, rock and/or wood. Beach material builds up on the downdrift side, where littoral drift is predominantly in one direction, creating a wider and a more plentiful beach, therefore enhancing the protection for the coast because the sand material filters and absorbs the wave energy. However, there is a corresponding loss of beach material on the updrift side, requiring that another groyne to be built there. Moreover, groynes do not protect the beach against storm-driven waves and if placed too close together will create currents, which will carry sand material offshore.

Groynes are extremely cost-effective coastal defence measures, requiring little maintenance, and are one of the most common coastal defence structures. However, groynes are increasingly viewed as detrimental to the aesthetics of the coastline, and face strong opposition in many coastal communities.

Many experts consider groynes to be a "soft" solution to coastal erosion because of the enhancement of the existing beach.

But groyne construction creates a problem known as Terminal Groyne Syndrome. The terminal groyne prevents longshore drift from bringing material to other nearby places. This is a common problem along the Hampshire and Sussex coastline in the UK; a perfect example is Worthing.

Sea Walls

Walls of concrete or rock, built at the base of a cliff or at the back of a beach, or used to protect a settlement against erosion or flooding. They are usually about 3–5 metres high. Older style vertical seawalls reflected all the energy of the waves back out to sea, and for this purpose were often given recurved crest walls which also increase the local turbulence, and thus increasing entrainment of sand and sediment. During storms, sea walls help longshore drift.

Modern seawalls aim to re-direct most of the incident energy, resulting in low reflected waves and much reduced turbulence and thus take the form of sloping revetments. Current designs use porous designs of rock, concrete armour (Seabees, SHEDs, Xblocs) with intermediate flights of steps for beach access, whilst in places where high rates of pedestrian access are required, the steps take over the whole of the frontage, but at a flatter slope if the same crest levels are to be achieved.

Care needs to be taken in the location of a seawall, particularly in relation to the swept prism of the beach profile, the consequences of long term beach recession and amenity crest level. These factors must be considered in assessing the cost benefit ratio, which must be favourable in order to justify construction of a seawall.

Sea walls can cause beaches to dissipate rendering them useless for beach goers. Their presence also scars the very landscape that they are trying to save.

Modern examples can be found at Cronulla (NSW, 1985-6), Blackpool (1986–2001), Lincolnshire (1992–1997) & Wallasey (1983–1993). The sites at Blackpool and Cronulla can be visited both by Google Earth and by local webcams (Cronulla, Cleveleys).

A most interesting example is the seawall at Sandwich, Kent, where the Seabee seawall is buried at the back of the beach under the shingle with crest level at road kerb level.

Sea walls are probably the second most traditional method used in coastal management.

Sea walls cost £10,000 per metre (depending on material, height and width) £10,000,000 per km (depending on material, height and width)

Revetments

Wooden slanted or upright blockades, built parallel to the sea on the coast, usually towards the back of the beach to protect the cliff or settlement beyond. The most basic revetments consist of timber slants with a possible rock infill. Waves break against the revetments, which dissipate and absorb the energy. The cliff base is protected by the beach material held behind the barriers, as the revetments trap some of the material. They may be watertight, covering the slope completely, or porous, to allow water to filter through after the wave energy has been dissipated. Most revetments do not significantly interfere with transport of longshore drift. Since the wall greatly absorbs the energy instead of reflecting, it erodes and destroys the revetment structure; therefore, major maintenance will be needed within a moderate time of being built, this will be greatly determined by the material the structure was built with and the quality of the product.

The *Cost* – Confirmed by material used; est. $2340 – $4000. Average $10 per metre built - around £6 GBP.

Rock Armour

Also known as riprap, rock armour is large rocks piled or placed at the foot of dunes or cliffs with native stones of the beach. This is generally used in areas prone to erosion to absorb the wave energy and hold beach material. Although effective, this solution is unpopular due to the fact that it is unsightly. Also, longshore drift is not hindered.

Rock armour has a limited lifespan, it is not effective in storm conditions, and it reduces the recreational value of a beach. The cost is around £3000 per metre, depending on the type of rocks used.

Gabions

Boulders and rocks are wired into mesh cages and usually placed in front of areas vulnerable to heavy erosion: sometimes at cliffs edges or jag out at a right angle to the beach like a large groyne. When the seawater breaks on the gabion, the water drains through leaving sediments, also the rocks and boulders absorb a moderate amount of the wave energy.

Gabions need to be securely tied to prevent abrasion of wire by rocks, or detachment of plastic coating by stretching. Hexagonal mesh distributes overloads better than rectangular mesh.

Offshore Breakwater

Enormous concrete blocks and natural boulders are sunk offshore to alter wave direction and to filter the energy of waves and tides. The waves break further offshore and therefore reduce their erosive power. This leads to wider beaches, which absorb the reduced wave energy, protecting cliff and settlements behind. The Dolos which was invented by a South African engineer in East London has replaced the use of enormous concrete blocks because the dolos is much more resistant to wave action and requires less concrete to produce a superior result. Similar concrete objects like the Dolos are the A-jack, Akmon, Xbloc and the Tetrapod, Accropode.

Cliff Stabilization

Cliff stabilization can be accomplished through drainage of excess rainwater of through terracing, planting, and wiring to hold cliffs in place. Cliff drainage is used to hold a cliff together using plants, fences and terracing, this is used to help prevent landslides and other natural disasters.

Entrance Training Walls

Rock or concrete walls built to constrain a river or creek discharging across a sandy coastline. The walls help to stabilise and deepen the channel which benefits navigation, flood management, river erosion and water quality but can cause coastal erosion due to the interruption of longshore drift. One solution is the installation of a sand bypassing system to pump sand under and around the entrance training walls.

Cost – Expensive - Gold Coast Seaway was a A$50M project in the 1980s and the adjacent sand bypassing project costs A$3M per year to pump 500,000 cubic metres of sand across the trained entrance.

Floodgates

Storm surge barriers, or floodgates, were introduced after the North Sea Flood of 1953 and are a prophylactic method to prevent damage from storm surges or any other type of natural disaster that could harm the area they "protect". They are habitually open and allow free passage, but close when the land is under threat of a storm surge. The Thames Barrier is an example of such a structure.

Soft Engineering Methods

Beach Replenishment: Beach replenishment or nourishment is one of the most popular soft engineering techniques of coastal defence management schemes. This involves importing sand off the beach and piling it on top of the existing sand. The imported sand must be of a similar quality to the existing beach material so it can integrate with the natural processes occurring there, without causing any adverse effects. Beach nourishment can be used alongside the groyne schemes. The scheme requires constant maintenance: 1 to 10-year life before first major recharge. *Cost* – est. £5,000-£200,000 per 100-metre, plus control structures, ongoing management and minor works.

Sand Dune Stabilization

Vegetation can be used to encourage dune growth by trapping and stabilising blown sand.

Cost – est. of £1.1 million per annum

Beach Drainage

Beach drainage or beach face dewatering lowers the water table locally beneath the beach face. This causes accretion of sand above the drainage system.

Grant (1946) – the elevation of the beach watertable had an important bearing on deposition and erosion across the foreshore. A high watertable coincided with periods of accelerated beach erosion, and conversely, a low watertable coincided with pronounced aggradation of the foreshore A lower watertable (unsaturated beach face) facilitates deposition by reducing flow velocities during backwash and prolonging laminar flow. In contrast, a high watertable results in condition favouring beach erosion. With the beach in a saturated state, Grant proposed that backwash velocity is accelerated by the addition of groundwater seepage out of the beach within the effluent zone. Turner and Leatherman (1997) moving from the origins and development of the dewatering concept to field and laboratory studies available at the time of writing concluded that there was too little evidence for being convinced that the systems had a positive effect. None of the case studies provide full scientific evidence of indisputable positive results regarding beach stabilisation although in some cases an overall positive performance was reported. In many cases no adequate long-term monitoring was undertaken at a frequency high enough to discriminate the response to high energy erosive events.

A useful side effect of the system is that the collected seawater is very pure because of the sand filtration effect. It may be discharged back to sea but can also be used to oxygenate stagnant inland lagoons /marinas or used as feed for heat pumps, desalination plants, land-based aquaculture, aquariums or seawater swimming pools.

Beach drainage systems have been installed in many locations around the world to halt and reverse erosion trends in sand beaches. Twenty four beach drainage systems have been installed since 1981 in Denmark, USA, UK, Japan, Spain, Sweden, France, Italy and Malaysia.

Costs

The costs of installation and operation per metre of shoreline protection will vary due to

- system length (non-linear cost elements)
- pump flow rates (sand permeability, power costs)
- soil conditions (presence of rock or impermeable strata)
- discharge arrangement /filtered seawater utilization
- drainage design, materials selection & installation methods
- geographical considerations (location logistics)
- regional economic considerations (local capabilities /costs)
- study requirements /consent process.

The costs associated with a beach drainage system are generally considerably lower than hard engineered structures. They also compare very favourably with beach nourishment projects, particularly when long-term project economics are considered (nourishment projects often have a limited life or a programme of re-nourishment).

Monitoring Coastal Zones

Coastal zone managers are faced with difficult and complex choices about how best to reduce property damage in the shorelines. One of the problems they face is error and uncertainty in the information available to them on the processes that cause erosion of beaches. Video-based monitoring lets collect data continuously at low cost and produce analyses of shoreline processes over a wide range of averaging intervals.

Event Warning Systems

Event warning systems, such as tsunami warnings and storm surge warnings, can be used to minimize the human impact of catastrophic events that cause coastal erosion. Storm surge warnings can also be used to determine when to close floodgates to reduce the physical impact of such events.

Wireless sensor networks can be deployed quickly to set up a coastal erosion monitoring system, and scaled accordingly.

Shoreline Mapping

Defining the shoreline is a difficult task due to the dynamic nature of the coast and the intended application of the shoreline (Graham et al. 2003; Boak & Turner 2005). Given this idea the shoreline must therefore be considered in a temporal sense whereby the scale is dependent on the context of the investigation (Boak & Turner 2005). The following definition of the coast and shoreline is most commonly employed for the purposes of shoreline mapping. The coast comprises the interface between land and sea, and the shoreline is represented by the margin between the two (Woodroffe, 2002). Due to the dynamic nature of the shoreline coastal investigators adopt the use of shoreline indicators to represent the true shoreline position (Boak & Turner 2005).

Shoreline Indicator

The choice of shoreline indicator is a primary consideration in shoreline mapping. According to Leatherman (2003) it is important that indicators are easily identified in the field and on aerial photography. Shoreline indicators may be physical beach morphological features such as the berm crest, scarp edge, vegetation line, dune toe, dune crest and cliff or the bluff crest and toe. Alternatively, non-morphological features may also be used. These indicators are based on water level including the high water line, mean high water line, wet/dry boundary, and the physical water line (Pajak & Leatherman 2000).

The high water line (HWL), defined as the wet/dry line is the most commonly used shoreline indicator because it is visible in the field, and can be interpreted on both colour and grey scale aerial photographs

(Leatherman, 2003; Crowell et al. 1991). The HWL represents the landward extent of the most recent high tide and is characterised by a change in sand colour due to repeated, periodic inundation by high tides. The HWL is portrayed on aerial photographs by the most landward change in colour or grey tone (Boak & Turner 2005).

Importance and Application

The location of the shoreline and its changing position over time is of fundamental importance to coastal scientists, engineers and managers (Boak & Turner 2005; Pajack & Leatherman 2002). Present day shoreline monitoring campaigns provide information about historic shoreline location and movement, and about predictions of future change (Appeaning Addo et al. 2008). More specifically the position of the shoreline in the past, at present and where it is predicted to be in the future is useful for in the design of coastal protection, to calibrate and verify numerical models to assess sea level rise, map hazard zones and formulate policies to regulate coastal development. Accurate and consistent delineation of the shoreline is integral to all of these tasks. The location of the shoreline also provides information regarding shoreline reorientation adjacent to structures, beach width, volume and rates of historical change (Boak & Turner 2005; Pajack & Leatherman 2002).

Data sources

A variety of data sources are available for examining shoreline position however, the availability of historical data is limited at many coastal sites and so the choice of data source is largely limited to what is available for the site at a given time (Boak & Turner 2005). Shoreline mapping techniques applied to data sources have moved towards automation in association with technological advances and the need to reduce uncertainty. Although these changes have resulted in improvement in coastal data processing and storage capabilities, the frequent change in technology has prevented the emergence of one standard method of shoreline mapping. This has occurred because each data source and associated method have their own unique capabilities and shortcomings (Moore 2000). A number of the data sources used for shoreline mapping and their associated advantages and disadvantages are discussed below.

Historical Maps

In the event that a study requires the shoreline position to be mapped before the development of aerial photographs, or if the location has poor photograph coverage it is necessary to employ historical maps in order to detail shoreline position (Moore 2000). The main advantage and reason for using historical maps is that they are able to provide a historic record that is not available from other data sources. Many potential errors however are associated with historical coastal maps and charts. Such errors may be associated with scale, datum changes, distortions from uneven shrinkage, stretching, creases, tears and folds, different surveying standards, different publication standards, and projection errors (Boak & Turner 2005). The severity of these errors depends on the accuracy standards met by each map and the physical changes that have occurred since the publication of the map (Anders & Byrnes 1991). The oldest reliable source of shoreline data in the United States dates back to the early-to-mid-19th century and is the U.S Coast and Geodetic Survey/National Ocean Service T-sheets (Morton 1991). In the United Kingdom, many maps and charts were deemed to be inaccurate until around 1750. The founding of the Ordnance Survey in 1791 has since improved the accuracy of the mapping.

Aerial Photographs

Aerial photographs have been used since the 1920s to provide topographical information about an area. They are therefore a good database for compilation of historical shoreline change maps. Aerial photographs are the most commonly used data source in shoreline mapping because many coastal areas have extensive aerial photo coverage therefore providing a valuable record of shoreline position (Moore 2000). In general, aerial photographs provide good spatial coverage of the coast however temporal coverage is very much site specific depending on the flight path of the aeroplane. A second disadvantage associated with aerial photography is that the interpretation of the shoreline position is subjective given the dynamic nature of the coastal environment. This combined with various distortions inherent in aerial photographs can lead to significant error levels (Moore 2000). The minimisation of further errors is discussed below.

Object Space Displacements

Conditions outside of the camera can cause objects in an image to be displaced from their true ground position. Such conditions may include ground relief, camera tilt and atmospheric refraction.

Relief displacement is prominent when photographing a variety of elevations. This situation causes objects above ground level to be displaced outward from the centre of the photograph and objects below ground level to be displaced toward the centre of the image. The severity of the displacement is affected negatively with decreases in flight altitude and as radial distance from the centre of the photograph increases. This distortion can be minimised by photographing numerous swaths and creating a mosaic of the images. This technique will create a focus for the centre of each photograph where distortion is minimised. It is important to note that this error is not common in shoreline mapping is the relief is fairly constant. It is however important to consider when mapping cliffs (Moore 2000).

Ideally aerial photographs are taken so the optical axis of the camera is perfectly perpendicular to the ground surface thereby creating a vertical photograph. Unfortunately this is not often the case and virtually all aerial photographs experience tilt whereby up to 3° is not uncommon (Camfield et al. 1996). In this situation the scale of the image will be larger on the upward side of the tilt axis and smaller on the downward side. Moore, (2000) notes that many coastal researchers have not realised the severity of this error and therefore do not consider it in their methods.

Radial Lens Distortion

Lens distortion varies as a function of radial distance from the iso-centre of the photograph meaning that the centre of the image is relatively distortion free, but as the angle of view increases the distortion becomes more prominent. This is a significant source of error in earlier aerial photography but as technology has increased and camera lens have become more refined it has become less of an issue with later photographs. Such a distortion is impossible to correct for without knowing the make and model of the lens used to capture the image. However if overlapping images have been acquired one can digitize the centre portions of the aerial photographs (Crowell et al. 1991).

Delineation of The Shoreline

The dynamic nature of the coast has meant that accurate mapping of an instantaneous shoreline position has been associated with significant uncertainty. This uncertainty arises because at any given time the position of the shoreline is influenced by the short-term effect of the tide and a wide variety of long term effects such as relative sea-level rise and along shore littoral sediment movement. Not only does this affect the accuracy of computed historic shoreline position but also any predicted future positions (Appeaning Addo et al. 2008). As mentioned earlier the HWL is most commonly used as a shoreline indicator. This can usually be seen as a significant tonal change on aerial photographs. There are however many errors associated with using the wet/dry line as a proxy for the HWL and shoreline. The errors of largest concern are the short term migration of the wet/dry line, interpretation of the wet/dry line on a photograph and measurement of the interpreted line position (Leatherman 2003; Moore 2000). Systematic errors such as the migration of the wet/dry line may arise from tidal and seasonal changes. Storm-induced erosion is another factor which may cause the wet/dry line to migrate landward. Field investigations have shown that these changes can be minimised by using only summertime data (Moore 2000; Leatherman 2003). Furthermore, the error bar can be significantly reduced by using the longest record of reliable data to calculate erosion rates (Leatherman 2003). Finally it is important to note that errors may arise due to the difficulty of measuring a single line on a photograph. For example where the pen line is 0.13 mm thick this translates to an error of ±2.6 m on a 1:20000 scale photograph.

Beach Profiling Surveys

Beach profiling surveys are typically repeated at regular intervals along the coast in order to measure short-term (daily to annual) variations in shoreline position and beach volume. (Smith & Zarillo 1990). Beach profiling is a very accurate source of information however measurements are generally subject to the limitations of conventional surveying techniques. Shoreline data derived from beach profiling is often spatially and temporally limited due to the high cost associated with such a labour intensive activity. Shorelines are generally derived by interpolating between a series of discrete beach profiles. It is important to note however that the distance between the profiles is usually quite large and so the accuracy of the interpolating becomes compromised. In contrast to aerial photographs, survey data is limited to smaller lengths of shoreline generally less than ten kilometres (Boak & Turner 2005). Beach profiling data is commonly available in from regional councils in New Zealand such as those compiled by the Hawkes Bay Regional Council.

Remote Sensing

Technological advancement over the last decade has led to the development of a range of airborne, satellite and land based remote sensing techniques (Smith & Zarillo 1990). Some of the remotely sensed data sources are listed below:

- Multispectral and hyperspectral imaging
- Microwave sensors
- Global positioning system (GPS)
- Airborne light detection and ranging technology (LIDAR)

Remote sensing techniques are attractive as they are cost effective, reduce manual error and remove the subjective approach of conventional field techniques (Maiti et al. 2009). Remote sensing is a relatively new concept and so extensive historical observations are unavailable. Given this idea, it is important that coastal morphology observations are quantified by coupling remotely sensed data with other sources of information detailing historic shoreline position from archived sources (Appeaning Addo et al. 2008).

Video Analysis

Video analysis provides quantitative, cost-effective, continuous and long-term monitoring beaches (Turner et al. 2004). The advancement of coastal video systems over the past 15 years has resulted in the extraction of large amounts of geophysical data from images. Such data includes that about coastal morphology, surface currents and wave parameters. The main advantage of video analysis lies in the ability to reliably quantify these parameters with high resolution and coverage in both space and time. This in particular highlights their potential importance as an effective coastal monitoring system and an aid to coastal zone management (Van Koningsveld et al. 2007). Interesting case studies have been carried out using video analysis. Turner et al. (2004) used a video-based ARGUS coastal imaging system to monitor and quantify the regional-scale coastal response to sand nourishment and construction of the world-first Gold Coast artificial (surfing) reef in Australia. In addition, Smit et al. (2007) demonstrated the added value of high resolution video observations for making short-term predictions of near shore hydrodynamic and morphological processes, at temporal scales of metres to kilometres and days to seasons.

Construction Engineering

Construction engineering is a professional discipline that deals with the designing, planning, construction, and management of infrastructures such as highways, bridges, airports, railroads, buildings, dams, and utilities. Construction Engineers are unique such that they are a cross between civil engineers and construction managers. Construction engineers learn the designing aspect much like civil engineers and construction site management functions much like construction managers. The primary difference between a construction engineer and a construction manager is that the construction engineer has the ability to sit for the Professional Engineer license (PE) whereas a construction manager cannot. At the educational level, construction managers are not as focused on design work as they are on construction procedures, methods, and people management. Their primary concern is to deliver a project on time, within budget, and of the desired quality.

The difference between a construction engineer and civil engineer is only at the educational level as both disciplines are able to sit for the PE exam giving them the same title of engineer. Civil engineering students concentrate more on the design work, gearing them toward a career as a design professional. This essentially requires them to take a multitude of design courses. Construction engineering students take design courses as well as construction management courses. This allows them to understand both the design functions as well as the building requirements needed to design and build today's infrastructures.

Work Activities

Depending on which career the construction engineer has chosen to follow, an entry-level design engineer normally provides support to project managers and assist with creating conceptual designs, scopes, and cost estimates for the planning and construction of approved projects. It should be noted that a career in design work does require a professional engineer license (PE). Individuals who pursue this career path are strongly advised to sit for the Engineer In Training exam (EIT) while in college as it takes five years (4 years in USA) post graduate to obtain the PE license.

Entry-level construction manager positions are typically called project engineers or assistant project engineers. They are responsible for preparing purchasing requisitions, processing change orders, preparing monthly budgeting reports, and handling meeting minutes. The construction management position does not necessarily require a PE license; however possessing one does make the individual more marketable, as the PE license allows the individual to sign off on temporary structure designs.

Abilities

Construction engineers are problem solvers, they help create infrastructure that best meets the unique demands of its environment. They must be able to understand infrastructure life cycles and have the perspective to solve technical challenges with clarity and imagination. Therefore individuals should have a strong understanding of maths and science, but many other skills are required, including critical and analytical thinking, time management, people management and good communication skills.

Educational Requirements

Individuals looking to obtain a construction engineering degree must first ensure that the programme is accredited by EAC or Technology Accreditation Commission (TAC) of the Accreditation Board for Engineering and Technology (ABET). ABET accreditation is assurance that a college or university programme meets the quality standards established by the profession for which it prepares its students. In the US there are currently twenty-five programmes that exist in the entire country so careful college consideration is advised.

A typical construction engineering curriculum is a mixture of engineering mechanics, engineering design, construction management and general science and mathematics. This usually leads to a Bachelor of Science degree. The B.S. degree along with some design or construction experience is sufficient for most entry level positions. Graduate schools may be an option for those who want to go further in depth of the construction and engineering subjects taught at the undergraduate level. In most cases construction engineering graduates look to either civil engineering, engineering management, or business administration as a possible graduate degree. For authority to approve any final designs of public projects (and most any project), a construction engineer must have a professional engineers (P.E.) license.

Job Prospects

Job prospects for construction engineers generally have a strong cyclical variation. For example, starting in 2008 - continuing until at least 2011 - job prospects have been poor due to the collapse of housing bubbles in many parts of the world. This sharply reduced demand for construction, forced construction professionals towards infrastructure construction and therefore increased the competition faced by established and new construction engineers. This increased competition, and a core reduction in quantity demand is in parallel with a possible shift in the demand for construction engineers due to the automation of many engineering tasks, overall resulting in reduced prospects for construction engineers. In early 2010 the United States construction industry had a 27% unemployment rate, this is nearly three times higher than the 9.7% national average unemployment rate. The construction unemployment rate (including tradesmen) is comparable to the United States 1933 unemployment rate - the lowest point of the Great Depression - of 25%.

Remuneration

The average salary for a civil engineer in the UK depends on the sector, and more specifically the level of experience of the individual. A 2010 survey of the remuneration and benefits of those occupying jobs in construction and the built environment industry showed that the average salary of a civil engineer in the UK is £29,582. The average salary varies depending on experience, for example the average annual salary for a civil engineer with between 3 and 6 years experience is £23,813. For those with between 14 and 20 years experience the average is £38,214.

Earthquake Engineering

Earthquake engineering is the scientific field concerned with protecting society, the natural and the man-made environment from earthquakes by limiting the seismic risk to socio-economically acceptable levels. Traditionally, it has been narrowly defined as the study of the behaviour of structures and geo-structures subject to seismic loading, thus considered as a subset of both structural and geotechnical engineering. However, the tremendous costs experienced in recent earthquakes have led to an expansion of its scope to encompass disciplines from the wider field of civil engineering and from the social sciences, especially sociology, political science, economics and finance.

The main objectives of earthquake engineering are:

- Foresee the potential consequences of strong earthquakes on urban areas and civil infrastructure.
- Design, construct and maintain structures to perform at earthquake exposure up to the expectations and in compliance with building codes.

A properly engineered structure does not necessarily have to be extremely strong or expensive. It has to be properly designed to withstand the seismic effects while sustaining an acceptable level of damage.

Seismic Loading

Seismic loading means application of an earthquake-generated excitation on a structure (or geo-structure). It happens at contact surfaces of a structure either with the ground, with adjacent structures, or with gravity waves from tsunami.

Seismic Performance

Earthquake or seismic performance defines a structure's ability to sustain its main functions, such as its safety and serviceability, *at* and *after* a particular earthquake exposure. A structure is normally considered *safe* if it does not endanger the lives and well-being of those in or around it by partially or completely collapsing. A structure may be considered *serviceable* if it is able to fulfill its operational functions for which it was designed.

Basic concepts of the earthquake engineering, implemented in the major building codes, assume that a building should survive a rare, very severe earthquake by sustaining significant damage but without globally collapsing. On the other hand, it should remain operational for more frequent, but less severe seismic events.

Seismic Performance Assessment

Engineers need to know the quantified level of the actual or anticipated seismic performance associated with the direct damage to an individual building subject to a specified ground shaking. Such an assessment may be performed either experimentally or analytically.

Experimental Assessment

Experimental evaluations are expensive tests that are typically done by placing a (scaled) model of the structure on a shake-table that simulates the earth shaking and observing its behaviour. Such kinds of experiments were first performed more than a century ago.Only recently has it become possible to perform 1:1 scale testing on full structures. Due to the costly nature of such tests, they tend to be used mainly for understanding the seismic behaviour of structures, validating models and verifying analysis methods. Thus, once properly validated, computational models and numerical procedures tend to carry the major burden for the seismic performance assessment of structures.

Analytical/Numerical Assessment

Seismic performance assessment or seismic structural analysis is a powerful tool of earthquake engineering which utilizes detailed modelling of the structure together with methods of structural analysis to gain a better understanding of seismic performance of building and non-building structures. The technique as a formal concept is a relatively recent development.

In general, seismic structural analysis is based on the methods of structural dynamics. For decades, the most prominent instrument of seismic analysis has been the earthquake response spectrum method which also contributed to the proposed building code's concept of today.

However, such methods are good only for linear elastic systems, being largely unable to model the structural behaviour when damage (i.e., non-linearity) appears. Numerical *step-by-step integration* proved to be a more effective method of analysis for multi-degree-of-freedom structural systems with significant non-linearity under a transient process of ground motion excitation.

Basically, numerical analysis is conducted in order to evaluate the seismic performance of buildings. Performance evaluations are generally carried out by using nonlinear static pushover analysis or nonlinear time-history analysis. In such analyses, it is essential to achieve accurate non-linear modelling of structural components such as beams, columns, beam-column joints, shear walls etc. Thus, experimental results play an important role in determining the modelling parameters of individual components, especially those that are subject to significant non-linear deformations. The individual components are then assembled to create a full non-linear model of the structure. Thus created models are analyzed to evaluate the performance of buildings.

The capabilities of the structural analysis software are a major consideration in the above process as they restrict the possible component models, the analysis methods available and, most importantly, the numerical robustness. The latter becomes a major consideration for structures that venture into the non-linear range and approach global or local collapse as the numerical solution becomes increasingly unstable and thus difficult to reach. There are several commercially available Finite Element Analysis software's such as CSI-SAP2000 and CSI-PERFORM-3D which can be used for the seismic performance evaluation of buildings. Moreover, there is research-based finite element analysis platforms such as OpenSees, RUAUMOKO and the older DRAIN-2D/3D, several of which are now open source.

Research for Earthquake Engineering

Research for earthquake engineering means both field and analytical investigation or experimentation intended for discovery and scientific explanation of earthquake engineering related facts, revision of conventional concepts in the light of new findings, and practical application of the developed theories.

The National Science Foundation (NSF) is the main United States government agency that supports fundamental research and education in all fields of earthquake engineering. In particular, it focuses on experimental, analytical and computational research on design and performance enhancement of structural systems.

The Earthquake Engineering Research Institute (EERI) is a leader in dissemination of earthquake engineering research related information both in the U.S. and globally.

A definitive list of earthquake engineering research related shaking tables around the world may be found in Experimental Facilities for Earthquake Engineering Simulation Worldwide. The most prominent of them is now E-Defence Shake Table in Japan.

Environmental Engineering

Environmental engineering is the integration of science and engineering principles to improve the natural environment, to provide healthy water, air, and land for human habitation and for other organisms, and to remediate pollution sites. Further more it is concerned with finding plausible solutions in the field of public health, such arthropod-borne diseases, implementing law which promote adequate sanitation in urban, rural and recreational areas. It involves waste water management and air pollution control, recycling, waste disposal, radiation protection, industrial hygiene, environmental sustainability, and public health issues as well as a knowledge of environmental engineering law. It also includes studies on the environmental impact of proposed construction projects.

Environmental engineers study the effect of technological advances on the environment. To do so, they conduct hazardous-waste management studies to evaluate the significance of such hazards, advise on treatment and containment, and develop regulations to prevent mishaps. Environmental engineers also design municipal water supply and industrial wastewater treatment systems as well as address local and worldwide environmental issues such as the effects of acid rain, global warming, ozone depletion, water pollution and air pollution from automobile exhausts and industrial sources. At many universities, Environmental Engineering programmes follow either the Department of Civil Engineering or The Department of Chemical Engineering at Engineering faculties. Environmental "civil" engineers focus on hydrology, water resources management, bioremediation, and water treatment plant design. Environmental "chemical" engineers, on the other hand, focus on environmental chemistry, advanced air and water treatment technologies and separation processes.

Additionally, engineers are more frequently obtaining specialized training in law (J.D.) and are utilizing their technical expertise in the practices of Environmental engineering law.. About four percent of environmental engineers go on to obtain Board Certification in their speciality area(s) of environmental engineering (Board Certified Environmental Engineer or BCEE).

Most jurisdictions also impose licensing and registration requirements.

Development

Ever since people first recognized that their health and well-being were related to the quality of their environment, they have applied thoughtful principles to attempt to improve the quality of their environment. The ancient Harappan civilization utilized early sewers in some cities. The Romans constructed aqueducts to prevent drought and to create a clean, healthful water supply for the metropolis of Rome. In the 15th century, Bavaria created laws restricting the development and degradation of alpine country that constituted the region's water supply.

The field emerged as a separate environmental discipline during the middle third of the 20th century in response to widespread public concern about water and pollution and increasingly extensive environmental quality degradation. However, its roots extend back to early efforts in public health engineering. Modern environmental engineering began in London in the mid-19th century when Joseph Bazalgette designed the first major sewerage system that reduced the incidence of waterborne diseases such as cholera. The introduction of drinking water treatment and sewage treatment in industrialized countries reduced waterborne diseases from leading causes of death to rarities.

In many cases, as societies grew, actions that were intended to achieve benefits for those societies had longer-term impacts which reduced other environmental qualities. One example is the widespread application of the pesticide DDT to control agricultural pests in the years following World War II. While the agricultural benefits were outstanding and crop yields increased dramatically, thus reducing world hunger substantially, and malaria was controlled better than it ever had been, numerous species were brought to the verge of extinction due to the impact of the DDT on their reproductive cycles. The story of DDT as vividly told in Rachel Carson's "Silent Spring" (1962) is considered to be the birth of the modern environmental movement and the development of the modern field of "environmental engineering."

Conservation movements and laws restricting public actions that would harm the environment have been developed by various societies for millennia. Notable examples are the laws decreeing the construction of sewers in London and Paris in the 19th century and the creation of the U.S. national park system in the early 20th century.

Scope

Solid Waste Management: Solid waste management is the collection, transport, processing or disposal, managing, and monitoring of solid waste materials. The term usually relates to materials produced by direct or indirect human activity, and the process is generally undertaken to reduce their effect on health, the environment, or aesthetics. Waste management is a distinct practice from resource recovery, which focuses on delaying the rate of consumption of natural resources. The management of wastes treats all materials as a single class, whether solid, liquid, gaseous, or radioactive substances, and the objective is to reduce the harmful environmental impacts of each through different methods.

Environmental Impact Assessment and Mitigation

Scientists have developed air pollution dispersion models to evaluate the concentration of a pollutant at a receptor or the impact on overall air quality from vehicle exhausts and industrial flue gas stack emissions. To some extent, this field overlaps the desire to decrease carbon dioxide and other greenhouse gas emissions from combustion processes. They apply scientific and engineering principles to evaluate if there are likely to be any adverse impacts to water quality, air quality, habitat quality, flora and fauna, agricultural capacity, traffic impacts, social impacts, ecological impacts, noise impacts, visual (landscape) impacts, etc. If impacts are expected, they then develop mitigation measures to limit or prevent such impacts. An example of a mitigation measure would be the creation of wetlands in a nearby location to mitigate the filling in of wetlands necessary for a road development if it is not possible to reroute the road.

In the United States, the practice of environmental assessment was formally intitiated on January 1, 1970, the effective date of the National Environmental Policy Act (NEPA). Since that time, more than 100 developing and developed nations either have planned specific analogous laws or have adopted procedure used elsewhere. NEPA is applicable to all federal agencies in the United States.

Water Supply and Treatment

Engineers and scientists work to secure water supplies for potable and agricultural use. They evaluate the water balance within a watershed and determine the available water supply, the water needed for various needs in that watershed, the seasonal cycles of water movement through the watershed and they develop systems to store, treat, and convey water for various uses. Water is treated to achieve water quality objectives for the end uses. In the case of a potable water supply, water is treated to minimize the risk of infectious disease transmission, the risk of non-infectious illness, and to create a palatable water flavour. Water distribution systems are designed and built to provide adequate water pressure and flow rates to meet various end-user needs such as domestic use, fire suppression, and irrigation.

Waste Heat Conveyance and Cause

There are numerous wastewater treatment technologies. A wastewater treatment train can consist of a primary clarifier system to remove solid and floating materials, a secondary treatment system consisting of an aeration basin followed by flocculation and sedimentation or an activated sludge system and a secondary clarifier, a tertiary biological nitrogen removal system, and a final disinfection process. The aeration basin/activated sludge system removes organic material by growing bacteria (activated sludge). The secondary clarifier removes the activated sludge from the water. The tertiary system, although not always included due to costs, is becoming more prevalent to remove nitrogen and phosphorus and to disinfect the water before discharge to a surface water stream or ocean outfall.

Air Pollution Management

Scientists have developed air pollution dispersion models to evaluate the concentration of a pollutant at a receptor or the impact on overall air quality from vehicle exhausts and industrial flue gas stack emissions. To some extent, this field overlaps the desire to decrease carbon dioxide and other greenhouse gas emissions from combustion processes.

Carrying out These Key Tasks

The U.S. Environmental Protection Agency (EPA) is one of the many agencies that work with Environmental Engineers to solve key issues. An important component of EPA's mission is to protect and improve air, water, and overall environmental quality in order to avoid or mitigate the consequences of harmful effects.

Education

Courses aimed at developing graduates with specific skills in environmental systems or environmental technology are becoming more common and fall into broads classes:

- *Mechanical engineering* that designs machines and mechanical systems for the environmental used such as water treatment facility, pumping stations, garbage segregation plants and other mechanical facilities.
- *Environmental engineering or environmental systems* courses oriented towards a civil engineering approach in which structures and the landscape are constructed to blend with or protect the environment;
- *Environmental chemistry, sustainable chemistry* or *environmental chemical engineering* courses oriented towards understanding the effects (good and bad) of chemicals in the environment. Focus on mining processes, pollutants and commonly also cover biochemical processes;
- *Environmental technology* courses oriented towards producing electronic or electrical graduates capable of developing devices and artifacts able to monitor, measure, model and control environmental impact, including monitoring and managing energy generation from renewable sources.

7

Construction Surveying

Construction surveying (otherwise known as "lay-out" or "setting-out") is to stake out reference points and markers that will guide the construction of new structures such as roads or buildings. These markers are usually staked out according to a suitable coordinate system selected for the project.

History of Construction Surveying

- The nearly perfect squareness and north-south orientation of the Great Pyramid of Giza, built c. 2700 BC, affirm the Egyptians' command of surveying.
- A recent reassessment of Stonehenge (c.2500 BC) suggests that the monument was set out by prehistoric surveyors using peg and rope geometry.
- In the sixth century BC geometric based techniques were used to construct the tunnel of Eupalinos on the island of Samos.

Elements of the Construction Survey

- Survey existing conditions of the future work site, including topography, existing buildings and infrastructure, and underground infrastructure whenever possible (for example, measuring invert elevations and diameters of sewers at manholes);
- Stake out reference points and markers that will guide the construction of new structures
- Verify the location of structures during construction;
- Conduct an As-Built survey: a survey conducted at the end of the construction project to verify that the work authorized was completed to the specifications set on plans.

Coordinate Systems Used in Construction

Land surveys and surveys of existing conditions are generally performed according to geodesic coordinates. However for the purposes of construction a more suitable coordinate system will often be used. During construction surveying, the surveyor will often have to convert from geodesic coordinates to the coordinate system used for that project.

Chainage or Station

In the case of roads or other linear infrastructure, a *chainage* (derived from Gunter's Chain - 1 chain is equal to 66 feet or 100 links) will be established, often to correspond with the centre line of the road or pipeline. During construction, structures would then be located in terms of *chainage*, *offset* and *elevation*. *Offset* is said to be "left" or "right" relative to someone standing on the *chainage line* who is looking in the direction of increasing *chainage*. Plans would often show *plan* views (viewed from above), *profile* views (a "transparent" section view collapsing all section views of the road parallel to the *chainage*) or *cross-section* views (a "true" section view perpendicular to the *chainage*). In a *plan* view, *chainage* generally increases from left to right, or from the bottom to the top of the plan. *Profiles* are shown with the chainage increasing from left to right, and *cross-sections* are shown as if the viewer is looking in the direction of increasing *chainage* (so that the "left" *offset* is to the *left* and the "right" *offset* is to the *right*).

"Chainage" may also be referred to as "Station".

Building Grids

In the case of buildings, an arbitrary system of grids is often established so as to correspond to the rows of columns and the major load-bearing walls of the building. The grids may be identified alphabetically in one direction, and numerically in the other direction (as in a road map). The grids are usually but not necessarily perpendicular, and are often but not necessarily evenly spaced. Floors and basement levels are also numbered. Structures, equipment or architectural details may be located in reference to the floor and the nearest intersection of the arbitrary axes.

Other Coordinate Systems

In other types of construction projects, arbitrary "north-south" and "east-west" reference lines may be established, that do not necessarily correspond to true coordinates.

Equipment and Techniques Used in Construction Surveying

Surveying equipment, such as levels and theodolites, are used for accurate measurement of angular deviation, horizontal, vertical and slope distances. With computerisation, electronic distance measurement (EDM), total stations, GPS surveying and laser scanning have supplemented (and to a large extent supplanted) the traditional optical instruments.

The builder's level measures neither horizontal nor vertical angles. It simply combines a spirit level and telescope to allow the user to visually establish a line of sight along a level plane. When used together with a graduated staff it can be used to transfer elevations from one location to another. An alternative method to transfer elevation is to use water in a transparent hose as the level of the water in the hose at opposite ends will be at the same elevation.

Equipment and Techniques Used in Mining and Tunneling

Total stations are the primary survey instrument used in mining surveying.

Underground Mining

A total station is used to record the absolute location of the tunnel walls (stopes), ceilings (backs), and floors as the drifts of an underground mine are driven. The recorded data is then downloaded into a CAD programme, and compared to the designed layout of the tunnel.

The survey party installs control stations at regular intervals. These are small steel plugs installed in pairs in holes drilled into walls or the back. For wall stations, two plugs are installed in opposite walls, forming a line perpendicular to the drift. For back stations, two plugs are installed in the back, forming a line parallel to the drift.

A set of plugs can be used to locate the total station set up in a drift or tunnel by processing measurements to the plugs by intersection and resection.

Professional Status of Construction Surveyors

Building Surveying emerged in the 1970s as a profession in the United Kingdom by a group of technically minded General Practice Surveyors. Building Surveying is a recognized profession within Britain and Australia. In Australia in particular, due to risk mitigation/ limitation factors the employment of surveyors at all levels of the construction industry is widespread. There are still many countries where it is not widely recognized as a profession. The Services that Building Surveyors undertake are broad but include:

- Construction design and building works
- Project Management and monitoring
- CDM Co-ordinator under the Construction (Design & Management) Regulations 2007
- Property Legislation adviser
- Insurance assessment and claims assistance
- Defect investigation and maintenance adviser
- Building Surveys and measured surveys
- Handling Planning applications
- Building Inspection to ensure compliance with building regulations
- Undertaking pre-acquisition surveys
- Negotiating dilapidations claims

Building Surveyors also advise on many aspects of construction including:

- design
- maintenance
- repair
- refurbishment
- restoration.

Clients of a building surveyor can be the public sector, Local Authorities, Government Departments as well as private sector organisations and work closely with architects, planners, homeowners and tenants groups. Building Surveyors may also be called to act as an expert witness. It is usual for building surveyors to undertake an accredited degree qualification before undertaking structured training to become a member of a professional organisation. For Chartered Building Surveyors, these courses are accredited by the Royal Institution of Chartered Surveyors. Other professional organisations that have building surveyor members include CIOB, ABE, HKIS and RICS.

With the enlargement of the European community, the profession of the Chartered Building Surveyor is becoming more widely known in other European states, particularly France. Chartered Building Surveyors, where many English speaking people buy second homes.

Distinction From Land Surveyors

In the United States, Canada, the United Kingdom and most Commonwealth countries land surveying is considered to be a distinct profession. Land surveyors have their own professional associations and licencing requirements. The services of a licenced land surveyor are generally required for boundary surveys (to establish the boundaries of a parcel using its legal description) and subdivision plans (a plot or map based on a survey of a parcel of land, with boundary lines drawn inside the larger parcel to indicated the creation of new boundary lines and roads).

Geotechnical Engineering

Geotechnical engineering is the branch of civil engineering concerned with the engineering behaviour of earth materials. Geotechnical engineering is important in civil engineering, but is also used by military, mining, petroleum, or any other engineering concerned with construction on or in the ground. Geotechnical engineering usually uses principles of soil mechanics and rock mechanics to investigate subsurface conditions and materials; determine the relevant physical/ mechanical and chemical properties of these materials; evaluate stability of natural slopes and man-made soil deposits; assess risks posed by site conditions; design earthworks and structure foundations; and monitor site conditions, earthwork and foundation construction.

A typical geotechnical engineering project begins with a review of project needs to define the required material properties. Then follows a site investigation of soil, rock, fault distribution and bedrock properties on and below an area of interest to determine their engineering properties including how they will interact with, on or in a proposed construction. Site investigations are needed to gain an understanding of the area in or on which the engineering will take place. Investigations can include the assessment of the risk to humans, property and the environment from natural hazards such as earthquakes, landslides, sinkholes, soil liquefaction, debris flows and rockfalls.

Ground Improvement refers to a technique that improves the engineering properties of the soil mass treated. Usually, the properties that are modified are shear strength, stiffness and permeability. Ground improvement has developed into a sophisticated tool to support foundations for a wide variety of structures. Properly applied, i.e. after giving due consideration to the nature of the ground being improved and the type and sensitivity of the structures being built, ground improvement often reduces direct costs and saves time.

A geotechnical engineer then determines and designs the type of foundations, earthworks, and/or pavement subgrades required for the intended man-made structures to be built. Foundations are designed and constructed for structures of various sizes such as high-rise buildings, bridges, medium to large commercial buildings, and smaller structures where the soil conditions do not allow code-based design.

Foundations built for above-ground structures include shallow and deep foundations. Retaining structures include earth-filled dams and retaining walls. Earthworks include embankments, tunnels, dikes and levees, channels, reservoirs, deposition of hazardous waste and sanitary landfills.

Geotechnical engineering is also related to coastal and ocean engineering. Coastal engineering can involve the design and construction of wharves, marinas, and jetties. Ocean engineering can involve foundation and anchor systems for offshore structures such as oil platforms.

The fields of geotechnical engineering and engineering geology are closely related, and have large areas of overlap. However, the field of geotechnical engineering is a speciality of engineering, where the field of engineering geology is a speciality of geology.

History

Humans have historically used soil as a material for flood control, irrigation purposes, burial sites, building foundations, and as construction material for buildings. First activities were linked to irrigation and flood control, as demonstrated by traces of dykes, dams, and canals dating back to at least 2000 BCE that were found in ancient Egypt, ancient Mesopotamia and the Fertile Crescent, as well as around the early settlements of Mohenjo Daro and Harappa in the Indus valley. As the cities expanded, structures were erected supported by formalized foundations; Ancient Greeks notably constructed pad footings and strip-and-raft foundations. Until the 18th century, however, no theoretical basis for soil design had been developed and the discipline was more of an art than a science, relying on past experience.

Several foundation-related engineering problems, such as the Leaning Tower of Pisa, prompted scientists to begin taking a more scientific-based approach to examining the subsurface. The earliest advances occurred in the development of earth pressure theories for the construction of retaining walls. Henri Gautier, a French Royal Engineer, recognized the "natural slope" of different soils in 1717, an idea later known as the soil's angle of repose. A rudimentary soil classification system was also developed based on a material's unit weight, which is no longer considered a good indication of soil type.

The application of the principles of mechanics to soils was documented as early as 1773 when Charles Coulomb (a physicist, engineer, and army Captain) developed improved methods to determine the earth pressures against military ramparts. Coulomb observed that, at failure, a distinct slip plane would form behind a sliding retaining wall and he suggested that the maximum shear stress on the slip plane, for design purposes, was the sum of the soil cohesion, , and friction , where is the normal stress on the slip plane and is the friction angle of the soil. By combining Coulomb's theory with Christian Otto Mohr's 2D stress state, the theory became known as Mohr-Coulomb theory. Although it is now recognized that precise determination of cohesion is impossible because is not a fundamental soil property, the Mohr-Coulomb theory is still used in practice today.

In the 19th century Henry Darcy developed what is now known as Darcy's Law describing the flow of fluids in porous media. Joseph Boussinesq (a mathematician and physicist) developed theories of stress distribution in elastic solids that proved useful for estimating stresses at depth in the ground; William Rankine, an engineer and physicist, developed an alternative to Coulomb's earth pressure theory. Albert Atterberg developed the clay consistency indices that are still used today for soil classification. Osborne Reynolds recognized in 1885 that shearing causes volumetric dilation of dense and contraction of loose granular materials.

Modern geotechnical engineering is said to have begun in 1925 with the publication of *Erdbaumechanik* by Karl Terzaghi (a mechanical engineer and geologist). Considered by many to be the father of modern soil mechanics and geotechnical engineering, Terzaghi developed the principle of effective stress, and demonstrated that the shear strength of soil is controlled by effective stress. Terzaghi also developed the framework for theories of bearing capacity of foundations, and the theory for prediction of the rate of settlement of clay layers due to consolidation. In his 1948 book, Donald Taylor recognized that interlocking and dilation of densely packed particles contributed to the peak strength of a soil. The interrelationships between volume change behaviour (dilation, contraction, and consolidation) and shearing behaviour were all connected via the theory of plasticity using critical state soil mechanics by Roscoe, Schofield, and Wroth with the publication of "On the Yielding of Soils" in 1958. Critical state soil mechanics is the basis for many contemporary advanced constitutive models describing the behaviour of soil.

Geotechnical centrifuge modelling is a method of testing physical scale models of geotechnical problems. The use of a centrifuge enhances the similarity of the scale model tests involving soil because the strength and stiffness of soil is very sensitive to the confining pressure. The centrifugal acceleration allows a researcher to obtain large (prototype-scale) stresses in small physical models.

Municipal or Urban Engineering

Municipal or urban engineering applies the tools of science, art and engineering in an urban environment.

Summary

Municipal engineering is concerned with municipal infrastructure. This involves specifying, designing, constructing, and maintaining streets, sidewalks, water supply networks, sewers, street lighting, municipal solid waste management and disposal, storage depots for various bulk materials used for maintenance and public works (salt, sand, etc.), public parks and bicycle paths. In the case of underground utility networks, it may also include the civil portion (conduits and access chambers) of the local distribution networks of electrical and telecommunications services. It can also include the optimizing of garbage collection and bus service networks. Some of these disciplines overlap with other civil engineering specialties, however municipal engineering focuses on the coordination of these infrastructure networks and services, as they are often built simultaneously (for a given street or development project), and managed by the same municipal authority.

History

Modern municipal engineering finds its origins in the 19th-century United Kingdom, following the Industrial Revolution and the growth of large industrial cities. The threat to urban populations from epidemics of waterborne diseases such as cholera and typhus lead to the development of a profession devoted to "sanitary science" that later became "municipal engineering".

A key figure of the so-called "public health movement" was Edwin Chadwick, author of the parliamentary report "The Sanitary Condition of the Labouring Population", published in 1842.

Early British legislation included:

- Burgh Police Act 1833 - powers of paving, lighting, cleansing, watching, supplying with water and improving their communities.
- Municipal Corporations Act 1835
- Public Health Act 1866 – formation of drainage boards
- Public Health Act 1875 known at the time as the Great Public Health Act

This legislation provided local authorities with powers to undertake municipal engineering projects and to appoint borough surveyors (later known as "municipal engineers").

In the U.K, the Association of Municipal Engineers, (subsequently named Institution of Municipal Engineers), was established in 1874 under the encouragement of the Institution of Civil Engineers, to address the issue of the application of sanitary science. By the early 20th century, Municipal Engineering had become a broad discipline embracing many of the responsibilities undertaken by local authorities, including roads, drainage, flood control, coastal engineering, public health, waste management, street cleaning, water supply, sewers, waste water treatment, crematoria, public baths, slum clearance, town planning, public housing, energy supply, parks, leisure facilities, libraries, town halls and other municipal buildings.

In the UK, the development of different strands of knowledge necessary for the management of municipal infrastructure led to the emergence of separate specialised institutions, including:

- For drainage: Chartered Institution of Water and Environmental Management, 1895
- For town planning: Town Planning Institute 1914 ... subsequently becoming the Royal Town Planning Institute
- For street lighting: Association of Public Lighting Engineers, 1934...subsequently becoming the Institution of Lighting Engineers
- For highway engineering: Institution of Highways and Transportation, 1930
- For public housing: Institute of Housing, 1931

In 1984 the Institution of Municipal Engineers merged with the Institution of Civil Engineers.

Since the 1970s, there has been a global trend toward increasing privatisation and outsourcing of municipal engineering services.

In the UK in the 1990s a change in management philosophy brought the demise of the traditional organisational structure of boroughs where the three functions of town clerk, borough treasurer and borough engineer were replaced by an administrative structure with a larger number of specialised departments.

In the late 1990s and early 21st century there was increasing dissatisfaction over what was perceived to be fractured and dysfunctional public services designed along narrow specialties. A more holistic approach to urban engineering began to emerge as an alternative concept. Critics of the specialised approach included the Commission for Architecture and the Built Environment that complained that the specialised approach to management of the public realm focussed too much on the on efficient movement of vehicles rather than the more general interests of local communities.

Professional Practice

In the United Kingdom there is no longer any formal professional qualification in municipal engineering although there are degree courses available in urban engineering.

A professional certificate in Urban Engineering is available from through the Institution of Incorporated Engineers via the Public Realm Information and Advice Network.

The British Institution of Civil Engineers (ICE) caters to practitioners employed in the public sector, private consultancy and academia through its Proceedings Journal Municipal Engineer. The journal, first published in 1873, has a global scope and covers the whole life cycle of municipal services addressing technical, political and community issues. In addition an Expert Panel responds on behalf of ICE to Government consultations and is represented on the International Federation of Municipal Engineering.

International Organisation

The International Federation of Municipal Engineering (IFME) is an organisation comprising professional municipal engineers from all round the world. IFME's mission is to connect municipal engineers, public works professionals, public agencies, institutions and businesses around the world in order that they can share a global pool of knowledge and experience. The aim is to foster continued improvement in the quality of public works and wider community services.

The inaugural meeting was held in 1960 at the UNESCO headquarters in Paris. Membership has grown steadily and in 2009 comprised representatives from national associations in: Australia, Canada, Denmark, Estonia, Finland, Italy, Israel, The Netherlands, New Zealand, Norway, Southern Africa (South Africa, Botawana, Namibia & Zimbabwe), Sweden, UK (England, Scotland, Wales & Northern Ireland) and USA. Belgium and San Marino are presently Corresponding Members.

Related Engineering Disciplines

Municipal or urban engineering combines elements of environmental engineering, water resources engineering and transport engineering.

Relationship to Urban Design or Urban Planning

Today, municipal engineering may be confused with urban design or urban planning. Whereas the urbanist or urban planner may design the general layout of streets and public places, the municipal engineer is concerned with the detailed design. For example, in the case of the design of a new street, the urbanist may specify the general layout of the street, including landscaping, surface finishings and urban accessories, but the municipal engineer will prepare the detailed plans and specifications for the roads, sidewalks, municipal services and street lighting. However Municipal Engineering as practiced a century ago fully embraced the function of urban design and urban planning, even though the terms had yet to be coined.

Transport Engineering

Transportation engineering is the application of technology and scientific principles to the planning, functional design, operation and management of facilities for any mode of transportation in order to provide for the safe, efficient, rapid, comfortable, convenient, economical, and environmentally compatible movement of people and goods (transport). It is a sub-discipline of civil engineering and of industrial engineering. Transportation engineering is a major component of the civil engineering and mechanical engineering disciplines, according to specialisation of academic courses and main competences of the involved territory. The importance of transportation engineering within the civil and industrial engineering profession can be judged by the number of divisions in ASCE (American Society of Civil Engineers) that are directly related to transportation. There are six such divisions (Aerospace; Air Transportation; Highway; Pipeline; Waterway, Port, Coastal and Ocean; and Urban Transportation) representing one-third of the total 18 technical divisions within the ASCE (1987).

The planning aspects of transport engineering relate to urban planning, and involve technical forecasting decisions and political factors. Technical forecasting of passenger travel usually involves an urban transportation planning model, requiring the estimation of trip generation (how many trips for what purpose), trip distribution (destination choice, where is the traveller going), mode choice (what mode is being taken), and route assignment (which streets or routes are being used). More sophisticated forecasting can include other aspects of traveller decisions, including auto ownership, trip chaining (the decision to link individual trips together in a tour) and the choice of residential or business location (known as land use forecasting). Passenger trips are the focus of transport engineering because they often represent the peak of demand on any transportation system.

A review of descriptions of the scope of various committees indicates that while facility planning and design continue to be the core of the transportation engineering field, such areas as operations planning, logistics, network analysis, financing, and policy analysis are also important to civil engineers, particularly to those working in highway and urban transportation. The National Council of Examiners for Engineering and Surveying (NCEES) list online the safety protocols, geometric design requirements, and signal timing.

Transportation engineering, as practiced by civil engineers, primarily involves planning, design, construction, maintenance, and operation of transportation facilities. The facilities support air, highway, railroad, pipeline, water, and even space transportation. The design aspects of transport engineering include the sizing of transportation facilities (how many lanes or how much capacity the facility has), determining the materials and thickness used in pavement designing the geometry (vertical and horizontal alignment) of the roadway (or track).

Before any planning occurs the Engineer must take what is known as an inventory of the area or if it is appropriate, the previous system in place. This inventory or database must include information on (1) population, (2) land use, (3) economic activity, (4) transportation facilities and services, (5) travel patterns and volumes, (6) laws and ordinances, (7) regional financial resources, (8) community values and expectations. These inventories help the engineer create business models to complete accurate forecasts of the future conditions of the systemReview.

Operations and management involve traffic engineering, so that vehicles move smoothly on the road or track. Older techniques include signs, signals, markings, and tolling. Newer technologies involve intelligent transportation systems, including advanced traveller information systems (such as variable message signs), advanced traffic control systems (such as ramp metres), and vehicle infrastructure integration. Human factors are an aspect of transport engineering, particularly concerning driver-vehicle interface and user interface of road signs, signals, and markings.

Highway Engineering

Engineers in this specialization:

- Handle the planning, design, construction, and operation of highways, roads, and other vehicular facilities as well as their related bicycle and pedestrian realms.
- Estimate the transportation needs of the public and then secure the funding for the project.
- Analyze locations of high traffic volumes and high collisions for safety and capacity.
- Use civil engineering principles to improve the transportation system.
- Utilizes the three design controls which are the drivers, the vehicles, and the roadways themselves.

Railroad Engineering

Railway engineers handle the design, construction, and operation of railroads and mass transit systems that use a fixed guideway (such as light rail or even monorails). Typical tasks would include determining horizontal and vertical alignment design, station location and design, and construction cost estimating. Railroad engineers can also move into the specialized field of train dispatching which focuses on train movement control.

Railway engineers also work to build a cleaner and safer transportation network by reinvesting and revitalizing the rail system to meet future demands. In the United States, railway engineers work with elected officials in Washington, D.C. on rail transportation issues to make sure that the rail system meets the country's transportation needs.

Port and Harbor Engineering

Port and harbor engineers handle the design, construction, and operation of ports, harbors, canals, and other maritime facilities. This is not to be confused with marine engineering.

Airport Engineering

Airport engineers design and construct airports. Airport engineers must account for the impacts and demands of aircraft in their design of airport facilities. These engineers must use the analysis of predominant wind direction to determine runway orientation, determine the size of runway border and safety areas, different wing tip to wing tip clearances for all gates and must designate the clear zones in the entire port.

Cost Overrun

A cost overrun, also known as a cost increase or budget overrun, is an unexpected cost incurred in excess of a budgeted amount due to an underestimation of the actual cost during budgeting. Cost overrun should be distinguished from cost escalation, which is used to express an *anticipated* growth in a budgeted cost due to factors such as inflation.

Cost overrun is common in infrastructure, building, and technology projects. For IT projects, an industry study by the Standish Group found that the average cost overrun was 43 percent; 71 percent of projects were over budget, exceeded time estimates, and had estimated too narrow a scope; and total waste was estimated at $55 billion per year in the US alone.

Many major construction projects have incurred cost overruns. The Suez Canal cost 20 times as much as the earliest estimates; even the cost estimate produced the year before construction began underestimated the project's actual costs by a factor of three. The Sydney Opera House cost 15 times more than was originally projected, and the Concorde supersonic aeroplane cost 12 times more than predicted.

The Channel Tunnel between the UK and France had a construction cost overrun of 80 percent, and a 140-percent financing cost overrun.

Causes

Three types of explanation for cost overrun exist: technical, psychological, and political-economic. Technical explanations account for cost overrun in terms of imperfect forecasting techniques, inadequate data, etc. Psychological explanations account for overrun in terms of optimism bias with forecasters. Scope creep, where the requirements or targets rises during the project, is common. Finally, political-economic explanations see overrun as the result of strategic misrepresentation of scope or budgets.

Prevention and Mitigation

In IT projects (essentially meaning software development projects in this context), the traditional approach to try to control costs is the use of project management techniques, such as PRINCE2 - though the use of such techniques has *not* prevented cost overruns in all cases. In the 21st century, a newer family of approaches, collectively termed agile software development, have grown in popularity for IT projects - although conventional project management is still very widely used, and in some cases has merely been inaccurately "rebranded" as agile.

Agile development does *not* claim to guarantee perfect on-time and on-budget delivery of the original expectations (which may not be even realistic or suitable to meet user needs). However, in many cases it may be able to:

- converge faster on a suitable solution
- meet user needs faster (users may even be able to use a partially-implemented system and therefore obtain economic benefit from it during the project's implementation, depending on the nature of the project)
- catch bugs faster, maybe even when they only exist in the primordial form of requirements deficiencies, and hence be able to fix them more cheaply on average (because studies have shown bugs are more expensive to fix the later they are found)
- trim away unnecessary or even unwanted "nice to haves" from the list of features planned to be implemented, in order to cut costs (in this setting, the traditional software engineering term "requirements" is clearly seen to be something of a misnomer, as many so-called requirements aren't actually requirements at all)
- avoid the worst-case scenario: project cancellation, in which all the money is wasted (except possibly that portion of the money spent on reusable code and/or reusable software components, if they are considered to be worth reusing)

It has been claimed that agile development did not prevent cost and time overruns in the UK government's Universal Credit IT project, but there are serious doubts as to whether the Universal Credit software development project was in fact following a proper agile process in the first place.

Describing Cost Overruns

Cost overrun can be described in multiple ways.

- As a percentage of the total expenditure

- As a total percentage including and above the original budget
- As a percentage of the cost overruns to original budget

For example, consider a bridge with a construction budget of $100 million where the actual cost was $150 million. This scenario could be truthfully represented by the following statements.

- The cost overruns constituted 33% of the total expense.
- The budget for the bridge increased to 150%.
- The cost overruns exceeded the original budget by 50%.

The final example is the most commonly utilized as it specifically describes the cost overruns exclusively whereas the other two describe the overrun as an aspect of the total expense. In any case care should be taken to accurately describe what is meant by the chosen percentage so as to avoid ambiguity.

Cost-effectiveness Analysis

Cost-effectiveness analysis (CEA) is a form of economic analysis that compares the relative costs and outcomes (effects) of two or more courses of action. Cost-effectiveness analysis is distinct from cost-benefit analysis, which assigns a monetary value to the measure of effect. Cost-effectiveness analysis is often used in the field of health services, where it may be inappropriate to monetize health effect. Typically the CEA is expressed in terms of a ratio where the denominator is a gain in health from a measure (years of life, premature births averted, sight-years gained) and the numerator is the cost associated with the health gain. The most commonly used outcome measure is quality-adjusted life years (QALY). Cost-utility analysis is similar to cost-effectiveness analysis. Cost-effectiveness analyses are often visualized on a cost-effectiveness plane consisting of four-quadrants. Outcomes plotted in Quadrant I are more effective and more expensive, those in Quadrant II are more effective and less expensive, those in Quadrant III are less effective and less expensive, and those in Quadrant IV are less effective and more expensive.

General Application

The concept of cost effectiveness is applied to the planning and management of many types of organized activity. It is widely used in many aspects of life. In the acquisition of military tanks, for example, competing designs are compared not only for purchase price, but also for such factors as their operating radius, top speed, rate of fire, armor protection, and caliber and armor penetration of their guns. If a tank's performance in these areas is equal or even slightly inferior to its competitor, but substantially less expensive and easier to produce, military planners may select it as more cost effective than the competitor. Conversely, if the difference in price is near zero, but the more costly competitor would convey an enormous battlefield advantage through special ammunition, radar fire control and laser range finding, enabling it to destroy enemy tanks accurately at extreme ranges, military planners may choose it instead—based on the same cost effectiveness principle.

Cost effectiveness analysis is also applied to many other areas of human activity, including the economics of automobile usage.

CEA in Pharmacoeconomics

In the context of pharmacoeconomics, the cost-effectiveness of a therapeutic or preventive intervention is the ratio of the cost of the intervention to a relevant measure of its effect. Cost refers to the resource expended for the intervention, usually measured in monetary terms such as dollars or pounds. The measure of effects depends on the intervention being considered. Examples include the number of people cured of a disease, the mm Hg reduction in diastolic blood pressure and the number of symptom-free days experienced by a patient. The selection of the appropriate effect measure should be based on clinical judgement in the context of the intervention being considered.

A special case of CEA is cost-utility analysis, where the effects are measured in terms of years of full health lived, using a measure such as quality-adjusted life years or disability-adjusted life years. Cost-effectiveness is typically expressed as an incremental cost-effectiveness ratio (ICER), the ratio of change in costs to the change in effects. A complete compilation of cost-utility analyses in the peer reviewed medical literature is available from the Cost-Effectiveness Analysis Registry website.

A 1995 study of the cost-effectiveness of over 500 life-saving medical interventions found that the median cost per intervention was $42,000 per life-year saved. A 2006 systematic review found that industry-funded studies often concluded with cost effective ratios below $20,000 per QALY and low quality studies and those conducted outside the US and EU were less likely to be below this threshold. While the two conclusions of this article may indicate that industry-funded ICER measures are lower methodological quality than those published by non-industry sources, there is also a possibility that, due to the nature of retrospective or other non-public work, publication bias may exist rather than methodology biases. There may be incentive for an organization not to develop or publish an analysis that does not demonstrate the value of their product. Additionally, peer reviewed journal articles should have a strong and defendable methodology, as that is the expectation of the peer-review process.

Cost-minimization Analysis

Cost-minimization is a tool used in pharmacoeconomics and is applied when comparing multiple drugs of equal efficacy and equal tolerability. Therapeutic equivalence must be referenced by the author conducting the study and should have been done prior to the cost-minimization work. Since equal efficacy and equal tolerability is already demonstrated, there is no requirement to find a common efficacy denominator as would be the case when conducting a cost-effectiveness study. The author is not precluded from doing so through the use of "cost/cure" or "cost/year of life gained". If efficacy and tolerability is demonstrated, however, then a simple comparison of "cost/course of treatment" can suffice for the purpose of comparing two or more therapeutically equivalent treatment alternatives.

When conducting a cost-minimization study, the author needs to measure all costs (resource expenditures) inherent to the delivery of the therapeutic intervention and that are relevant to the pharmacoeconomic perspective. It is the simplest method It is used to compare costs of alternative therapies that have: identical clinical effectiveness (including adverse reactions, complications and duration of therapy), BUT Different costs Choose the least cost alternative among equivalent or equally efficacious alternatives

Value Management Techniques for Building Design and Construction

There are a number of techniques which are commonly used in the conduct of value management (VM) studies. Some of these techniques are:

1. Function analysis.
2. Function analysis system technique (FAST).
3. Cost/worth.
4. SMART methodology (Simple Multi-Attribute Rating Technique).
5. Value drivers.

6. Value benchmarking (or value profiling).
7. Options selection.
8. Weighting techniques.
9. Creative techniques.
10. Evaluation techniques.
11. Scenarios technique.
12. Target costing.
13. Function performance specification (FPS).

Function Analysis

Function analysis is a method for analysing the functions of the constituent parts of a project. There are many approaches to function analysis, some very structured (such as the function system analysis technique) and others less formal (such as value trees or mind maps).

One of the key principles of the VM process is that it focuses on achieving successful outcomes rather than on the process of getting there. Functional analysis provides a very powerful tool to identify intended outcomes. In developing a functional model, the team is forced to make a very clear definition of the project by considering key questions such as:

- What are we trying to achieve?
- What must we get right if we are trying to achieve it?
- What considerations do we need to bear in mind while designing it?
- How do various design solutions contribute towards achieving the desired outcome?

8

Functional Analysis Systems Technique (FAST)

This technique relies on logically linking functions and allows people from different technical backgrounds to use a common language to describe and link the functions of complex systems to build a FAST diagram. In order to produce the FAST diagram, the team will have to interact and communicate with one another effectively to arrive at a logical diagram that they can all understand and agree with.

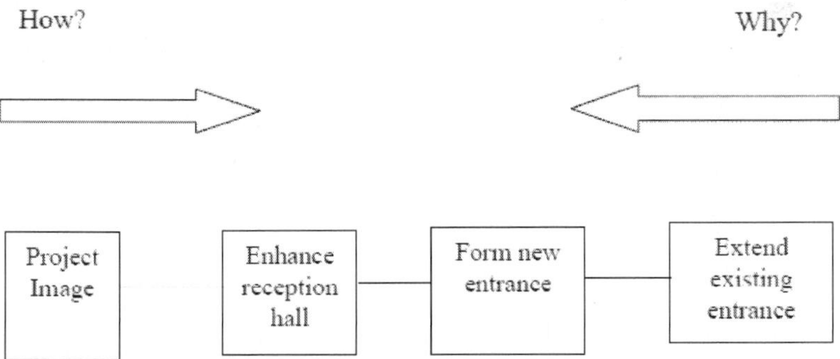

The how/why logic provides the key to developing a logic-linked function diagram. Randomly generated functions (as used in function analysis) can be logically linked through the use of questions "how" and "why". The level of abstraction, gradually diminishes from left to right. This also reflects "dependencies", where a function of lesser abstraction is dependent upon higher-level abstraction functions. Thus, changing the higher order functions will effectively change the outcome. While looking for innovations or improvement ideas, it is therefore necessary to address functions of higher-level abstractions.

In addition to the "how" and "why", other key words that are used for producing FAST diagrams include "when" (to identify things that occur simultaneously with an identified function), "and" (to indicate when two dependent functions happen simultaneously) and "or" (eventually either one dependent function will happen or another, depending upon circumstances).

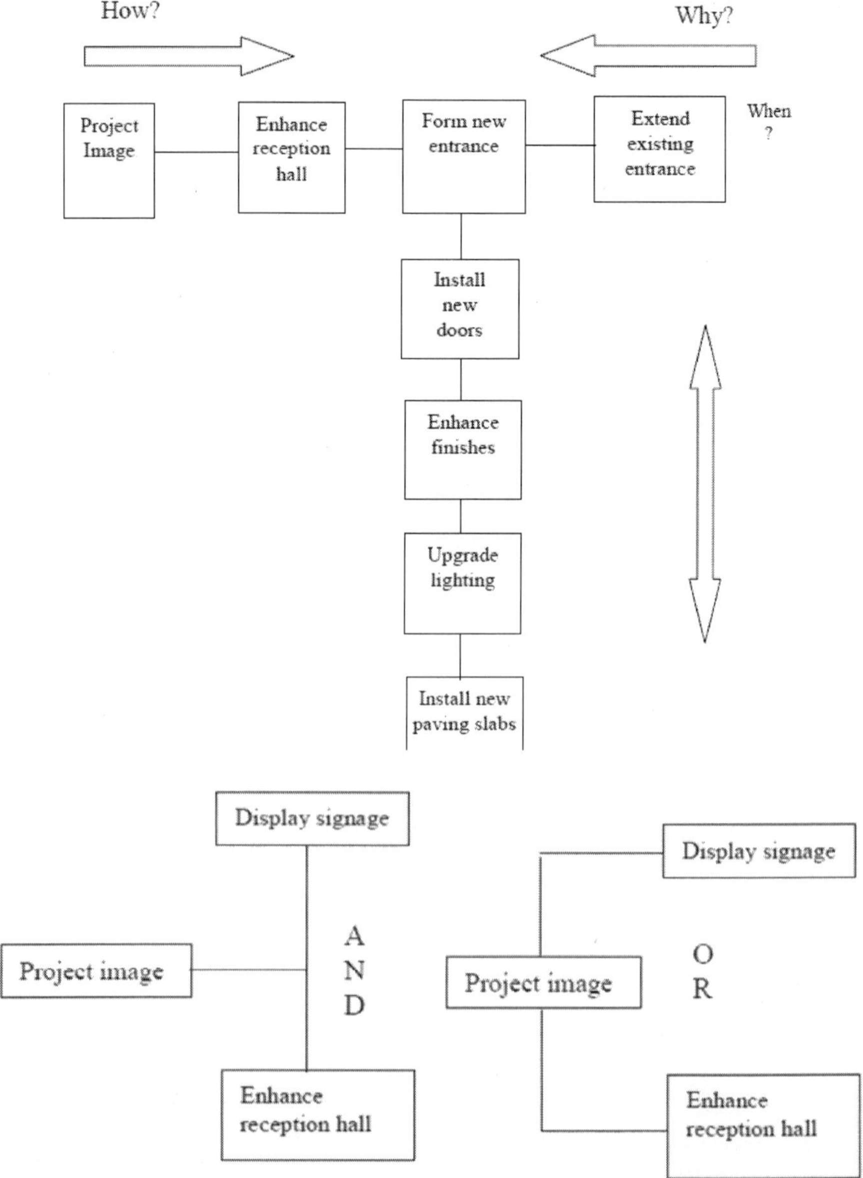

Cost / worth

A key principle of VM is to analyse each of the functions and to assess what it actually costs to perform the function, using a functional cost matrix. For comparison, the team assesses the lowest cost at which the function can be performed, referred to as the function's "worth". A comparison of the two diagrams gives an indication of the "cost/worth" of the function being examined. The functions whose cost significantly exceeds their worth may warrant further study to explore whether they can be performed in a different way at less cost. However, this approach must be understood with the caveat that it is absolutely critical that all functions performed by each component must be taken into account. For example, the basic function of granite paving may be to support pedestrians. This function can also be performed by using concrete paving slabs at a much lower cost. However, there are other functions that the granite paving will have contributed to, not least of which is the aesthetics of the area. Similarly, granite performs an additional function "resisting wear" considerably better than its concrete equivalent. It is vital, therefore, that in considering the basic function of a component, other functions to which it contributes are taken into account to assess its true "worth".

SMART Methodology (Simple Multi-Attribute Rating Technique)

The SMART (Simple Multi-Attribute Rating Technique) methodology, introduced in the mid 1990's generated two evolutionary concepts from FAST methodology. The first of these was the value tree. Instead of expressing the essential components necessary to fulfil the project objectives by means of two three word functions, this methodology uses the concept of a value tree to link functions. The second innovation was to create an importance hierarchy for the functions.

The value tree is similar to the FAST diagram in that it normally begins on the left hand side with a statement of project objectives. The answer to the question "how" is expressed in simple value-adding attributes required to deliver the project objective. Each of these is broken down into the attributes that add value to that branch, thus building a tree of decreasing abstraction from left to right. The figure below illustrates an example of a value tree for a school.

The second aspect of the SMART method requires the client to rank the value adding attributes in order of their importance in achieving project objectives. Under the SMART value tree the weighting for each of the values is expressed as a decimal of less than 1, such that for any level of abstraction for any single attribute, the total weighting adds to 1.

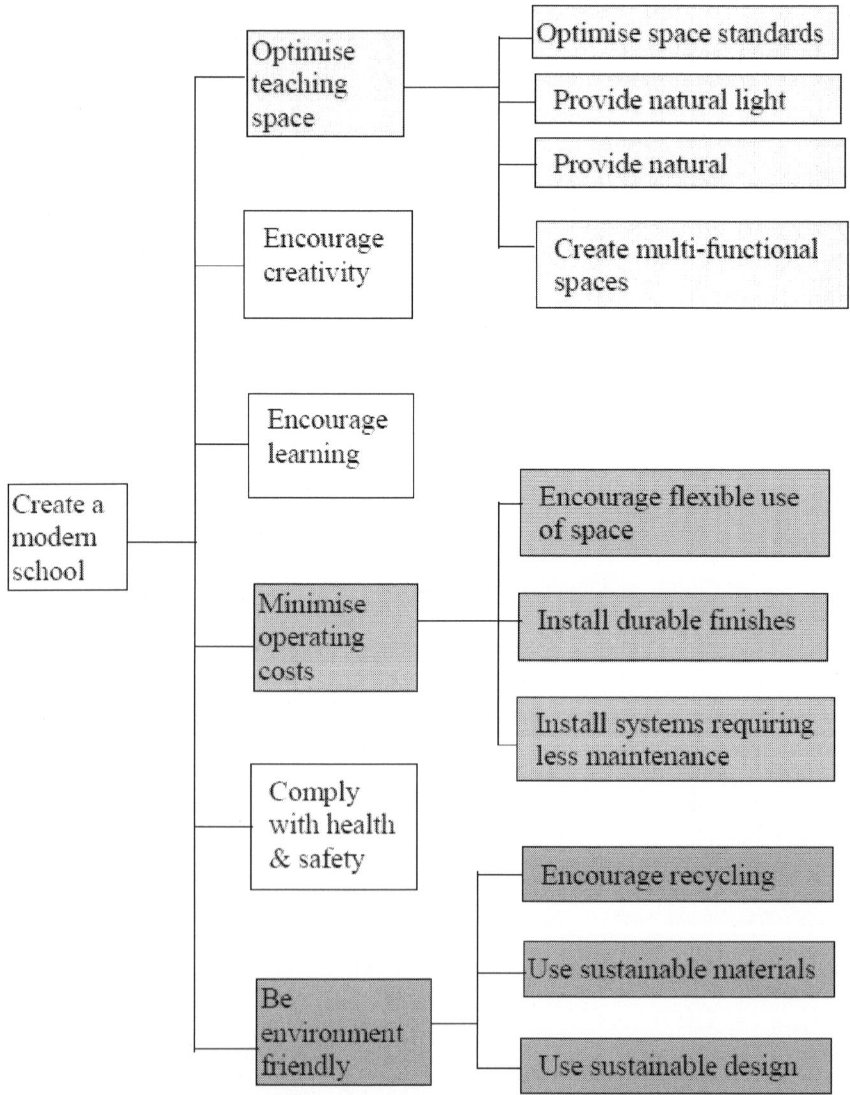

By attributing costs to the value tree it is possible to assess the cost of undertaking a function relative to its importance in the overall project, and to consider different approaches to undertaking the same function for fewer resources.

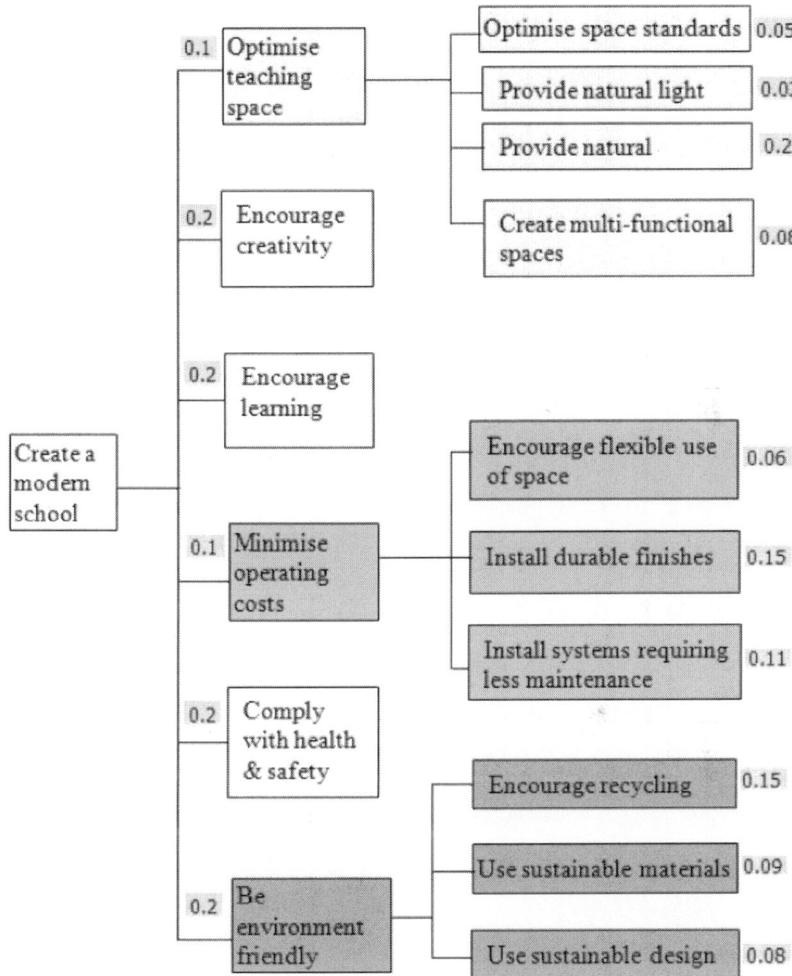

Value Drivers

Many of the functions in construction projects are not physical in nature. Since these abstract functions are essential to adequately describe a project, the concept of "value driver", instead of primary function, is often used. Value drivers are those things which contribute to the value of the building and are readily understood.

Development of generic value drivers offers an advance on the generation of random value drivers for each and every project. While random value drivers may be just as effective for the purposes of VM, the resulting function analysis would be unique to the particular project and the circumstances in which they were developed. Use of generic value drivers creates the advantage of comparability, where projects with similar objectives can be benchmarked against one another.

Value Benchmarking (or Value Profiling)

Utilising the value driver tool, it is possible to describe the client's value priorities, which form the project's value benchmark or value profile. This, in turn, creates a way of identifying those parts of the project which provide most potential for adding value and shaping the project.

Value benchmarking should take place at the beginning of a VM study. Using the weighted value drivers, the client team (excluding client consultants and advisers, but including the end users) produces the value profile. The VM team, in conjunction with the client team, creates an acceptable range for each value driver using objective matrices (for example, using a scale of 1 to 10, where 1 is unacceptable and 10 is ideal).

The VM team, with the client team, may also identify targets within each range for the VM objective to achieve. These targets will help to benchmark the exercise and the project, by clearly contrasting current performance values against the target (benchmark) values.

Options Selection

A weighted value driver model provides an objective way of making decisions. By using an options evaluation matrix, it is possible to assess the relative benefits of each option using the weighted value drivers as evaluation criteria. The best option will be the one that satisfies the value drivers the most.

A value score for each option is obtained by multiplying the weighting of each value driver by the degree to which the options satisfy it. It is recommended that a scale of 1 to 4 is used, where 1 is poor and 4 is excellent. It is better to use a 4 point score than a more common 5 point scale, as there is a tendency for groups to pick the midpoint number 3 on the 5 point scale, whereas on a 4 point scale the group is forced to select above or below the mean by choosing 3 or 2. Adding all the value scores across all functions for each option gives a total value score for that option. The option with the highest score is that which best satisfies the requirements in the project objectives.

Value for Money

Value for Money (VfM) is a further sophistication of this technique, used for option selection. VfM is calculated by dividing the value score by the total cost of the option. This helps to differentiate between two options, each of which has a high value score, but where one costs significantly more than the other.

NB It is recommended that a sensitivity analysis be performed as well, since small changes in the weighting of each option against the value drivers will have an impact on the end result. Even when scientific methods are used to assess weightings or assessing how well each option satisfies a particular function, there remains an aspect of subjectivity. A sensitivity analysis varies both the importance weightings and satisfaction assessments to ensure that the process is robust.

Weighting Techniques

There are a number of different weighting techniques with varying degrees of complexity which are commonly used in VM studies. These include:

- Dots.
- Distribution of points.
- Paired comparisons.

'Dots' is perhaps the most simplistic technique and the least scientific, but can be the quickest way to assess the relative importance of a number of items. Here, the VM team simply allocates dots to their preferred choices. There should be some guidance as to how many favourites can be selected. The number should not be more than one third of the items under consideration. The item with the most dots is ranked most important and so on.

A more statistically sound way to assign weightings is to ask the team to allocate a fixed number of points between the items (distribution of points). Each person can put as many points as they wish against any one item, but must use all their points and no more. The points against each item are added up and divided by the total number of contributors to give an average score for each item. Then these scores are normalised to arrive at a percentage weighting for each.

However, the outcome of this technique can be biased if the VM team does not have representatives from the whole project team. Furthermore, sometimes there may be a significant divergence in individual weightings across the team. In this situation, the average will not be representative of all the members' views. Convergence tools such as the Delphi technique (Harold A. Linstone, Murray Turoff (1975) (in English), The Delphi Method: Techniques and Applications, Reading, Mass.: Adison-Wesley, ISBN 9780201042948) or similar can be utilised in these situations. A further technique is 'paired comparison', where direct comparisons are made between each of the attributes. In this technique, each item is judged against the others. Scales of assessing by how much one attribute is better than another vary. A 3-point scale (1 being low and 3 being high) is most commonly used. The score for each attribute is calculated by adding up the total number of times it appears in the matrix, with each entry being multiplied by the scale factor if applicable. The weighting is then calculated by normalising the scores on a percentage basis.

Creative Techniques

One of the fundamental concepts underpinning VM is to encourage innovative solutions. Functional analysis can be used to generate and foster innovation and creativity.

Ideas can be generated simply by asking questions such as "how can the component be made better, efficient and cheaper", particularly in terms of value drivers. This is based on the fundamental assumption that there will always be more than one way to solve a problem.

Creative techniques such as brainstorming (McFadzean, E. S. (1997), "Improving Group Productivity with Group Support Systems and Creative Problem Solving Techniques", Creativity and Innovation Management, Vol. 6, No. 4, pp. 218-225.) can be used to generate and foster ideas.

It is also necessary to develop processes to evaluate the ideas generated, by creating common evaluation criteria so that ideas can be ranked and suitable implementation proposals developed.

It may also be necessary to undertake scenario appraisals to risk assess the selected ideas.

Target Costing

VM techniques can be used to establish not only what functionality the client wants, but also how much the client is willing to pay for it.

Construction, being a fiercely competitive market, operates in an environment where, broadly, the price is dictated by the customer. Historically, the industry operates on the following commercial basis:

Cost + profit = price

Designers will produce a design based on the client's requirements; quantity surveyors price the design based on market testing and experience (which contain unstated risk allowances). All too often the client is not willing to pay the price and through competition, where the suppliers cut their margins, alternative (often inferior) specifications are adopted and scope (functionality) is reduced to arrive at the price that the client is willing to pay.

The application of VM techniques from the outset of the project will establish the functionality required by the client and the necessary margins to sustain a profitable business for all the suppliers involved:

Price – profit = cost

If the resulting cost is lower than the estimate, the functional cost model will identify the areas of discrepancy. The client will then be in a position to work with the designers and suppliers to align cost with their required functionality without creating adversarial or confrontational circumstances.

Functional Performance Specification (FPS)

A specification is a documentm that describes a designer's or a user's intentions to a provider of the item being specified. Specifications can be broadly categorised as:

1. Absolute specifications. Here the specifier describes exactly what is required in detail and the scope for innovation or alternative options is non-existent.
2. Performance specifications describe the output required from a component or subsystem, but do not indicate or dictate the means of delivering that output. For example, the specification may require the internal environment in a room to be 21 ±2 °C throughout the year, with an occupancy of up to 50 people. There are a variety of air conditioning and heating systems that could achieve this and the choice is left to the provider. This type of specification provides scope for innovation and genuine competitive bidding.
3. Function performance specifications (FPS) take this one step further. The specifier defines user requirements by what the item must do rather than what it must be. In the previous example, the specification might read 'the room shall facilitate comfortable gatherings for the users at all times', where the function of the room is to enable meetings to take place. The definition of "comfortable" is flexible and could be negotiated with the users. Similarly, the number of people attending can also vary. This gives the provider ultimate flexibility and the ability to devise a very innovative and competitive solution.

The FPS comprises a thorough functional description of the system or subsystem being specified as it relates to the user (a user-related function - URF). To each function it attaches measurable attributes (known as Compliance Criteria - CC). Each CC is assigned a target level which can be quantitative or qualitative. Each target level is provided with a degree of flexibility by defining tolerance bands.

The requires a function analysis of user's needs, identification of measurable CCs, and agreement of the target levels and acceptable degrees of freedom. Having completed the FPS it is possible to explore trade-offs between the CC for different functions. This enables identification of the most competitive offering that complies with the specification.

Value Management in Building Design and Construction

History of Development

Value Management (VM) and Value Engineering (VE) are techniques concerned with defining, maximising and achieving "value for money" (VfM). These are systematic team-based collaborative approaches, initially pioneered by United States practitioners during the Second World War, to secure maximum output from limited resources.

At the initial stages of a project, value management provides an exceptionally powerful tool to explore a project's objectives and aspirations from the client's perspective.

Whilst the process originated in the manufacturing industry, the key initiating question ("what function does a component perform and how else can this function be performed") is equally applicable to a wide range of disciplines, including construction, and within 10 years of the concept emerging, the US Department of Defence incorporated VfM in the delivery of its very extensive construction programme.

Although its use was widespread in the US from the 1950's, it took another three decades for the concept to be applied in Europe, with its first ever application in the UK in 1983 by the American company Xerox. One of the reasons for this slow uptake was probably due to the fact that the US approach to VfM required a separate team to audit the incumbent design team's proposals. The design team was then expected to implement the audit team's proposals. This predictably opened up numerous problems relating to design responsibility, legal complications and even professional rivalry.

However, with the growing spread of the quality movement in the 1980's and shift of the initial focus from materials to cost and quality, the concept was eventually accepted in the UK and Europe, where the incumbent design team became a key part of the team undertaking the value audit.

With time, there was a realisation that materials, cost and quality, as governed by the specification, are not enough. Products had to respond to the needs of the customer. Emphasis therefore shifted to a more rounded appreciation of value, encapsulating cost, time, performance, knowledge and technical competency. At the same time, the scope of the studies has also grown, to capture processes as well as products, with the focus being on expressing and measuring value in such a way that the project team can respond with the most effective solutions.

A key differentiator between the value management concept and many other processes is that value management focuses on the expected outcome from a project. Only once the outcome is clearly established, understood, agreed and defined, does the process address the question of how it will be delivered. The aspired outcomes from a project are represented in a statement of the project objectives, expressed in terms of the expected benefits to the business. These are linked through "value drivers" (defined as a functional attribute that is necessary to fully deliver the expected benefits from a project – equivalent to a primary function) to the design intent. Later, as the project evolves, these relate directly to the design solutions and what is built.

Process

Value management is a team-based approach used to define the client's objectives and ensure that best value, whole-life solutions are selected to satisfy those objectives. It is not necessarily about cost cutting.

To achieve maximum benefit, value management should be carried out from the very early stages of a project, not simply introduced when problems occur. The process of value management includes value engineering, which is a more systematic approach to ensuring that specific functions are satisfied to the required standard for the least cost. It assess a range of possible solutions against the values required by the client.

Value management exercises can also be used to recover cost divergence (costs diverging from the budget) that may become apparent when design reports are prepared. Under these circumstances, the client may have to choose priorities, or decide to increase the budget.

It may be possible to:

- Identify items that can be omitted.
- Identify items that can have their specification changed.
- Identify items that could be re-instigated later in the programme if the budget allows.
- Identify enabling works that can be incorporated into the design, allowing elements to be added during later phases of construction.

The client and the full consultant team should take part, along with the contractor, construction manager or management contractor if appointed.

Value Management Techniques.

The history section of this article is based on VALUE MANAGEMENT IN CONSTRUCTION, by Saleem Akram, Andrzej Minasowicz, Bartosz Kostrzewa, Arnab Mukherjee and Piotr Nowak. The original manual was published in 2011. It was developed within the scope of the LdV programme, project number: 2009-1-PL1-LEO05-05016 entitled "Common Learning Outcomes for European Managers in Construction".

It is reproduced here in a slightly modified form with the kind permission of the Chartered Institute of Building.

Approximate bill of Quantities

An approximate bill of quantities (sometimes referred to as a notional bill of quantities or provisional bill of quantities) can be used on projects where it is not possible to prepare a firm bill of quantities at the time of tendering. Generally, the design will be relatively complete, but there is either insufficient time or information to determine the exact quantities and so a conventional bill of quantities cannot be prepared.

Tendering on the basis of an approximate bill of quantities can allow early selection of the contractor and so an early start on site. However the approximate nature of the bill of quantities will tend to result in more variations during construction and so less price certainty when the investment decision is made. This means that even if it is not possible to determine exact quantities, it is sensible to try to ensure quantities are as accurate as possible.

Some contracts allows for re-measurement of approximate quantities (for example, this is common on cut and fill on roadworks).

Here, quantities are simply revised and payments made accordingly without the need to instruct a variation.

If an approximate quantity turns out not to have been a realistic estimate of the quantity actually required, this may constitute a relevant event giving rise to claims for an extension of time and loss and expense.

Approximate bills of quantities can also be used during the design process as a tool for controlling design costs. They are then sometimes included in the tender documents as a guide with a caveat stating that responsibility for measuring quantities lies with the contractor, and drawings and specifications take priority over any description in the approximate bills.

An approximate quantities cost plan is, in effect, a priced approximate bill of quantities. It is a development of the elemental cost plan, but unlike the elemental cost plan (in which the cost of elements is broken down from the overall construction cost, based on the experience of the cost consultant and known costs of similar completed projects) the approximate quantities cost plan is a first attempt to measure defined quantities from drawings. It presents a more accurate picture of where costs are distributed, in particular it draws to the attention of designers those elements of the design that are standard and those that are not and as a consequence may be more expensive. The approximate quantities cost plan should form a solid base for an effective value engineering exercise. From the point that the approximate quantities cost plan has been approved, cost control can be introduced by treating changes as if they are variations.

Approximate Quantities Cost Plan

There are very many different names given to cost planning documents. Cost plans are generally prepared by cost consultants (often quantity surveyors). They evolve through the life of the project, developing in detail and accuracy as more information becomes available about the nature of the design, and then actual prices are provided by specialist contractors, contractors and suppliers. They range from very early initial cost appraisals through to tender pricing documents and the final account.

As a consequence there are a great number of names that can be used for key cost planning information. On Designing Buildings Wiki we have standardised these as follows:

- Initial cost appraisals (studies of options prepared during the feasibility study stage).

- Elemental cost plan (prepared during the project brief stage and developed all the way through to detailed design).
- Approximate quantities cost plan (from the end of detailed design through to tender).
- Pre-tender estimate (prepared alongside tender documentation).
- Tender pricing document (strictly speaking this is not a priced document, but is part of the tender documentation issued to the contractor for pricing).
- Contract sum (agreed with the contractor during the tender period and adjusted during the construction period).
- Contract sum analysis (a break down of the contract sum prepared by the contractor on design and build projects).
- Final account (agreed during the defects liability period).

Other than initial cost appraisals, these all relate to the construction cost of the project (rather than wider project costs that the client might incur, which could include; fees, equipment costs, furniture, the cost of moving staff, contracts outside of the main works, and so on). It is important that the client makes clear what costs should be monitored by the cost consultant and what will remain within the control of the client organisation.

The approximate quantities cost plan is a development of the elemental cost plan. Unlike the elemental cost plan in which the cost of elements is broken down from the overall construction cost, based on the experience of the cost consultant and known costs of similar completed projects, the approximate quantities cost plan is a first attempt to to measure defined quantities from drawings. It presents a more accurate picture of where costs are distributed, in particular it draws to the attention of designers those elements of the design that are standard and those that are not and as a consequence may be more expensive. In effect it is a priced approximate bill of quantities.

The approximate quantities cost plan should form a solid base for an effective value engineering exercise.

From the point that the approximate quantities cost plan has been approved, cost control can be introduced by treating changes as if they are variations.

Pre-tender Estimate

There are very many different names given to cost planning documents. Cost plans are generally prepared by cost consultants (often quantity surveyors). They evolve through the life of the project, developing in detail and accuracy as more information becomes available about the nature of the design, and then actual prices are provided by specialist contractors, contractors and suppliers. They range from very early initial cost appraisals through to tender pricing documents and the final account.

As a consequence there area a great number of names that can be used for key cost planning information. On Designing Buildings Wiki we have standardised these as follows:

- Initial cost appraisals (studies of options prepared during the feasibility study stage).
- Elemental cost plan (prepared during the project brief stage and carried through to detailed design).
- Approximate quantities cost plan (from the end of detailed design through to tender).
- Pre-tender estimate (prepared alongside tender documentation).
- Tender pricing document (strictly speaking this is not a priced document, but is part of the tender documentation issued to the contractor for pricing).
- Contract sum (agreed with the contractor during the tender period and adjusted during the construction period).
- Contract sum analysis (a break down of the contract sum prepared by the contractor on design and build projects).
- Final account (agreed during the defects liability period).

Other than initial cost appraisals, these all relate to the construction cost of the project (rather than wider project costs that the client might incur, which could include; fees, equipment costs, furniture, the cost of moving staff, contracts outside of the main works and so on). It is important that the client makes clear what costs should be monitored by the cost consultant and what will remain within the control of the client organisation.

The pre-tender estimate (PTE) is the final estimate of the likely cost of the works that are described in the completed tender documents (the pre-tender estimate is not included in the tender documents). It gives a basis for assessing and comparing tenders when they are returned (having clarified all matters and qualifications with tenderers), provides a final comparison with the budget, and along with the cash flow estimate enables the client to confirm that sufficient funds area available before committing to tender.

If the pre-tender estimate exceeds the approved budget, an explanation should be provided for the client to consider and issue instructions.

As with the tender documents, the pre-tender estimate should be broken down into a series of packages (even if there will only be one main contract), this will allow easy appraisal of tenders received, which are likely to prepared by contractors based on prices of packages received form sub-contractors.

Provisional Sum

A provisional sum is an allowance, usually estimated by the cost consultant, that is inserted into tender documents for a specific element of the works that is not yet defined in enough detail for tenderers to price. This, together with a brief description, allows tenderers to apply mark up and attendance costs within their overall tender price and make allowance for the work in the contract programme.

An example of a situation where a provisional sum might be appropriate is when work is required below an existing structure, where the ground conditions cannot be determined until the existing structure is demolished and the ground opened up.

Provisional sums can be 'defined' or 'undefined':

- Defined provisional sums are considered to have been accounted for within the contractor's price and programme. In effect the contractor is taking the risk that their estimate will be sufficient.
- Undefined provisional sums are not accounted for in the contractor's price and programme. This means that the client is taking the risk for the works and the contractor may be entitled to an extension of time and additional payments.

Provisional sums are provided for in different ways in different forms of contract, and some forms of contract can be a little vague about how provisional sums should be handled, in particular regarding adjustments to the programme.

Provisional sums place either the contractor or the client at risk of unexpected costs or delays. Agreeing the cost of such work or extensions of time that might be claimed can result in tension between the contractor and client. For this reason, they should only be used as a last resort, they should not be an easy fall-back position for consultants (who are not bearing any of the risk) when designs are incomplete or information is difficult to obtain. The risks are significant enough that the NEC Engineering and Construction Contract (NEC3) does not have any allowance for provisional sums.

Provisional sums should not be confused with prime cost sums, which are allowances for the supply of work or materials to be provided by a contractor or supplier nominated by the client. Prime cost sums might include items that have already been purchased by the client, such as equipment, or a specific installation by a company with a strong existing relationship with a client organisation.

Rate Relief Schemes

Small Business Rate Relief: You will be eligible for a discount under the small business rate relief scheme in England if you only occupy one property and it has a rateable value below £12,000.

The Government has temporarily doubled the level of relief available. Between 1 October 2010 and 31 March 2013, eligible rate payers will receive small business rate relief at 100 per cent on properties up to £6,000 (rather than 50 per cent), and a tapering relief from 100 per cent to 0 per cent for properties up to £12,000 in rateable value for that period.

The temporary Small Business Rate Relief increase will therefore apply throughout the whole of the 2012-13 billing year. The relief was originally doubled by the government until September 2011, but this was extended by the Budget in March 2011, and then extended again in the 2011 Autumn Statement to take account of economic conditions.

If you have more than one business property, the discount is only available if the rateable value of each of the other properties is below £2,600. If this is the case, the rateable values of all the properties will be combined and the relief is applied to the main property based on the total rateable value.

However, if you occupy a property with a rateable value below £18,000 (£25,500 in London), and you are not receiving a different mandatory relief, you will be eligible to have your bill calculated using the small business multiplier, regardless of the number of properties you occupy.

The Government has also simplified the process for claiming the relief by removing the legal requirement for an application form in order to claim the relief. However, if you are not receiving the relief and you think that you are eligible, you should contact your local billing authority.

Small Business Rate Relief in Wales

You will be eligible for small business rate relief if your rateable value is below certain levels:

- If you have business premises with a 2010 rateable value up to £2,400 (except beach huts, adverts or car park spaces, sewage works or communication sites), your bill will be reduced by 50 per cent.
- If you have business premises with a 2010 rateable value between £2,401 and £7,800 (excluding beach huts, adverts or car park spaces, sewage works or communication sites), your bill will be reduced by 25 per cent.
- If you have a post office with a 2010 rateable value up to £9,000, your bill will be reduced by 100 per cent.
- If you have a post office with a 2010 rateable value between £9,001 and £12,000, your bill will be reduced by 50 per cent.
- If you have registered child-care premises with a 2010 rateable value up to £12,000, your bill will be reduced by 50 per cent.
- If you have retail premises with a 2010 rateable value between £7,801 and £11,000 (including restaurants, pubs and petrol filling stations), your bill will be reduced by 25 per cent. If you occupy more than one property, only one can be chosen to receive relief.
- If you have a property occupied by a registered Credit Union with a 2010 rateable value up to £9,000, your bill will be reduced by 50 per cent.

There are a small number of instances where businesses received a higher rate of relief under the scheme operating before 1 October 2010 than under the current scheme - in these instances they will receive the rate of relief that is most beneficial to them.

The following will not be affected by the temporary changes:

- Premises with rateable value between £10,501 and £11,000 in receipt of 25 per cent retail relief.
- Post offices in receipt of 100 per cent or 50 per cent relief.
- Registered child care premises with rateable value £9,001 - £12,000 in receipt of 50 per cent relief.

Project Plan

The feasibility studies stage considers the options for satisfying the client's needs, enabling the client to prepare a business case for the preferred option and deciding whether to proceed with the project. It is possible to make an outline planning application during this stage if the risk to the project of not receiving planning permission is high, or if delays in receiving planning permission would be problematic.

In this work plan we suggest the construction manager is appointed on completion of concept design. Earlier or later appointment will result in some activities being re-allocated between the consultant team and the construction manager (for example the role of cost consultant).

A. Updating the project documents.
   1. The client updates the preliminary business case and strategic brief to reflect comments made at the end of the previous stage: Construction management: business justification.
   2. The client collates site information ready to issue to the consultant team.

B. Appointing a consultant team.
   1. The client appoints the consultant team and other advisers (such as independent client advisers). Go to work stage: Construction management: appointment.
   2. The client chairs a consultant team start-up meeting to issue information (such as the strategic brief and site information to the consultant team. This is also an opportunity to establish collaborative practices and agree a programme.
   3. The CDM co-ordinator (if appointed) checks the client is aware of their duties under the CDM regulations.

C. Developing the strategic brief so that feasibility studies can be carried out and the preferred options selected.
   1. The consultant team work with the client to help them develop the strategic brief sufficiently for feasibility studies and options appraisals to be carried out.
   2. The consultant team assess the site information issued to them by the client, and undertake site appraisals.
   3. The consultant team obtain any further information about the site that might be required to undertake feasibility studies, such as; site surveys, information about site services, site access conditions, legislative constraints, existing planning consents etc. Where necessary, approval should be sought from the client (for example site surveys requiring additional expenditure).

4. The lead consultant co-ordinates the preparation of feasibility studies to establish whether the project is viable, and to identify feasible options.
5. The client considers the feasibility studies, and agrees which options the consultant team should develop.

D. Preparing an options review report.
   1. The lead designer co-ordinates the identification of any further site surveys or site information required in order to carry out options appraisals and where appropriate seeks approval from the client.
   2. The lead designer co-ordinates the preparation of diagrammatic options studies.
   3. The CDM co-ordinator (if appointed at this stage) assesses the risks of the options in relation to the CDM regulations.
   4. The architect co-ordinates consultations with the local authority and other statutory authorities, and assesses possible planning permission requirements and other statutory requirements (such as the need for an environmental impact assessment for the options).
   5. The cost consultant prepares initial cost appraisals of the options.
   6. The lead consultant co-ordinates the preparation of a draft options review report.

E. Preparing a business case and project execution plan for the preferred option.
   1. The lead consultant co-ordinates further assessment of the preferred option in order to assist the client in preparing a business case and project execution plan.
   2. The lead designer establishes requirements for statutory approvals and other regulations with which the preferred option must comply.
   3. The lead designer co-ordinates consultations with utility providers.
   4. The lead consultant co-ordinates an assessment of the need for specialist advice to develop the preferred option and advises the client.
   5. With the benefit of assessments carried out by the consultant team, the client develops the preliminary business case into

a business case and project execution plan for the preferred option.

6. The client considers, and if appropriate, approves the business case and project execution plan for the preferred option and gives instructions to proceed to the next stage along with any other instructions that may be necessary.

Project Brief

This stage is concerned solely with preparing the project brief. We use the term 'project brief' here and throughout the rest of this site to mirror the terminology used in guidance for public projects and to reflect the fact that the brief tends to be a single document that evolves.

In this work plan we suggest the construction manager is appointed on completion of concept design. Earlier or later appointment will result in some activities being re-allocated between the consultant team and the construction manager (for example the role of cost consultant).

A. Starting the work stage and appointing additional members of the consultant team if necessary.
   1. The client updates the business case and project execution plan to reflect comments made at the end of the previous stage.
   2. The lead consultant co-ordinates a start-up meeting attended by the consultant team and the client to issue the revised project execution plan (and business case or part of it if appropriate), to pass on comments made at the end of the previous stage, and to agree the programme for the stage.
   3. The consultant team or the client may identify a requirement to appoint additional consultants or specialist designers. Go to work stage: Construction management: appointment.

B. Preparing the project brief.

1. The client and consultant team discuss the required contents of the project brief and consider who the consultant team may need to consult in the preparation of the project brief. It may be appropriate to prepare a project directory of contact details and perhaps a stakeholder map.
2. The client informs user panels, champions and other stakeholders that will be involved in the development of the project brief that they should make time available to meet with the consultant team.

3. The lead consultant co-ordinates the consultant team to carry out consultations with user panels, champions and other stakeholders and feeds back the outcome of consultations to the client.
4. The lead consultant co-ordinates the consultant team to prepare a draft project brief.
5. The client begins preparing, or arranges for the consultant team to begin preparing, a site waste management plan. At this stage, this is a means of recording decisions made to minimise the consumption of resources and to minimise the generation of waste.
6. The cost consultant highlights areas of potential cost savings and areas of potential cost problems apparent in the draft project brief and prepares an elemental cost plan.
7. The client considers advice from the cost consultant and instructs the consultant team to amend the draft project brief if necessary.
8. The client issues the revised project brief to the user panels, champions and other stakeholders who may propose further revisions.
9. The client considers the proposed amendments and instructs any necessary revision of the project brief.
10. The cost consultant amends the elemental cost plan if necessary.
11. The client considers and approves the project brief
12. If necessary the client revises the business case and project execution plan. This might include: additional value management and risk assessment exercises, re-assessment of the budget and re-assessment of the procurement route.

Bibliography

Anbuvelan, K. : *Management Concepts for Civil Engineers*, Laxmi Publications, Delhi, 2005.

Avallone, E.A., Baumeister, T.: *Marks' Standard Handbook for Mechanical Engineers,* McGraw-Hill, Inc., New York, 1997.

Basu, S.K. : *Global Dictionary of Civil Engineering*, Global Vision, Delhi, 2012.

Bansal, R.K. : *Basic Civil Engineering and Engineering Mechanics*, Laxmi Publications, Delhi, 2011.

Bennett, S.: *A History of Control Engineering: 1800-1930*, IEE Press, London, 1979.

Bhavikatti, S. S. : *A Textbook on Elements of Civil Engineering and Engineering Mechanics*, New Age International , Delhi, 2011.

Booker, P. J.: *A History of Engineering Drawing*, Chatto & Windus, London, 1963.

Calhoun, Daniel H. : *The American Civil Engineer: Origins and Conflict.* Cambridge: MIT Press, 1960.

Chen, W.F.: *Civil Engineering Handbook.* Boca Raton, FL: CRC Press, 1995.

David Fisher: *Rules of Thumb for Engineers and Scientists*, Gulf Pub, Houston, 1991.

Davison, C. S. C. B.: *Engineering Heritage*, Institute of Mechanical Engineers, London, 1963.

Domminghaus, H.: *Plastics for Engineers: Materials, Properties, Applications*, Hanser Publishers, Munich, 1993.

Dym, J.B.: *Product Design with Plastics: A Practical Manual*, Industrial Press, New York, 1983.

Edward H. Smith: *Mechanical Engineer's Reference Book,* Butterworth-Heinemann, Oxford, 1994.

Emerson, Howard P.: *Origins of Industrial Engineering: The Early Years of a Profession.* Institution of Industrial Engineers, 1988.

Fernandez, Martin : *Dictionary of Civil Engineering*, A P H, Delhi, 2011.

Fitchen, John: *Building Construction Before Mechanization.* MIT Press, 1986.

Florman, S.: *The Civilized Engineer*, St. Martin's Press, New York, 1979.

Groover, Mikell P.: *Fundamentals of Modern Manufacturing*, John Wiley & Sons, INC, New York, 2002.

Gupta, J.P. : *A T B of Engineering Mech. and Basic Civil Engineering*, S. Chand Publishing, Delhi, 2011.

Hasan, Syed Danish : *Civil Engineering Materials and Their Testing*, Narosa, Delhi, 2011.

Howard B., Cary,: *Modern Welding Technology*, Pearson Education, Chicago, New Jersey, 2005.

Joshi, Jagat Pati : *Harappan Architecture And Civil Engineering*, Rupa Pub, Delhi, 2008.

Kapoor, R : *Encyclopedia of Civil Engineering*, SBS Pub, Delhi, 2007.

MacCollum, David V.: *Construction Safety Planning*. New York, NY: Van Nostrand Reinhold, 1995.

Mendel, Otto: *Practical Piping Handbook*. Tulsa, OK: PennWell Books, 1981.

Nicholas P.: *Handbook of Chemical Engineering Calculations*, McGraw-Hill, New York, 2004.

Punmia, B.C.; Ashok Kr. Jain and Arun Kr. Jain: *Basic Civil Engineering*, Laxmi Publications, Delhi, 2003.

Richard Valentine: *Motor Control Electronics Handbook,* McGraw-Hill, New York, 1998.

Robert C. Rosaler: *Standard Handbook of Plant Engineering,* McGraw-Hill, New York, 1995.

Seely, Bruce E: *Building the American Highway System: Engineers as Policy Makers*. Philadelphia: Temple University Press, 1987.

Singh, Gurcharan : *Standard Handbook of Civil Engineering*, Standard Pub, Delhi, 2003.

Thomas Sixsmith & R. Hanselka: *Handbook of Thermoplastic Piping System Design*. Marcel Dekker Ltd, London, 1997.

Weman, Klas: *Welding Processes Handbook*, CRC Press, New York, 2003.

Index

G

I

J

L

M

N

O

P

Q

R

S

T

U

V

W

❑❑❑